CHICHESTER
FESTIVAL THEATRE
at Fifty

Dear Keith (and Jenny, of course)

You are one of the reasons, CFT is the place it is today. Actor, director and CEO, thank you so much for your help and support at the booth. I hope you enjoy...

All best wishes Kate —

Also by Kate Mosse

FICTION
Eskimo Kissing
Crucifix Lane
Labyrinth
Sepulchre
The Winter Ghosts

NON-FICTION
Becoming a Mother
The House: Behind the Scenes at the Royal Opera House, Covent Garden

PLAYS
Syrinx
Endpapers
Dodger

CHICHESTER FESTIVAL THEATRE
at Fifty

1962-2012 • A CELEBRATION

KATE MOSSE

Foreword by Dame Joan Plowright, The Lady Olivier

unbound

For my father
Richard Mosse
1924 – 2011

**Richard McCabe,
Derek Griffiths and
Nicholas Le Prevost
in *The Critic*, 2010.**
Photo: Manuel Harlan

Chichester Festival Theatre at Fifty
This special limited edition first published in 2012

unbound

32-38 Scrutton Street, Shoreditch, London, EC2A 4RQ
www.unbound.co.uk

Book Design by Graham Smith
Cover by Dan Mogford

All rights reserved
© Mosse Associates Ltd 2012

The right of Kate Mosse to be identified as the author of this work has been asserted
in accordance with Section 77 of the Copyright, Designs and Patents Act 1988

A CIP record for this book is available from the British Library

ISBN 978-1-908717-23-8
Print production by Arnold Moon Limited

ARNOLD
MOON
www.arnoldmoon.com

Contents

Interviews

(April 2010 – September 2011)

As a journalist and author, the interview is the bedrock of what I do. Few assignments have provided such a rich tapestry as the 35 individuals who generously gave their time to tell me of their life and times at Chichester. The interviews with artistic directors, directors, actors, stage crew, designers and many others from the Board to the bar comprised around 100 hours. As many hours were devoted to transcribing them to achieve not just the best anecdotes, but more importantly the many perspectives that show what makes CFT a landmark theatre through five decades.

Over time memories can dull and recollections of CFT's triumphs and disasters often contradict. A willing, but forgetful subject admitted: 'You seem to know rather more about my time here than I do.' At times the process was like detective work; constantly expanding the list of 'witnesses', one person leading to another, to provide the compelling 'evidence' of what actually happened and to help capture the essence of what made a performer or a production special or infamous. Sadly, there are highly entertaining anecdotes that cannot appear for legal reasons and considerations of taste – many of them featuring Rex Harrison!

However valid the existing written sources and records are, these are the live voices and this was research of the most rewarding kind.

Rex Harrison in *Monsieur Perrichon's Travels*, 1976.

Photo: Zoë Dominic

TIM BOUQUET
Chichester, January 2012

Acknowledgements

'I can no other answer make, but, thanks, and thanks.'

TWELFTH NIGHT
William Shakespeare

This book is a group effort. Rather than just one voice, it is a collection of the stories, thoughts and memories of many of the women and men who, over the past half century, have played their own part in the history of Chichester Festival Theatre.

The local author and journalist, Tim Bouquet, carried out a series of formal in-depth interviews between April 2010 and September 2011. The list, drawn up by the current artistic directors, includes all but one of their living predecessors, as well as leading actors, directors, board members past and present, theatre critics and others with an association that has spanned much – or all – of CFT's fifty-year history. Tim then provided me with selected written transcripts of his recorded interviews. On behalf of Chichester Festival Theatre, Tim and myself, I would like formally to thank those 35 women and men who gave so generously of their time. We could only use a fraction of the wonderful material, but their verbatim words form the bedrock of this book: Sarah Badel, Janet Bakose, Michael Billington, Jonathan Church, Max Davies, Christopher Doman, Martin Duncan, David Evershed-Martin, Alan Finch, Tony French, John Gale, Patrick Garland, Phil Hewitt, Clifford Hodgetts, Sir Derek Jacobi, Penelope Keith CBE, Ruth Mackenzie OBE, Keith Michell, John McKerchar, Sam Mendes CBE, Holly Mirams, Richard Mosse, Andy Neal, Paul Rogerson, Dale Rooks, Patricia Routledge CBE, David Shalit, Sophie Shalit, the Duke of Richmond, Charles Spencer, Peter Stevens, Andrew Welch, Duncan Weldon, Brian Wingate and the Rt Hon Lord Young of Graffham.

John Standing and Sarah Badel in *The Farmer's Wife*, 1967.
Photo: John Timbers/ArenaPAL

Committee in session.

Arundel Castle Ball programme, May 1961. West Sussex Record Office

CENTRE

42nd Street, 2010.

Photo: Johan Persson

In addition to the substantial and in-depth interviews, I am grateful to Dame Joan Plowright, the Lady Olivier, for agreeing to write the Foreword. There is a pleasing symmetry to this and one that illustrates the family nature of CFT. In the two books written by Leslie Evershed-Martin OBE – *The Impossible Theatre* (1971) and *The Miracle Theatre* (1987) – the Forewords were both written by Sir Laurence Olivier. I am grateful to the publishers for allowing me to quote from both titles.

It is a reflection, perhaps, of the achievements of many of those who appear in *Chichester Festival Theatre at Fifty* that there should be rather a lot of titles and gongs to contend with! So as not to get in the way of the story, I have used a person's title in full when they first appear in the text, but thereafter taken the liberty of sticking to first names and surnames. Lack of space is the enemy in a celebratory book such as this, so I hope readers will be tolerant of this wobbly etiquette.

Unfortunately, there is no official archive and there are many gaps in the materials kept or filed. We have been dependent on the memory of individuals and their willingness to help. So, in addition to those thanked above, I'd like to pay tribute to the many others who gave support, provided images, shared letters, stories, background information from personal archives – or those of their families. No one more so than Jill Evershed-Martin, who most kindly allowed us access to the Evershed-Martin archive; Keith Michell and Jeanette Sterke were wonderfully supportive, both with their time and their generosity in providing material; Duncan Weldon was kind with his time and assistance in allowing us access to his substantial archive. Andy Neal's help with backstage images, not available anywhere else, was much appreciated. Special thanks also go to Barbara Mosse, Lisel Gale and Helena Michell Eden for their help and contributions during the interview process.

I'd like to pay tribute to all those who answered questions or took the time to share with us – either in person or via email/post – personal photographs and memorabilia, in particular: Tim Andrews, Bill Bray, Andy Brereton, Barry Evershed-Martin, Tony French, David Goodman, Clifford Hodgetts, Pamela Howard OBE, Edward Milwood-Oliver, Amanda Mirams, Victoria Ponnelle, Nigel Purchase, Roger Redfarn, Denise Roberts, Gerald Scarfe CBE, David Shalit and Sophie Shalit. Sharon Meier's research skills and extraordinary knowledge of CFT has been invaluable, as were her unsurpassed proof-reading skills. We would like to thank Simon Annand, Catherine Ashmore, Robert Day, Zoë Dominic, Mike Eddowes, Adrian Gatie, Manuel Harlan, John Haynes, Tristram Kenton, Michael Le Poer Trench, Alistair Muir, Johan Persson and John Swannell who have generously donated their photographs for use within the book.

We have been able to use only a fraction of the material available – and apologies to those who might be disappointed not to find their favourite

photographs (or their own names) included in these pages. I hope that, even though not every single festival production, concert, fringe event or person can be mentioned by name in the text, readers will nonetheless feel we have made our choices wisely to capture the beating heart of CFT over the past fifty years. Lists of Main House and Minerva Festival productions are provided from page 244 onwards and full photo/image credits are listed on page 254. Additional testimonies and the complete lists of productions, players and creative teams over the past fifty years are available on the Chichester Festival Theatre website (cft.org.uk).

At Unbound, I'd like to thank Dan Kieran, John Mitchinson, Justin Pollard, Xander Cansell, Jane Fitz-Gerald and Graham Smith for his heroic work; my agent, Mark Lucas, at LAW, was as always wonderfully supportive (and very decent about the whole book-as-gift scenario!); thanks too to the archivists and staff at West Sussex Record Office, particularly Clare Snoad; the National Theatre Archives; staff at *The Chichester Observer*; *The Argus, Brighton* and *The News, Portsmouth*. As always, my love and thanks to my husband, Greg Mosse – without his support and enthusiasm, little of anything much would be possible.

Last, but by no means least, a massive thank you to everybody at CFT who contributed to this book in whatever way – detective work, muscle power, dusty hours spent searching through boxes in their attics (or in the CFT store, never a pleasant experience). It is impossible to mention everyone by name – and I apologise for leaving anybody out – but special mention must go to those who gave me support and friendship during my two stints working at the theatre (1979 – 1981, 1998 – 2001): Janet Bakose, Jessica Blake-Lobb, Lucy Brett, Janet Capelin, Peter Clayton, Doreen Eastment, Alan Finch, Sally Garner-Gibbons, Sam Garner-Gibbons, Sarah Hammet, Colin Hedgecock, Barrie Hodgson, Wanda Hurley, Pat Kemp, John Knight, Sarah Mansell, Sally Mason, Karl Meier, Sharon Meier, James Morgan, Annemarie Nichols, Pat Packham, Debbie Plentie, the legendary Paul Rogerson, Dale Rooks, Rupert Rowbotham, Jan Saunders, Barbara Sherlock, Marian Stapley and Adrian Whitaker.

The fact that so many people have been so generous with their time, serves to illustrate the great affection and esteem in which CFT is held. But the final plaudits must go to two people – efficient, good humoured, inspiring – without whom the book could not have been written: Tim Bouquet, whose support and dogged hard work in carrying out the interviews, not to mention wrestling the thousands of words into manageable text, was invaluable and essential; and Project Administrator, Diane Goodman, who spent every waking hour tracking down photographs, copyright holders, images, newspaper cuttings and coordinating the project on behalf of CFT. She has been a star.

To all, my thanks.

Penelope Keith in *Entertaining Angels*, 2006.

Photo: Robert Day

Foreword

On March 17 1961 I was married to Laurence Olivier and we were living in New York, both acting in plays on Broadway – he in *Becket* and I in *A Taste of Honey* – when the letter arrived. It came from an optician in Chichester who said he was about to build a theatre and would Sir Laurence consider becoming its first Artistic Director. Neither of us knew Chichester and at any other time in the life of a world-famous actor/director such a request would have elicited only a polite refusal. However, by a million-to-one chance this seemingly impossible shot in the dark found its target. It caught Larry at the moment he had started saying 'what can I find that is new and challenging?' And came, as he described it, 'like God's gift from heaven'.

On our first visit to Chichester we were met by Leslie Evershed-Martin, the author of the letter, who took us to Oaklands Park where we gazed at a big muddy hole in the ground with six upright drain pipes marking the hexagonal shape of the theatre-to-be. As the building took shape, Larry threw himself tirelessly into the details of planning and of choosing the plays for the first season and the actors to perform in them. Some were famous, some destined to be so, all delighted to be part of such an exciting adventure.

By 1962 the Festival Theatre, looking picturesque in its parkland setting, was ready to open its doors. When we stepped onto the stage on the first day of rehearsal there was a sudden feeling of apprehension as we realised how exposed we were going to be. Gone was the safety of the proscenium

Joan Plowright and Laurence Olivier at the Chichester Festival Theatre Thanksgiving service, June 3 1962.

Photo: Chichester Photographic Collection/ West Sussex Record Office

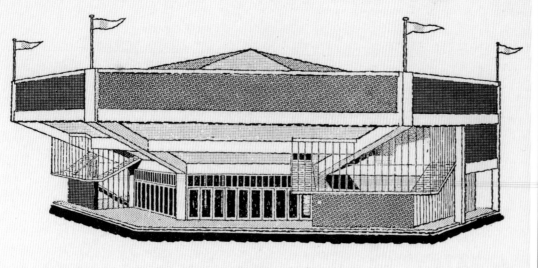

WHEN the Theatre is completed (early in 1962) you will see a building of great charm and originality, perfectly related to its parkland setting. But it will also be a building of great importance in the world of drama to-day.

The design is unique—hexagonal in plan, with the auditorium cantilevered over the foyer and a remarkable single-span roof. The seating will be for 1,400 and no member of the audience will be more than 20 rows from the stage.

If you would like to know more about this exciting theatre, call at the Theatre Centre (by the Cross) where you can see a scale model and plans, and where you will be given full information about the various committees, the Society, and future activities. Or write for a brochure to: The Appeal Secretary, Chichester Festival Theatre, South Street, Chichester.

An information tent is also available here to-day for your enquiries.

Arundel Castle Ball programme, May 1961.

Image: West Sussex Record Office

Joan Plowright in *Saint Joan*, 1963.

Photo: Angus McBean

arch where you could turn your back on the audience to deal with an escaping hairpiece or to hide a fit of the giggles. Everything could be seen by somebody somewhere.

The first play of the opening season was a forgotten Restoration comedy, *The Chances*, which had been a favourite of Samuel Pepys and was a riot of colour, movement and music. I played Constantia but, as I was carrying my second child, my gynaecologist was appalled to see me hurtling down the steps of one vomitorium and up the steps of the other and dancing a jig on the stage. The audience enjoyed the evening but the critics did not share Mr Pepys' enthusiasm. The second play, *The Broken Heart* by John Ford, fared even worse with the critics. There was a general feeling of hurt, puzzlement and despondency in the company, for it seemed as

if the new theatre itself was being rejected, as well as the productions.

So it was in the spirit of 'Custer's Last Stand' that we waited to go on for the opening night of *Uncle Vanya*. Someone had asked Larry that day if he had slept well the night before. 'Oh yes,' he replied, 'like the man in the condemned cell, I spent a night untroubled by hope.' As it turned out he need not have been so hard on himself. The evening was a triumph, vindicating the Theatre and saving Larry's reputation and returning to packed houses for a second season.

Looking back on fifty years many a reputation has been built at Chichester. I have many happy memories of returning, particularly to play *Saint Joan*, as Katherina opposite Anthony Hopkins [in Jonathan Miller's production of *The Taming of the Shrew*] and with Maggie Smith in

The Way of the World. Chichester has become a favourite place for young actors and directors to do innovative or experimental work, often resulting in transfers to London, feeding the West End theatres and going on tours across the UK and abroad. It is also the place where actors who found fame in film and television, such as Patrick Stewart, can flex their muscles, go back to 'the real stuff' and do an acclaimed Macbeth.

Chichester has this marvellous opportunity to present six or seven new shows a year and this turnover of plays keeps the audience engaged and enthusiastic. The announcement of every new Festival season is awaited with as much anticipation and excitement as Larry's first – and I say that as somebody who was part of that first season and is now a frequent visitor to the Festival Theatre.

This book is the story of the many people who made the first fifty years of Chichester Festival Theatre so remarkable. That muddy hole has become a successful theatre complex and a landmark that has put a lovely city on a wider map. I wish that the next half century will be just like the 2011 season, with critical acclaim, a wide variety of plays, wonderful actors, writers, directors and choreographers and all enjoyed by packed houses.

Happy anniversary and here's to the next fifty.

Joan Plowright

DAME JOAN PLOWRIGHT,
The Lady Olivier

Joan Plowright and Laurence Olivier in *Uncle Vanya,* **1962.**
Photo: Angus McBean

Joan Plowright and Anthony Hopkins in *The Taming of the Shrew,* **1972.**
Photo: John Timbers/ArenaPAL

Prologue

'We do not remember days; we remember moments.'

THE BURNING BRAND
Cesare Pavese

This book is a love letter. My affair with Chichester Festival Theatre – CFT, as it's affectionately known – has lasted my whole life. I was born a couple of months after the foundation stone was laid in 1961 and moved to Chichester, with my parents, a couple of months after the first season in 1962. In 1963, my father Richard Mosse, once an actor and now a junior partner in a law firm, walked across from his office in West Street, knocked on the door of the Theatre's Founder, Leslie Evershed-Martin, and offered his services. He became Company Secretary to the Board in 1965 and from that point onwards, the Theatre was part of our day-to-day lives.

The Festival Theatre was where I saw my first live play, with real moving and breathing actors on a stage. It was where I first performed – inadequately on the recorder, not so badly on the violin – in local school concerts and youth orchestra galas. It was the place of my first 'proper' paid job in 1979 – as an usherette front of house selling ice creams and programmes during my A levels. And, as chance would have it, my last proper job too, as Administrative Director from 1998 – 2001. Now, in 2012, this book.

My affection for CFT, the way it's always been there as a backdrop to life, is not unusual – audience members and actors, directors and designers, production staff, board members, critics, autograph hunters, local businessmen and women, parents and grandparents, most everybody remembers

Chichester Festival Theatre Foyer, 1975.

Photo: Sam Lambert

the first time they came to CFT and what they saw. On every page, this warmth for the Theatre, the sense of it being special, different, unique, comes up time and again. It's partly to do with the fairytale nature of the founding and building of the Theatre, a glorious dream made a reality in concrete and glass. But mostly, I'd say, the enduring affection Cicestrians (by birth or adoption) feel for their 'impossible theatre' is down to the fact that it was, and remains, a theatre built by the community, for the community. As the current Artistic Director Jonathan Church says: 'the ownership spreads out from the stage and into the auditorium'. And it was done on a shoestring, the art of the possible, a theatre constructed brick by brick from the bottom up as and when the money came in.

So what makes CFT so special? The ambition of it, the dazzling and brave architectural design of it; the glory of the open-latticed steelwork of the lighting rig above the audience's head ('the night sky'), the open-plan auditorium where each face is visible to the actors and to the rest of the audience; the magnificent thrust stage fashioned from Canadian maple wood, protruding like sides of a 50-pence piece, into the purple and green; the wonderful production photographs that decorate the foyer; the seaside white-wooden clapperboard and strips of glass; the rough concrete pillars and painted soffit-stepped ceiling; the way the shadows dance along the façade at night.

In the old days, the foyer of the Festival Theatre was grey-vinyl tile rather than carpet – the sounds of the bar and ladies' high heels snapped sharp and obtrusive in the auditorium – but the atmosphere, the smell of it, the hushed welcome hasn't changed so very much in fifty years. The memory of the moment when

Set design for 'Scott writes', Terra Nova', 1980.

Designer: Pamela Howard

I was six, walking up through the vomitorium of Door 1 to see *An Italian Straw Hat* [1967]. Small hands in large, wearing a red-velvet party dress and black-patent party shoes. That sense of excitement and expectation at being on the verge of a different world, a world where time stands suspended – like the Pevensey children stepping into Narnia – has not faded. And more than fifty years later, looking around at the audience on a Saturday matinee, you spy that same glint of reminiscence on other people's faces and wonder if they too, perhaps, are remembering the first time they came to CFT and sat in the auditorium and waited for the house lights to go down. The ghosts of all those who have walked in these same spaces are all around. The air echoing with the memory of voices, with footsteps long gone.

Over the past half century there have, of course, been changes, though the spirit of CFT remains steadfast. The Minerva Theatre, with 283 seats (as against 1206 – originally 1360 – in the Main House) opened in 1989. Gunter's – the iconic white hut at the entrance to the site where, in the 1960s and 1970s, audiences chose from a smorgasbord of open sandwiches – has been replaced by bespoke rehearsal rooms. There's a restaurant and an upstairs cafe in the Minerva building instead, where the Learning and Participation and Youth Theatre offices can also be found. But the view up along and across Oaklands Park, the mixture of hawthorn and hazel, blackthorn, rowan and oak, remains much the same as on that blowsy day in May 1961 when Princess Alexandra came to lay the foundation stone.

The particular life and times of CFT holds a mirror up to the story of post-war British theatre.

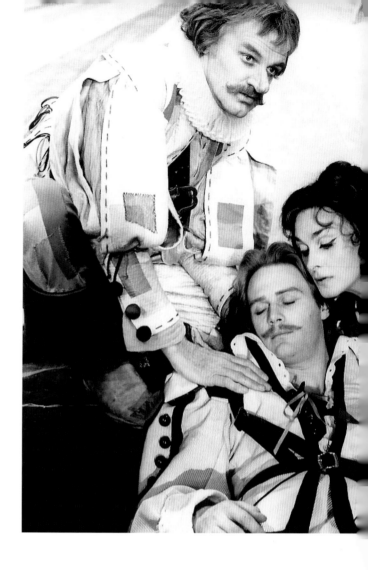

The struggles to make ends meet, the tension between public funding and private philanthropy, the fashioning of entertainment in a world where competition for the leisure pound grew stiffer, blunter, with each passing decade. Here too, writ large, are the perennial battles between commercial success and artistic excellence, how best to balance the books, how to keep satisfied your loyal audience at the same time as encouraging new faces to venture into the concrete-and-glass foyer. There are principals and supporting players, heroes and villains on (and off) the stage, backroom boys and girls – without whom no show would ever go on. Across the pages stride the major characters of British theatre – and some from further afield. Those who started their careers here and moved on, as well as those who have given much of their working life to Chichester through good times

and bad, the glory days and the dog days. Actors and directors, of course, but also set designers, lighting and sound and fight directors, choreographers, wardrobe mistresses and wig masters, those who care for the building and those who keep watch at stage door. What they have in common is each shares the same belief that there is something special about CFT.

Of course everyone has their favourite productions, the shows that mean most to them. Hundreds of moments, memories of a particular scene that sent a shiver down the spine: for me, they include Sarah Badel in *An Italian Straw Hat* [1967]; Keith Michell in *Oedipus Tyrannus* [1974], alone on that vast and open stage with bloodied eyes; the glint and clash of swords in *Cyrano de Bergerac* [1975] and Michele Dotrice's wistful Viola in *Twelfth Night* [1976]; the awful beauty of Ted Tally's *Terra Nova* [1980], watched

most nights from inside Door 6; the wild despair of Alan Bates in *A Patriot for Me* [1983]; the clear-eyed idealism of Anna Carteret in George Bernard Shaw's *Major Barbara* [1988], the glamour of Natalia Makarova in *Tovarich* [1991] and Zoe Wanamaker's astonishing *Electra* [1996].

Back working again at CFT as Administrative Director from 1998-2001, the joy of *Song of Singapore* [1998] with Issy van Randwyck and a nifty ukulele, David Hare's *Racing Demon*, the glorious community spirit on stage in Roger Redfarn's *The Barchester Chronicles* or Joss Ackland's towering performance as Captain Shotover. Later, Edward Kemp's superb adaptation of *The Master and Margarita* [2004], Michael Feast gloriously camp and diabolical as the Devil; begging a house seat in the Minerva to see Patrick Stewart in *Macbeth* [2007]; or one of only a handful of watchers at the first preview of Lucy Prebble's astonishing *ENRON* [2009], a play that was to go on to take Chichester and London by storm. Most recently, *Top Girls* and the aching pathos of *The Deep Blue Sea* and the perfection of *Singin' in the Rain* [2011].

But, this is not a history. Those hoping for in-depth analysis of figures and funding settlements, arguments or graphs detailing box office receipts (and losses!) will be disappointed. It is, rather, an affectionate portrait in words and pictures. A celebration of moments, in the first fifty years of the wonderful – the impossible – theatre that is CFT.

Kate Mosse.

KATE MOSSE, Chichester, April 2012

The Story Begins

'So to put it very simply, I started it off, John Clements made it good, future directors may swing its fortunes this way or that, but the credit for the fact that the place exists at all will always belong to the man who wrote the book that follows.'

PROLOGUE
The Impossible Theatre
Laurence Olivier

T he story of the founding of Chichester Festival Theatre is well known, at least to those with an affection or long relationship with the Theatre. But fifty years after that first Summer Season – under the auspices of the first (of nineteen) Artistic Directors, Laurence Olivier – it is worth reminding ourselves of quite how extraordinary an achievement it is that a world-class theatre should have been built in Chichester, a modest cathedral city on the south coast of England, some 60 miles south of London.

On the evening of Sunday 4 January 1959, Leslie Evershed-Martin – a local ophthalmic surgeon and former Mayor of Chichester – was at home with his wife Carol and his grown-up sons, David and Barry. A blustery sou' westerly was whistling over the rooftops of West Street, the fire was lit. Then, the voice of Huw Weldon talking to the Theatre Producer, Tyrone Guthrie about a new theatre in Stratford, Ontario. Evershed-Martin put down his book and gave the documentary his undivided attention as Guthrie explained how their theatre had come about, step by step and brick by brick. 'If they can do that in Canada,' he said when the programme was over, 'why can't we do it here in Chichester?'

In *The Impossible Theatre* and *The Miracle Theatre*, Evershed-Martin writes of how the ember of that idea sparked and caught light. How over the next two-and-a-half years, endless meetings with the Town Clerk and Chichester City Council, with Tyrone Guthrie, with townspeople and landed gentry, fire officers

All quotations in this chapter from Evershed-Martin and Olivier, unless otherwise specified, are taken from *The Impossible Theatre* or *The Miracle Theatre*.

Actor Andre Morell and Joan Greenwood, *Tatler*, 4 July 1962.

Courtesy of Tatler/ Mary Evans Picture Library

The Theatre Shop by the Cross, Arundel Castle Ball programme, May 1961.

West Sussex Record Office

David and Sophie Shalit, 1960.

Courtesy of Mr and Mrs Shalit

and publicity officers, he and a small band of advocates worked tirelessly to gain support, to acquire land, to raise money, to win hearts and minds.

To build a theatre.

His vision was for a seasonal festival of theatre held over the summer, taking place in a modern, ambitious, dynamic space, inspired by the revolutionary design of the theatre in Canada. The site chosen, eventually, was in parkland to the north of the city, with a car park to be situated on grassland on the traditional location of Sloe Fair Field.

In August 1959, Evershed-Martin had a meeting with the architect son of a Canon of the cathedral. Philip Powell and his partner Hidalgo Moya had devised the prize-winning symbol for the 1951 Festival of Britain – the glorious Skylon on London's South Bank – and, after a certain amount of 'will they, won't they?', they agreed to come up with a design.

'The only brief I gave was that it must be a building to hold at least 1400; it must be an amphitheatre with a thrust type of stage with the audience on at least two sides; and it must be as cheap as possible, because I should have to obtain all the money from the public.'

The idea was that the performance space should combine ancient Greek and Roman precedents with elements of Elizabethan theatre. It was to be, as Laurence Olivier later was to say: 'an actor's theatre'. And all this in the county town of West Sussex, a city only by virtue of its cathedral, its history writ large in its Roman remains and Georgian red brick façades. Folly or madness or 'vaulting ambition, which o'erleaps itself,' only time would tell.

During 1960 and 1961, raising money was the name of the game. Secretaries and fundraisers, a Development Fund and a London Committee, this was to be a theatre for the community, built by the community. The legacy of this is still in evidence fifty years later, as the current Artistic Director, Jonathan Church, says:

'Many of the children of the people who raised

The roof structure being built, winter 1961.

West Sussex Record Office/Chichester Photographic Service

the money to build this theatre come back to this neck of the woods to raise their families. They then come to this theatre as 40-something-year-olds and they bring their children. There is a sense of ownership that the act of the community building a theatre has given down the generations and we benefit from that history.'

The names of the Founder Members – all of whom donated £100 – were inscribed on a board in the foyer, much as the names of the support-

ers of this book are printed in the back here. For Chichester, the principle of crowd funding – though in 1962 it was not a term anyone would have used – has held good. Now, as then.

The months went by in a helter-skelter dash to raise the £105,000 needed. The skeleton of what was to become the first Board of Trustees started to take shape, including Lord Bessborough, Teddy Smith, Alan Draycott and Henny Gestetner (mother of Sophie Shalit). Jumble sales, coffee

mornings, champagne teas, all organised by the ladies of the Theatre Society. In 1960, a Bonfire Night in Walberton and a Theatrical Night in Pulborough, where guests were served by Vivien Leigh and Ian Carmichael, Kenneth More and Norman Wisdom!

Conversations continued, with Peter Hall and his wife, Lesley Caron, with Peggy Ashcroft, with Alec Guinness and Anthony Quayle, as well as Dame Sybil Thorndike and Sir Lewis Casson, both of whom would go on to join the 1961 company.

In January 1961, having spent a few days in County Monaghan with Tyrone Guthrie and his wife, Evershed-Martin sat down to consider who might be approached as the inaugural Artistic Director. One of the names not on the list was Laurence Olivier. Evershed-Martin reports Guthrie as saying: 'Leslie, you keep on and on about only having the best of everything at Chichester, so why don't you go for the best... Ask him.'

A letter was sent, outlining the story so far. Weeks of silence followed until, in February, a response arrived from America, from Olivier himself asking if he would have full artistic freedom in the selection of the plays, directors and designers? Evershed-Martin said yes. Olivier also wished to know if he might have a say in the design of the actual stage area. Again, the answer was yes and Philip Powell was asked to provide detailed plans, information and sketches.

Over the next few weeks, more meetings – with agents, with lawyers – until, finally, an offer was made. A salary of £5000 per annum was proposed. Olivier would only accept £3000, saying to Evershed-Martin that he wanted to be: 'all-in-all with us in the adventure'.

On Tuesday 13 March, a press conference was held and the extraordinary news – that Sir Laurence Olivier was to be the Artistic Director of Chichester Festival Theatre – was announced. Lady Olivier, in her Foreword, explains how the timing was right and so the invitation fell upon receptive ears. When, later, he was asked why he had accepted the job, Olivier also said:

'I found it immensely touching in this day and age that perfectly private people could want a thing so badly as the people of Chichester wanted this theatre.'

Setbacks and triumphs, money and problems with building permissions, the cost of materials outstripping the funds available to pay for them, a week before Princess Alexandra was due to come to lay the foundation stone, arguments over guarantees to the builders were still threatening to derail the project. Trustees were, again, called upon to increase their liabilities. Again, they did.

Friday 12 May dawned bright and blue and glorious, the sort of early summer day that arrives in Sussex after a spell of grey weather. Schoolchildren and well wishers, wide-brimmed hats and gloves and the Band of the Royal Marines. One hundred pupils from Chichester High School for Girls, in their pleated bottle-green skirts, white-and-beige-striped shirts and ties. Laurence Olivier and his wife, Joan Plowright, were still in America, but in the line to be presented to Princess Alexandra by Evershed-Martin, were the poet and playwright, Christopher Fry, the Duke and Duchess of Norfolk, Lord and Lady Bessborough and the Lord Bishop of Chichester.

Martlet swordsmen and folk dancers ribboned in yellow and white. Actor John Neville – who was to be part of Olivier's inaugural 1962 Company – delivered a poem written for the occasion by Christopher Fry.

'Now here, in a bare place,
with one stone laid,
Suppose our theatre built,
you in your places,

In these few halting words a drama played,
And in my face a stage of actors' faces.'

Sonnet for the Oration
CHRISTOPHER FRY

Later that evening, a fundraising ball at Arundel Castle where the iconic design of Minerva's head, within a hexagon, was unveiled for the first time in the Gala Programme. The artist David Goodman[1], in a note explaining the choice of Minerva (the Roman counterpart of Athene), said she had been chosen both as a way of honouring the city's Roman past and the classical Greek design of the amphitheatre, but also

[1] David Goodman – a celebrated local artist and President and Founder (in 1983) of the Chichester Society - is one of only a handful of people remaining who have been involved with CFT since its founding.

Minerva, a symbol for the Theatre. Arundel Castle Ball programme, 1961.
West Sussex Record Office

OPPOSITE
Princess Alexandra performs stone-laying ceremony. 12 May 1961.
The Argus, Brighton/West Sussex Record Office

Vivien Leigh at Mason's, Pulborough fundraising event, 1961.
Courtesy of Evershed-Martin Family archive

**Laurence Olivier
at the topping
out ceremony,
November 1961.**

Chichester Photographic
Collection/West Sussex
Record Office

as she was the 'goddess of the arts and sciences and associated with skill, wit and intelligence.' There was also, for the cost of a 1/- raffle ticket, a 'Win a Bungalow' competition.

It was not until late June that Laurence Olivier and Joan Plowright came to Chichester to meet Leslie Evershed-Martin for the first time. It was the beginning of a long and enduring relationship, stormy at times, but built on mutual respect and admiration for one another's achievements. David Evershed-Martin[1], remembers Olivier:

'There were two sides to him. Jekyll and Hyde totally, but a marvellous man, absolutely fantastic man. I had terrific respect for him. Of course he played up to my mother all the time and she loved it! My father had to get on with him, but on the whole very successfully; just the odd blip.'

For the summer and autumn months of 1961, the building rose rapidly in the shadow of the horseshoe of 170-feet-tall elm trees in Oaklands Park. According to reports in the *Chichester Observer* in September 1961, it became something of a local pilgrimage site, especially at weekends. Picnickers and architectural tourists, daytrippers with sandwiches and flasks of coffee and Brownie Starflash cameras, coming to see how much had changed since the week before.

The next milestone was the topping out ceremony on Thursday 23 November. Photographs show a damp and misty day, Olivier sharing a cigarette with the workmen. Ladders and scaffolding, trailing wires and, beneath the spider's web of iron and steel, the distinctive hexagon of Powell and Moya's creation. The theatre flag was flying to show the highest point of the building had been reached as Olivier and Evershed-Martin climbed up, and up again, into the skeleton roof.

Olivier's vision was that the Theatre would run for a summer season – a festival – producing several shows to run in repertoire, sharing the same ensemble cast. On Wednesday 10 January 1962, almost three years to the day when Evershed-Martin had seen Tyrone Guthrie on television, the first Festival was announced. A nine-week season of three plays – *The Chances* by John Fletcher, John Ford's *The Broken Heart* and *Uncle Vanya* by Anton Chekhov – all directed by Olivier himself, who would also play in the last two. The Company was to include Lewis Casson, Fay Compton, Joan Greenwood, Rosemary Harris, Keith Michell, John Neville, Joan Plowright, Sir Michael Redgrave, Athene Seyler and Dame Sybil Thorndike.[2]

The following six months was a pell-mell headlong dash to appoint the creative teams – designers, make-up artists, front-of-house staff, the army of behind-the-scenes girls and boys responsible for delivering the opening season – and to find places for them to work. The costume department was a first-floor room at the Unicorn Hotel, at the end of East Street [now the offices of the *Chichester Observer*].

David Evershed-Martin remembers being allowed to go in and watch:

'There was nowhere to clean the costumes, so they painted and repainted them.'

One of the actors in Olivier's opening Company was Keith Michell, playing Don John to John Neville's Don Frederick in Fletcher's Jacobean comedy, *The Chances*. Michell remembers his first visit to see the Theatre taking shape:

'We [the Company] came to Chichester in a

---

[1] The oldest son of the Founder, David Evershed-Martin was involved with CFT for his entire life, both as a Trustee and a member of the Board. He died in 2010.

[2] Olivier's 1962 company, and those of 1963, 1964 and 1965, were to form the nucleus of the new National Theatre Company, based at the Old Vic Theatre from 1963 (until moving to their permanent home on London's South Bank in 1976). The news was announced in the press on the opening night of the Festival Theatre 1962 season and although Olivier's appointment as Artistic Director was not made public until 3 August, gossip was rife that he was to be offered the position.

bus, saw the Theatre and looked around. It was an incredibly exciting shape. It was built but not finished; they were still putting bits on like hinges and things. We had a good walk around inside and out, and then we rehearsed the plays in situ.'

In *The Impossible Theatre*, Evershed-Martin quotes a journalist from *The Times* writing about his first view of the auditorium in May 1962:

'To walk round Chichester Festival Theatre is to have the feeling that, when it opens, Sir Laurence Olivier's Company will enter from one side and the audience from another, to meet, as friends do, and to spend the evening together, as friends do, while the play lasts.'

On Monday 29 May, with the building completed and with rehearsals in full swing, another last-minute hiccup with the theatre license and compliance with the fire regulations. After weeks of snagging and banging, adapting and tweaking – and with the opening night weeks away – the magistrates refused to grant the licence.

Clifford Hodgetts, then a junior solicitor on the Chichester Committee in the 1960s[1], takes up the story:

'So Leslie [Evershed-Martin] came up with the idea that Olivier had better take the magistrates on a tour of inspection of the building, so that "they can understand and get to see what it is all about". This is where Olivier was at his absolute best and, of course, he had them eating out of his hand... We instructed a barrister, who also put on a great show, and they granted the licence no more than a week before it was due to open.'

As the Opening Night drew closer, the pressures on company and crew were immense. Keith Michell – who was to be the third Artistic Director of CFT – remembers the last few

---

[1] Hodgetts was to become a Trustee in the 1980s and in 1997 became Deputy Chairman of the Trust Company. In 2003, when the Productions and Trust Company Boards were merged, he was appointed Deputy Chairman of the Board, a position he still holds.

days of rehearsal and dress rehearsal:

'The stage was vast – although I have always loved that sense of space and the freedom it gives you – and the acoustics were not great, so you had to speak up, and you had to come to terms with acting with your back to a part of the audience at any one time. But that camaraderie in the Company was marvellous. We were all terribly focused on getting it right for that first night.'

All eyes were on Chichester, theatrical agents and commentators, ink-slingers and editors. On Sunday 1 July, T S Ferguson wrote in the *Sunday Telegraph*:

'Chichester's new Festival Theatre will open on Tuesday largely because Mr Leslie Evershed-Martin did not know that the whole thing was quite impossible... Of course it was impossible to build the theatre in Chichester, just because that's where Mr Evershed-Martin lives... but that's where it is. It was impossible to get the money for it... but the money has been raised. And when he asked who was the best man to run the theatre he was told "Sir Laurence Olivier, but that's probably impossible." Olivier is now in charge, working all the hours of the day, and with a cast list that reads like an extract from a theatrical *Who's Who*.'

On Monday 2 July, the dress rehearsal for *The Chances* was held in the restaurant set up by David Enders and John Glenn at the north-west corner of the site (known affectionately as Gunter's, after Payne & Gunter who took it over in 1984) serving smorgasbord (Danish open sandwiches) and strawberries and cream. For more than twenty years, the business of going to the restaurant in the interval to choose one's two choices, then arriving back after the show to find them waiting at the table, was a key part of the CFT experience.

The following day, Tuesday 3 July 1962 – with the world's press, local dignitaries and supporters in attendance – the Opening Night

Scenic artist
Vanessa Clarke
flat out after
hectic last-minute
preparations.
Tatler, 4 July 1962.

Courtesy of Tatler/Mary
Evans Picture Library

Photo: Chichester
Photographic Collection/
West Sussex Record Office

finally arrived. Memories of that evening remain sharp, distinct, for many who were there, including Barry Evershed-Martin, the younger son of CFT's Founder:

'We drove to the Theatre at six o'clock, wearing dinner jackets and the ladies in long evening dresses, where we were met by many excited people waiting to see the celebrities arrive… The voice of Laurence Olivier came through the loud speakers inviting everyone to take their seats. Everyone moved to the doors for the stairs. It was the first time most people had seen inside of the theatre, and marvelled at the space and the stage being so close.'

The demand for tickets could have filled the Theatre three times over. Outside, a chorus of well wishers, photographers and journalists thronged around on the pavements, diamond squares and block, spilled onto the grass and the spaces beneath the canopy.

Brian Wingate – then a 12-year-old autograph hunter, whose passion for CFT started when watching Princess Alexandra laying the foundation stone – was in the crowd. He has the signatures of virtually all cast members from the Olivier seasons and many of the visiting stars since then.

'I remember a limousine sweeping in containing John Mills and his family. Teddy Smith[1] arrived with his usual entourage in a Rolls. There

was a sea of dinner jackets and gowns, quite incredible to me. Chichester had never seen anything like it.'

The guests made their way into the foyer, seeing for the first time the bush-hammered exposed concrete pillars, the white painted board and stepped white ceiling, the bar and the box office straight ahead, positioned between Doors 1 and 2. Everything was perfect, except for the lack of refreshments after the performance, something the newspapers, needless to say, did not fail to point out.

David Evershed-Martin: 'Father did things in style. He had Christopher Fry write a Prologue to be printed in the programme, the Royal Sussex Regimental Band and fireworks afterwards, little things that made the evening so special.'

At four minutes to seven, the glittering First Night audience in black tie and cocktail dresses walked from the gentle early evening sunshine of the foyer into the hushed green and purple auditorium. In their hands, a black and white, red and gold souvenir programme listing the plays and players, the designers – Beatrice Dawson, Roger Furse, Sean Kenny and Malcolm Pride – and with an introduction to the theatre written by Olivier. Christopher Fry's poem was printed in full:

'A theatre, speaking for the age
We live in, has an ancient need;
The link between audience and stage
For which I come to intercede…
So for a time we meet and share
The passions and humours of the heart,
To recognise our natures there,
And, at the evening's end, to part.
Until that time, however we may fare

---

[1] A member of the original Board, AT – Teddy – Smith served as Chairman from 1965. His 15-year record is about to be equalled, in 2012, by the current Chairman of the Board, Lord Young of Graffham.

VIP guests leaving Gunter's for the First Night performance, 3 July 1962.

Photo: Chichester Photographic Collection/ West Sussex Record Office

Our work, our hopes, our selves, are in your care.'

Prologue for Chichester Festival Theatre
CHRISTOPHER FRY

Over the speakers, next, a roll from the side-drum and the muffled sound of seats snapping shut as everyone stood for the National Anthem. Leslie Evershed-Martin and his wife Carol in the fourth row back, E33 and E34, with their sons David and Barry. Elsewhere, members of the Board and the Theatre Society – Henny Gestetner, Lord and Lady Bessborough, David Goodman and the Duchess of Norfolk, mayors and aldermen, actors and theatrical agents.

Then, after the dying notes of the chord of G major had faded, the house lights were dimmed. The audience heard spoken the opening words of the first play, in the inaugural season at Chichester Festival Theatre:

'And some sit here, I doubt not, dare aver
Living he made that house a theatre
Which he pleased to frequent;'

The Chances
JOHN FLETCHER

The CFT journey had begun.

The 1960s

Artistic Directors
LAURENCE OLIVIER (1962 – 1965)
JOHN CLEMENTS (1966 – 1973)

*'The most difficult character in comedy is that of a fool,
and he must be no simpleton who plays the part.'*

DON QUIXOTE
Miguel De Cervantes

The choice of John Fletcher's Jacobean comedy, *The Chances*, as the opening play of the 1962 season did not please everyone. Written around 1617, the plot was 'borrowed' from the Spanish playwright and poet, Miguel de Cervantes and although it was reputed to be a favourite of Samuel Pepys, the play had rarely been staged since the 19th century. A fact picked up by several critics when the season was announced in January 1962, including Alan Dent, the London *News Chronicle*'s 'ace theatre critic', who wrote to Olivier:

'How cute and characteristic and "devilish-sly" of you, Sir Lucifer, to choose Fletcher's *The Chances* for your opening. For it is an old play that no one has seen or read, and one which even the dramatic critics can hardly *pretend* to know.'

The opening night was a triumph in terms of the marriage of the town and the Theatre, the well-deserved sense of achievement and celebration, the glamour and admiration for the building itself. However, reviews for *The Chances* were mixed (though Olivier described the box office takings as 'quite merry'). And both box office and reviews for the second play of the season, *The Broken Heart*, were poor. It was, Olivier admitted, 'a dreadful flop' and it never played to more than 50 per cent. According to Keith Michell, Olivier remained sanguine:

'He [Olivier] was always ready for the worst. From our time together at Stratford [RSC], and Chichester was no different, during rehearsals he would go through every critic of the time and would predict what they

Laurence Olivier directing *The Chances*, 1962.

Photo: Angus McBean

Keith Michell in
The Broken Heart,
1962.

Photo: Angus McBean

would say... He was always dead on!'

However, this meant the burden on the third and final play of the opening nine-week season was immense. Rumours that Olivier was to be Artistic Director of the National Theatre had led to some critics questioning his ongoing commitment to CFT. In his Foreword to *The Impossible Theatre*, he wrote:

'I had never in my life faced a first night with more certainty of failure than I did that of our third offering, *Uncle Vanya*.'

Duncan Weldon – CFT Theatre Director from 1995 – 1997 (and a major partner in transferring shows from Chichester to London) – was then a young photographer just starting out. He was sent by *Vogue* to photograph Olivier at CFT in August 1962.

'I remember the actors got changed under the

theatre stage with a sheet pinned to a washing line separating the male actors from the female. As a 21-year-old, who could fail to be impressed by the calibre of actors either side of that sheet?'

The quality of the company notwithstanding, it was with a spirit of 'Custer's Last Stand' – as Joan Plowright puts it in her Foreword – that they prepared to open *Uncle Vanya* on Monday 16 July. Patricia Routledge CBE, one of CFT's most loved and popular actresses, was in the audience that night.

'I remember the first night of *Uncle Vanya* vividly because you sensed that the fortunes of the Theatre depended on it; the last production in the first year... Well, it was overwhelmingly wonderful. I came out in the interval and had to be given a good, strong gin and tonic, it was so moving!'

David Shalit, whose association with CFT goes back to 1960[1], felt similarly: 'There is a scene in the middle of the third act where you had Olivier (who was married to Joan Plowright) and Michael Redgrave, both acting to Plowright, and the emotion went up in spirals. Tears were running down my face and I looked around and saw tears running down many of the faces in an English audience... It has never happened to me before or since in a theatre.'

Michael Billington[2], now the UK's longest serving drama critic, was then working as the public liaison officer for Lincoln Theatre Company. On a hot July's afternoon, he drove from one

---

[1] A Trustee for many years and a sponsor, Shalit joined the board of the Productions Company and the Trust Company from 1998 – 2003, then was a member of the Development Board.

[2] Billington worked at *The Times*, then became Theatre Critic of *The Guardian* in 1971 and for *Country Life* in 1986. He is also the author of *State of the Nation: British Theatre Since 1945*, biographies of Harold Pinter and Peggy Ashcroft and critical studies of Stoppard and Ayckbourn and Ken Dodd, among other writings.

GREAT TRIUMPH FOR ALL CONCERNED

WAVE after wave of applause which resounded round Chichester Festival Theatre last night at the end of the first public performance in the £100,000 building, signified a night of triumph for all concerned with the project.

The cast of 30 were unable to leave the stage for several minutes as the enthusiastic first-nighters paid homage to their skill—and heralded the arrival of a completely new conception of dramatic art in Britain.

The general mood was summed up by the man responsible for the Theatre's birth, its founder, Chichester businessman, Mr. Leslie Evershed-Martin.

As he toured the dressing rooms after the performance, a jubilant but somewhat over-whelmed and disbelieving figure, Mr. Evershed-Martin took time off to give his impressions to an Evening News reporter.

"Tonight has vindicated all our hopes and dreams," he declared "It has proved that the Festival Theatre just had to be." He added: "It has also illustrated what can be accomplished with an arena stage . . . . it is the opening of a new era."

Social occasion

The theatre opening was a gay and glittering social occasion. Ambassadors rubbed shoulders with city tycoons, film, stage, and television personalities chatted gaily with high-ranking clergymen, foreign diplomats, and the inevitable influx of American tourists.

One of the coolest of those responsible for the success was undoubtedly Sir Laurence Olivier, the Theatre director.

Having congratulated his actress wife Joan Plowright for her outstandingly successful performance in "The Chances," Sir Laurence told a long succession of enthusiastic well-wishers: "It has been very gratifying to see that everything has gone so well."

While Sir Laurence was chatting to old friends Mr. and Mrs. John Mills and their vivacious teen-age daughter, Hayley, herself an international star, Lady Olivier was being congratulated in her dressing room by Dame Sybil Thorndike, who will herself be appearing at the Theatre during the season. "You were wonderful," said Dame Sybil—an opinion shared by all members of the audience.

Replied Miss Plowright: "I feel relaxed for the first time in months. We all seem to have been working so hard for so long, and now that the first night is over I feel all the tension has lifted."

Among the audience were the Duchess of Norfolk, Lord and Lady Bessborough, Mr. George A. Drew (High Commissioner for Canada) and Mrs. Drew, Sir David Eccles (Minister of Education) and Lady Eccles, and the Bishop of Chichester (Dr. Roger Wilson) and Mrs. Wilson.

The Mayor and Mayoress of Chichester (Coun. and Mrs. J. Selsby) were hosts to the remaining 10 Mayors and Mayoresses in Sussex.

Telegrams

On a backstage notice board near the dressing rooms were pinned more than 30 good luck telegrams from theatre managements, stage personalities, and persons connected with the theatre's development.

Among the crowds who milled round the dressing rooms to congratulate the stars were many of the actors and actresses who will appear in the other two productions at the theatre this season.

Only one snag arose to mar the festivities—a celebration party for cast, staff, and invited guests, had to be cancelled at the last moment because the supply of drink failed to arrive.

Comments

The following were first-night comments given by members of the cast and audience to an Evening News reporter after the performance:—

John Neville (who portrayed Don Frederick): "One of the greatest experiences of my life. This Theatre is surely here to stay."

John Mills: "A wonderful first night. I wish I had been acting in it."

Hayley Mills (sipping a glass of water as Daddy chatted with Sir Laurence: "Simply smashing."

Kathleen Harrison: "Before the performance I felt very tense. The idea of performing on an arena stage with the audience so close was a little frightening, but now it is over I feel wonderfully happy."

Mr. Evershed-Martin: "Tonight's success has far exceeded all I dreamed for. Sir Laurence's direction added the touch of genius."

Mrs. Evershed-Martin: "I am too thrilled to even talk about it."

Dame Sybil Thorndyke at the C[hichester] [ope]ning night.—E.N.9027.

---

cathedral city to another for a matinee of *The Broken Heart* and an evening performance of *Uncle Vanya*.

'It's interesting, fifty years on, if anyone says to me what is the greatest production of your theatre-going lifetime, that is the one I always pluck from my memory... I can actually still hear the inflections of Redgrave's Vanya – "exquisite autumn roses" he cries – when he comes in and sees Astrov [Olivier] kissing Elena [Rosemary Harris]... It remains one of the golden memories.'

The critics agreed. Harold Hobson of the *Sunday Times* later described it as: 'the admitted master achievement in British twentieth-century theatre', while the *New Yorker* subsequently was to call it: 'probably the best *Vanya* in English we shall ever see'.

The sense of glamour promised on that Opening Night, took root once more as people queued for tickets. Journalists often wrote as much about the Theatre as the productions themselves. Scrutiny was sharp, as recorded in *The Stage*.

'Never before in modern times has such a theatre, with an open stage and a tiered auditorium in which all seats are virtually of equal value for one's enjoyment of the show, been built in a part of this country where no theatre ever stood before. And never have we known a new theatrical venture under the artistic direction of an actor-manager of the stature and experience of Olivier.'

There was a palpable sense of Chichester being, suddenly, at the glorious heart of things. The crowds at stage door began to grow, autograph hunter Brian Wingate among them:

'Olivier was my first autograph, he always signed "L. Olivier". He was quite aloof, would drive right up to the stage door and sweep into

Courtesy of *The News*, Portsmouth, 4 July 1962. West Sussex Record Office

the Theatre, very much the Artistic Director. Joan Plowright was much more approachable. Michael Redgrave always arrived carrying a briefcase, as though he was on his way to a meeting. John Neville would always ask me how I was.'

Christopher Doman, who took over as Company Secretary from my father, Richard Mosse, agrees that the Theatre changed the nature of the town: 'Chichester had been a small inward-looking place. The Theatre contributed greatly to it becoming an outward-looking place and even an international place, which it certainly wasn't when I was growing up.'

Everyone – the players and stage management, the theatre management and Board, the creative teams and backstage staff – knew they had, in the nick of time, a hit on their hands.

Both a critical triumph and a box office success, it would allow CFT to live to fight another day. A special Gala Performance in the presence of the Queen and Prince Philip, on Tuesday 31 July, helped reinforce the sense that CFT's fortunes were changing. However, the evening did not go entirely smoothly.

Derek Jacobi CBE – who, in addition to appearing in many productions at Chichester, was Joint Artistic Director with Duncan Weldon in 1995 and 1996 – remembers hearing stories of that Royal Visit.

'They decided they would give the two loos a lick of paint; one for her and one for the Duke of Edinburgh. They literally made them fit for a queen, then locked them so nobody would use them. During the interval, they decided they

Uncle Vanya **company and theatre staff, July 1962.**

Photo: Angus McBean

would indeed like to use the loos. Dame Sybil [Sybil Thorndike] was to escort the Duke and Olivier was to take the Queen. When they got to her loo, it was still locked and there was an urgent hunt for the keys. All very embarrassing. It took all of Olivier's powers of improvisation to fill the anxious wait with soothing words.'

Discomfort breaks notwithstanding, *Uncle Vanya* ran for 29 performances. Looking back, one can't help but imagine, on the final performance on Saturday 8 September, the sigh of relief, a catching of the breath, a dropping of the shoulders. And a wry smile on the faces of cast and crew backstage as Sonya's poignant closing lines floated out over the tannoy.

> 'We shall rejoice and look back at these troubles of ours with tenderness, with a smile, and we shall rest.'

Autumn came upon Chichester. The mag-nificent glass doors to the Theatre were shut, locked. The familiar brisk north wind chased leaves down the park, setting a drift of gold and copper and amber against the brown painted façade. The building was left alone, with only the horseshoe of sentinel elm trees keeping watch. The actors scattered, the directors, designers, creative teams, box office and bar staff, all went back to the lives they had been living before Chichester laid claim.

A theatre left abandoned is a desolate place. 'Rehearsal Call' notices left pinned on boards, messages in lipstick and greasepaint growing faint on dressing room mirrors, empty champagne bottles from the last-night party. Telegrams from theatrical agents and well wishes for productions now done, the memory of footsteps in the winding backstage corridors. No one left to read the 'Quiet Please' sign at the bottom of the stairs up to the stage, a sign which is still there in 2012.

Uncle Vanya, 1962.

Photo: Angus McBean

Alexander Hanson, Timothy West, Roger Allam, Dervla Kirwan, Maggie Steed, Lara Pulver and Anthony O'Donnell in *Uncle Vanya*, 2012.

Photo: Johan Persson

7 FRENCH SOLDIERS
✓✓ 7½/8 John Rogers
✓✓ 9 Michael Elphick
✓✓ 9 Martin Holdbrook
✓✓ 9 David Wood
✓✓ 9 Mark Penfold
✓✓ 9 Alex Funnell

✓ Cloak lining Brown 61 22yds
Brown Boots
✓ Ankle lights

MONKS
✓✓ 9½ Derek Jacobi, Brother Martin
✓✓ 6 Harry Lomax,
✓✓ 7½/8 John Rogers
✓✓ 8½ Peter O'Shaughnessy
✓✓ 8½ Richard Hampton
✓✓ 9 Peter Cellier
✓✓ 8½ Michael Rothwell
✓✓ 8 Keith Marsh
Sandals

TUNIC SKIRT
Lewis 23/9 48"
3½yds 4.3.2

✓ TUNIC
Burys S.I.S A90
6yds 19/6 60"
5.17.0

SLEEVES Etc.
Scopes 14sq.ft.app.
2/- per sq.ft.
18.0.0 app.

✓ CLOAK
Primavera

22yds

✓ ROBE
Russell &Chappell
5/-yd app.
31yds @ 36"
64yds @ 54"
24.14.7

✓ CLOAKS
D.&G. 15/9 54"
120yds app.
84.5.8

1963

Saint Joan costume swatch, 1963.

Designer Michael Annals/ National Theatre Archive

Michael Billington

Courtesy of *The Guardian*

The winter of 1962/1963 was the coldest on record. But even though the actors had gone, fundraising and promotion of CFT didn't stop. Built by the community, for the community, the need to keep momentum and raise enough money for next year's season – and the one after – kept the Trustees and members of the Theatre Society busy.

By January, Olivier was starting to put together his second Festival and immediately ran into difficulties with Leslie Evershed-Martin. Richard Mosse, Company Secretary to the Board [1965 – 1997], is one of several people who talk of the infamous row in the theatre restaurant between the two men, when Olivier announced his decision to revive his triumphant production of *Uncle Vanya*, with the same cast, for the 1963 season.

Richard Mosse: ' "I am adamant, you will not do it," Leslie told him. [Olivier] drew himself up and said: "Don't you tell me what to do in my theatre! The Artistic Director, whoever he is, has the final say in what is played on that stage and the Board cannot object." That was a rule laid down, and a very important rule in how the Theatre is run to this day.'

Olivier got his way and the season was announced, opening with George Bernard Shaw's *Saint Joan*, closing with John Arden's 1963 play *The Workhouse Donkey*, and the revival of *Uncle Vanya* as the middle production.

In general terms, the challenge for Olivier was two-fold. First, to build on the successes of the 1962 season without sacrificing the ambitions and aims that had inspired the project, but learn from the mistakes. Second, to use the extraordinary space to its best advantage to create exceptional theatre and persuade the 'head-waggers' that it was a stage for all seasons.

Michael Billington: '[CFT] was ahead of its time by introducing the dynamics of the thrust stage to British theatre... Now, of course, you wouldn't dream of building a theatre without that kind of space, but my point is Chichester was in the vanguard. Everyone was worried before the theatre opened that it was only going to be suitable for big epics. But what [*Vanya*] showed was, with an intelligent design, you could actually do a domestic play on that big stage too.'

There had been problems with the acoustics, a mixture of actors finding their feet and the pitch of their voices – several reviews of the 1962 season talk of the inaudibility of certain players – but also the 'dry, dead' atmosphere inside the auditorium in general. Three baffle boards were erected on each side of the stage. There was nothing to be done about the absence of an orchestra pit, something already seen as a

Joan Plowright in
Saint Joan, **1963.**
Photo: Angus McBean

Joan Plowright in
***Saint Joan**, 1963.*

Photo: Angus McBean

flaw in the design delivered on a shoestring, but over the winter various running repairs to the performance space were carried out.[1]

There was also the additional headache for the Board concerning Olivier's appointment as Artistic Director of the new National Theatre Company. Olivier gave assurances that he would remain in Chichester for a few seasons more, but everyone knew that his continuing association with CFT was essential to the Theatre's long-term survival. Patrick Garland, one of the heroes of the CFT story, was Artistic Director in 1981 – 1984, then again in 1991 – 1994:

'Olivier was a gigantic presence on and off stage, and a fascinating man. He had compulsive energy. It was like watching Garrick... Actors like him do not come along very often.'

During the course of March 1963, a series of meetings were held between Evershed-Martin and Lord Chandos (formerly Oliver Lyttelton), Chairman of the National Theatre Board, to hammer out a way of working between Chichester and London that would allow Olivier to be the Artistic Director of both for the next two seasons, but without either theatre losing its individualism or independence. The negotiations resulted in an agreement that, for the 1964 and 1965 seasons, Olivier would divide his time equally between the National and Chichester, although the terms and conditions of the collaboration were not announced until after the 1963 CFT season had finished. From the beginning of the 1964 season, the National was financially contributing to the CFT coffers.

Paul Rogerson – who came to CFT as Theatre Manager in 1965, then was General Manager & Licensee until 2001[2] – explains:

'Leslie [Evershed-Martin] always said: "my theatre has never been subsidised", but that is not strictly true. The deal was that, under Olivier, the National Theatre paid for the productions and there was a 70/30 per cent box office split in favour of the NT.'

But agreements about percentage splits were all a long way in the future. In the spring of 1963, while debates, business and building matters were on-going behind the scenes, Olivier was assembling his cast and creative teams. John Dexter – who was to become an Associate Director of the National under Olivier – was invited to direct Shaw's *Saint Joan* and Stuart Burge to direct John Arden's *The Workhouse Donkey*. Designers were Michael Annals and, as for 1962, Beatrice Dawson, Roger Furse and Sean Kenny.

Most of the leading players of the 1962 Company returned to Oaklands Park, with the exception of Rosemary Harris and John Neville, already on his way to the Nottingham Playhouse. New faces included Jeremy Brett, Robert Stephens, Frank Finlay and a young Derek Jacobi.

'[Olivier] was doing a tour of reps looking for promising young actors. Birmingham Repertory Theatre was celebrating its fiftieth anniversary by staging three Shakespeare plays they had never done. I was playing Henry VIII and he sum-

---

[1] The first major addition to the original building was in 1966, when a scene dock with a lift for scenery was constructed, with space for laundry and additional dressing rooms underneath. In 1967, the foyer was extended at one end to add another bar and a box-office area built at the other. Air conditioning was installed in 1969.

[2] One of the most popular figures in the history of CFT, Rogerson worked for London music impresario Wilfrid Van Wyck who responded to Olivier's request that Arthur Rubinstein play a recital at CFT in 1962. Rubinstein was paid £750. In his 30-plus years at CFT, Rogerson was responsible for programming an outstanding sequence of concerts including such world-class performers as Sir John Barbirolli, Janet Baker, Jane Glover, John Dankworth and Cleo Laine, the Hallé Orchestra, Alfred Brendl, the Royal Philharmonic Orchestra and the London Philharmonic Orchestra.

moned me to London, to the rehearsal room he used in Chelsea, and cast me as Brother Martin in *Saint Joan*. What a break that was! I was just twenty-five.'

David Wood, who was to appear as Bowers in 1980 in Ted Tally's *Terra Nova*, was also cast as an extra in *Saint Joan* and a police officer in *The Workhouse Donkey*. He had been encouraged to audition by his English master, Norman Siviter[1], at Chichester High School for Boys.

The 1963 season opened with *Saint Joan* on Monday 24 June, with a Royal Gala performance the following day. Like *Uncle Vanya* the previous season, it is another iconic production remembered with admiration by those who saw it.

Christopher Doman, Company Secretary to the Board 1998 – 2003: 'I will never forget Joan Plowright as Saint Joan, sitting alone in the middle of the stage surrounded by hooded interrogators.'

The navy blue souvenir programme for the 1963 season – full of production shots and interviews with the cast and creative teams – cost two shillings and sixpence. *Saint Joan* was also the first of George Bernard Shaw's plays to be staged at Chichester. In the past fifty years, Shaw has been the second most presented playwright at Chichester, after Shakespeare.

In the middle of the run, Jacobi had to go to the dentist with toothache. Not enough gas was used, so he came round in the middle of the operation and had to be rushed into hospital for five days.

Derek Jacobi: 'Every day, Dame Sybil Thorndike and Lewis Casson used to take their constitutional around Oaklands Park. When they heard I was in St Richard's, they decided to take a detour and arrived at the hospital to see me. Sybil brought a book of poetry and gave an impromptu poetry recital in the ward. I will always remember that.'

---

[1] Norman Siviter was to be a key figure in the Theatre Society, serving as Secretary for many years and playing a major part in fundraising and running the Society.

The Workhouse Donkey, 1963.

Photo: Angus McBean

Uncle Vanya was sold out, the queues for tickets and box-office returns vindicating Olivier's instincts to revive the production.

Critic Michael Billington returned to see the production again: 'When I start about *Vanya*, I don't stop, because I can still hear that incredible final speech of Joan Plowright trying to console Vanya, as the tears came to one's eyes. I have a theory that, whatever age you are at, you can always identify with that play... It gave me, I suppose, the Chichester bug really.'

Jacobi was understudying Michael Redgrave and Robert Stephens understudied Olivier. He remembers Olivier taking the understudy rehearsals once a week: 'We had our own costumes and we had to replicate the performances and mannerisms of our principals exactly. So if Michael sat in a certain way, at a certain point, I would sit in exactly the same way. That might sound restricting, but it wasn't; it gave us young actors an insight and helped us develop.'

The final play of the season was the premiere of John Arden's *The Workhouse Donkey*, directed by Stuart Burge (who would subsequently take over from John Neville at the Nottingham Playhouse in 1968). Frank Finlay played ex-Mayor Alderman Charlie Butterthwaite – 'the workhouse donkey' of the title – born in the workhouse and stubborn as a donkey.

Set in a northern town in the early 1960s, it's about corruption in local politics, a mock heroic tribute to the energy and vision of the anti-hero of the title. It was neither a critical nor a box-office success. Billington recalls sitting in the half empty auditorium on a Saturday afternoon, but with Laurence Olivier himself settled in the row in front.

'There was some noise from outside the Theatre, I think someone was playing a portable radio, and Olivier being Olivier, got up and sidled out of his seat and went to tell them to shut up. It says something about his hands-on care of any theatre he was in charge of. He wasn't going to have a performance interrupted by noises going off or the audience being disturbed.'

The Workhouse Donkey required a huge cast of actors in order to represent a whole community on stage. It also helped establish CFT, under Olivier, as a centre of innovation and courage, a modern theatre looking forward.

Billington again: 'It ended with Frank Finlay being carried shoulder high through the town. They processed up the aisle and out into the car park beyond. It was just an amazing event, certainly at that stage of my life. For me, it is one of the great epic post-war British plays.' Billington was in the minority, though, and the play never played to more than half full houses.

In those early days, there was a late-night train laid on from Chichester at 10:15pm, spe-cifically to take visitors from London home after the performance, remembered with affection by my father, among others. Richard Mosse: 'It was a common sight, at the end of the performance, to see the nervous crowd outside the theatre as everyone tried to get quickly onto the bus and back to the station on time.'

Like the auditorium itself, the London train made regular appearances in reviews and news-papers articles about CFT.

'If you don't like people who start conversa-tions with strangers in trains, take my advice and don't come back from Sir Laurence's pro-ductions at the Chichester Festival Theatre by Dr Beeching's[1] late-night theatre special. It is the chattiest, most un-British train that British Rail runs.' (*Daily Mail*)

As the end of the 1963 season approached, the talk backstage was all about who was going to be picked to be part of the new National Theatre Company.

Jacobi remembers 'the long walk': 'We assem-bled in the Theatre and one by one we were called over to Olivier's office, which was where the Minerva now stands. Ninety-eight of us were chosen, but it was awful waiting to be called. He gave people like me, Robert Stephens and Frank Finlay three-year contracts. It meant we could not do films or television, but it was a huge opportunity, which we all grasped.'

Once more, in September the Theatre set-tled down to its winter hibernation. Once more, maintenance and improvements. And once more, the business of continuing to raise money and working out how best to continue to attract the best actors, designers, directors, musicians, play-wrights to Chichester. How to keep the town proud and supportive of the Theatre.

---

[1] Dr Richard Beeching was Chairman of the British Transport Commission charged with making the railways pay. His solution, announced in March 1963, was mas-sive cuts. Some 2000 stations were closed and more than 67,000 jobs were lost.

1964

The seasons of 1964 and 1965 were presented in association with the National Theatre. Olivier was to divide his time equally between Chichester and London. In spirit, the Company was also divided, developing work at Chichester that would subsequently be presented in London and no doubt thinking of what was to come in the future.

In some respects, though, 1964 was the most successful of Olivier's four Festivals as Artistic Director of the Theatre. Priority booking stood at £24,000, double the figure for 1963 and four times that for 1962.

The season opened on Tuesday 7 July with Peter Shaffer's *The Royal Hunt of the Sun*, directed by John Dexter and with music by Marc Wilkinson. An epic play intended for a thrust stage, more than any production so far at CFT, it showed the extraordinary possibilities, as Bernard Levin put it, of 'the vast open stretches of the wide open stage'.

Written in 1959 – and only Shaffer's second play – it tells of the Spanish conquest of Peru in the 16th century. Conquistador Pizarro [Colin Blakely] entices recruits by the promise of riches, while the Church claims the cause for Christianity. The clash between the two cultures leaves thousands of unarmed Inca troops slaughtered and sparks an intense battle of

The Royal Hunt of the Sun, 1964.

Photo: Angus McBean

wills between the Sun God, Atahuallpa [Robert Stephens] and his captor.

Dexter rehearsed the cast in two separate spaces, so that Spanish would meet Incas, almost for the first time, on stage. Michael Annals designed a set to suggest multiple locations and the ceaseless, monstrous sweep of history. Its centre piece was a huge sun, symbolising the Inca empire. Annals collected hundreds of metal bottle tops and hammered them down to make his sun shimmer. During the course of the play, the gold was removed, leaving a dark, glowering hole. Brian Wingate remembers, as a 14 year old, unexpectedly finding himself in the auditorium on the opening night.

'A world premiere and I was there with my autograph book. I can clearly remember it was about two minutes before the play was due to start – I was there with a friend of mine – and this well-dressed couple arrived. They said some friends had let them down and would we like the tickets? I was expected home for tea, but we weren't going to pass up the chance to see the play. We were about four rows from the front, dressed in jeans and t-shirts, surrounded by people in their finery. It was incredibly atmospheric, a brilliant play. The stage lent itself to this vast production.'

Audiences loved it and the critics agreed, Milton Schulman in the *Evening Standard* describing it as: 'trailing success behind it like a fizzing rocket.' He also praised 'the intensity, maturity and intelligence of Shaffer's writing… and the exotic, imaginative, tempestuous effect of the production.'

The critic in the *Evening News* felt the same: 'Has any other spectacle achieved such visual excitement and… so touched the historical imagination? … Mr Shaffer has not dodged one blood-stained, gold-strewn mile of the fantastic journey.'

It was with great expectation that the production left Chichester for London in July 1964. It was the first new British play the National

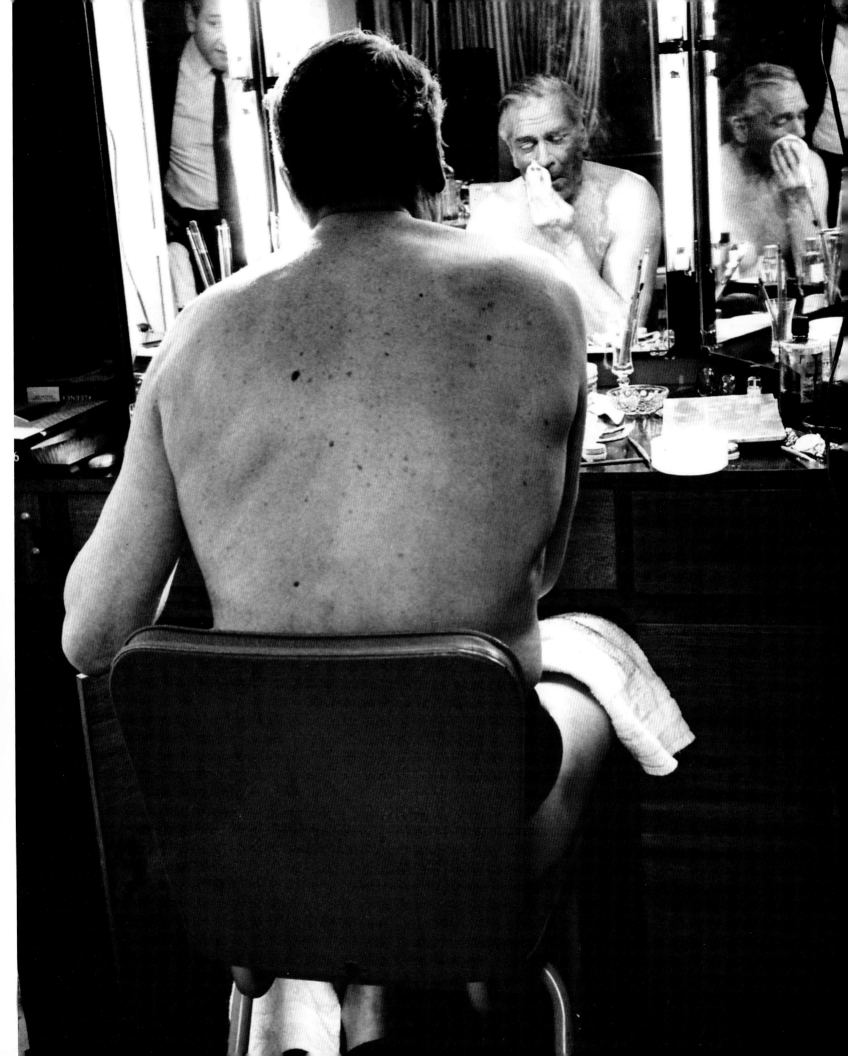

**Laurence Olivier,
Othello, 1964.**

Photo: Angus McBean

**Frank Finlay and
Laurence Olivier in
Othello, 1964.**

Photo: Angus McBean

Theatre was to stage at their temporary home at the Old Vic.

As well as those actors and actresses who would go to form the nucleus of the National Theatre Company – Olivier, Plowright, Stephens, Finlay, Jacobi, Maggie Smith, Edward Hardwicke, Edward Petherbridge – the Company also included Billie Whitelaw, Patricia Routledge and a young Christopher Timothy.

After the triumph of the opening production, the second play – John Marston's Jacobean *The Dutch Courtesan* – did respectably enough. The critics commented on the 'ripe' language, speculating that if it had not been written before the Censorship Act of 1737, it would have been a target for the Lord Chamberlain's blue pencil. In truth, the bawdy language notwithstanding, it was over-shadowed not only by the Shaffer, but also by what was to be one of the defining productions of Olivier's time at CFT, Shakespeare's *Othello.*

All seats were sold out within eight hours of the opening of public booking and over 2000 cheques had to be returned. From the Opening Night, Tuesday 21 July, there were queues at the box office stretching around the block. As the run continued, the local newspapers – the *Portsmouth Evening News* and the *Chichester Observer* – started to run photographs of people camping outside the Festival Theatre, sleeping bags, students and pensioners, all hoping for returns. The theatre built for the community, by the community, was creating new communities both on, and around, the stage.

Derek Jacobi, who was playing Cassio, remembers the atmosphere: 'One night, Olivier was in the restaurant and noticed them all bedding down for the night. He organised two cases of champagne for them, but he didn't just have them sent out. He carried one of the cases himself and went out with glasses dispensing champagne to them all.' A triumphant end to a triumphant Festival.

He just queued . . . and queued

Hans van Oortmerssen, a Dutch psychology student from Amsterdam University, queued for four days and nights for a ticket to see Sir Laurence Olivier in "Othello" at the Chichester Festival Theatre. Miss Jean Harrison, a prospective medical student from Bognor Regis, joined him for yesterday's performance.

1965

Olivier's final CFT season was announced on Thursday 28 January 1965, four plays rather than three – the last a double bill – beginning with Arden's Armstrong's *Last Goodnight*. A powerful and dramatic play, but the tremendous cast, Albert Finney included, struggled to make a Chichester audience warm to the broad Scots accents.

The 1965 company – joined by Ian McKellen and Geraldine McEwan among others – had more light-hearted fun with Pinero's 19th century romantic comedy, *Trelawny of the 'Wells'*. But the surprise hit was the double bill of Strindberg's *Miss Julie* and a new play from Peter Shaffer, *Black Comedy*.

Michael Billington was just embarking on his first job as a journalist on *The Times*. A friend, the actor John Savident, told him there was a coach going down from London for a National Theatre friends and supporters' dress rehearsal of the double bill, and invited him to come.

' "This could really be something," [Savident] said: "*Miss Julie* with Albert Finney and Maggie Smith." He said the other play, a new play by Peter Shaffer, was: "absolutely chaotic. They've had a terrible time in rehearsal, lots of rewrites etc, but never mind, come and see *Miss Julie*".

So I go down on this coach, this Sunday afternoon, and I see this perfectly respectable *Miss Julie* and then I suppose I was part of the first public audience that ever saw *Black Comedy*. And you can guess the rest, it just took off in the most extraordinary way. None of us knew what the premise of the play was and we were just dazzled and blown away by this comic event. I still think it's one of the great plays, great comic plays, of the post-War period.'

Based on an idea inspired by the Peking Opera – of performers acting in the light, thinking they

Maggie Smith in *Black Comedy*, 1965.

Photo: Angus McBean

Cutting courtesy of *The News*, Portsmouth, 28 July 1964/West Sussex Record Office

Maggie Smith and Jeanne Watts in *Miss Julie,* **1965.**

Photo: Angus McBean

Albert Finney and Derek Jacobi in *Black Comedy,* **1965.**

Photo: Angus McBean

were in the dark and vice-versa – audiences were entranced; they loved it.

Critic Graham Samuel: 'In an ideal world, this glorious farce would always be seen as we first saw it at Chichester. We knew nothing about it except its title and as first bewilderment and then surprise and then pure pleasure broke over us at the wit and sheer inspiration of Peter Shaffer's idea, a feeling of delight pervaded the theatre like nothing I have experienced before.'

So ended Olivier's time at Chichester Festival Theatre. When the summer ended, he and his company of actors departed for the National Theatre's temporary home at the Old Vic – the entire wardrobe department went with him – and Chichester got ready to welcome Sir John Clements, who had been announced as the new Artistic Director.

Clements' reputation notwithstanding, there was obviously an anxiety about how CFT would fare without Olivier at the helm.

As Billington puts it: '[Olivier's tenure] created the expectation that Chichester was always going to be great actors, in the great classics and extraordinary new work. I think it was then difficult for all the succeeding directors to live up to that standard. Chichester's reputation has fluctuated, but those early years of the 1960s were incredibly exciting. I think John Clements had a difficult role following Olivier.'

In the town, too, people were also wondering how the things might change.

Brian Wingate: 'In Olivier's day, huge Hollywood stars would come to Chichester to see him. Vivien Leigh was a frequent visitor, in her chauffeur-driven Rolls with its distinctive number plate – VL01... Other visitors I remember were Cary Grant, Greta Garbo, Julie Andrews, Mia Farrow, Gregory Peck, Henry Fonda and Montgomery Clift. I was a huge movie fan and I couldn't believe all these stars were in Chichester, but that was the drawing power of Olivier.' All eyes were on Oaklands Park.

1966

Sir John Clements, who lived in Brighton across the border in East Sussex, was a celebrated film star, one of the last of the great actor-managers. But Olivier's boots were big boots to fill. There were behind-the-scenes changes to make too. With a new man in charge at the top, it was a good moment to establish principles for running the theatre for the future. The dynamism and commitment that, from 1959 until 1964, had seen the money raised and the roof raised, the theatre built and the theatre established, were not necessarily the same skills required for running a festival of theatre year in, year out. Some members of the London Committee felt that their association with CFT had run its course. A new constitution and governance structures were put in place, looking to the future. In December 1964, Leslie Evershed-Martin stepped down as Chairman of the Productions Company Board (though he retained the Chairmanship of the Trust Company, responsible for the buildings) and was replaced, after a brief interregnum, by A T – Teddy – Smith.

Though forthright and a man of strong opinions, the common consent is that Smith was an excellent Chairman. Paul Rogerson, CFT General Manager from 1965 to 2001:

'On first nights, Teddy Smith would bring a party of sixty people down from London. He did a lot of good. Teddy Smith and Victor Behrens went among their friends, not just raising money, but getting them excited about this theatre.'

Smith also kept a tight hold on the purse strings. Paul Rogerson again: 'He was a very tough chairman. The accountant and I used to have to send twice-weekly reports to Teddy Smith and fierce letters would come back, saying: "These cleaning bills are absolutely outrageous. The staff should bring their own Hoovers! The electricity bill is monstrous. Have all bulbs changed to 40-watt." '

Keith Michell, Artistic Director (1974 – 1977) adds: 'In my experience at Chichester, if you wanted to get anything done, go straight to Teddy Smith.'

As well as putting together creative teams of actors, designers and directors, Clements also recruited his own people back of house, as Paul Rogerson recalls: 'He brought with him, as his General Manager, Doreen Dixon, who had been General Manager of the Royal Court Theatre and worked with him at the Intimate Theatre in Palmers Green in the mid-1930s.

Alastair Sim and Margaret Rutherford rehearsing a scene from *The Clandestine Marriage*, 1966.

Photo: Zoë Dominic

**Celia Johnson
(seated, centre) in
The Cherry Orchard,
1966.**

Photo: Zoë Dominic

They were a tough couple, but he put on eight wonderful seasons.'

Bill Bray, who worked at CFT from 1965 – 1993 (finishing his career in the position of Chief Electrician, as well as being the lighting designer on many shows) describes Dixon as: 'Clement's *Da Capo* – small... round... and terrifying.'

John Clements' first announcement as Artistic Director was that the season would be extended to 15 weeks and present four full productions rather than three. For 1966, the playbill read: *The Clandestine Marriage* by Colman & Garrick, followed by Anouilh's *The Fighting Cock*, Chekhov's *The Cherry Orchard* and, to close the season, *Macbeth* by Shakespeare.

Sarah Badel, one of the youngest of the 1966 company, was on tour in the States when the letter arrived from Clements inviting her to be part of the Company.

'I think Sir John was very apprehensive about Chichester, but after the huge success of Olivier, you would be, wouldn't you? He worried that people might think the glamour had gone out of the project. I remember him saying: "Getting actors to come is going to be difficult. So far, it's only Celia Johnson and me".'

Clements needn't have worried. The 1966 company included Tom Courtenay, Peter Egan, Ray McAnally, Margaret Rutherford, Alastair

Sim, John Standing, Clive Swift and a young Ben Kingsley, playing the servant in *The Clandestine Marriage* and first murderer in *Macbeth*.

Sarah Badel continues the story: 'Sir John was planning his first season[1]. He said he wanted a new play alongside the classics he was going to do. I went home and spoke to my father Alan and he said: "He should do an Anouilh. He should do *The Fighting Cock*." He'd got it on his shelves and said: "Give it to him, see what he feels about it. There's a wonderful part in it for him, an actor of his age."

'Next day, I knocked on the dressing room door and there was Sir John in his specs and cotton wool under the frames on the bridge of his nose so they wouldn't make a mark. "Come in! Come in!" he commanded. "I've found a new play for you," I said, passing him the script. "It's never been done in England before."

'The next day, his dresser Hal said: "Sir John would like to see you in the interval." I went down to see him and asked if he liked the play. "Yes! Yes!" he said. "Phoned the agent in Paris. Negotiated the rights. Doing it!"

'Initially, he was trying to get Alec Guinness to play the General, but in the end he did it and it was well received... John Standing, Sir John's stepson was in it, and there were very good parts for the whole company.'

Badel opened the 1966 season in the role of Miss Fanny in *The Clandestine Marriage*, with Alastair Sim:

'Alastair acted with his whole body. He was like a contortionist. I remember on the set there were two flights of stairs coming down to the stage, quite steep, and Sir John told him at one rehearsal: "Alastair, you are taking forever to come down there, old chap, can you make it a bit quicker?"

'"I can," he said rather threateningly, with those great hooded eyes, then proceeded to fall from top to bottom. Everyone gasped. But he was just having us on. It was the most spectacular

[1] Clements and Badel were appearing in the musical *Robert and Elizabeth* at the Lyric Theatre, Shaftesbury Avenue, London. Keith Michell was playing Robert Browning.

stage fall and he rose like a phoenix at the end of it. He was making a point that he knew best how to come down the stairs.' The pratfall stayed in the production, which was a roaring success.

'Sim's Lord Ogleby, all leers and palsy, kept going on pills and potions and the sight of pretty faces, is more of a buffoon strayed out of Molière than Garrick's eighteenth-century elder fop, but in every agonised step, each glittering fix of the eyes, a delicious performance.' (*Glasgow Herald*)

The Fighting Cock was also a box office success, though some of the off-stage arrangements broke down, as Paul Rogerson recalls: 'We had been promised a delivery of tables, chairs and umbrellas for outside the theatre, but they did not turn up until the afternoon *The Fighting Cock* was due to open. Doreen [Dixon] said that the crew should put them up the next day. This was not good enough for Clements. He came up from a tiring day's rehearsals at the Minerva Studios in Eastgate Square and, even though he was due on stage that evening, he said to me: "Come on, let's get those tables and chairs out," and he unpacked every single one. He was

the ultimate professional and hardworking and he was absolutely right.'[1]

The Cherry Orchard, directed by Lindsay Anderson, received respectable if not ecstatic notices. John McKerchar, a local chartered accountant who had recently joined the Board, remembers it as much for financial as for artistic reasons: 'I was amazed that he spent £3000 on three cherry trees in blossom... hardly an orchard!'

But this was very unusual. Mostly, as Rogerson says, John Clements is remembered for keeping a very tight control on costs: 'Getting a rise was very difficult. You didn't talk to him about rises, you talked to Doreen and she was the toughest negotiator, fearsome. And she would say: "I'll have to talk to Sir John about it, but he's busy in rehearsal." The star salary was £75 a week. Peter Egan lodged with us in St Paul's Road and

---

[1] A scene to be repeated some thirty years later, at the beginning of Andrew Welch's first season, when Paul Rogerson and I found ourselves frantically unpacking the tables and chairs the catering company should have organised, as the audience was beginning to arrive. *Plus ça change.*

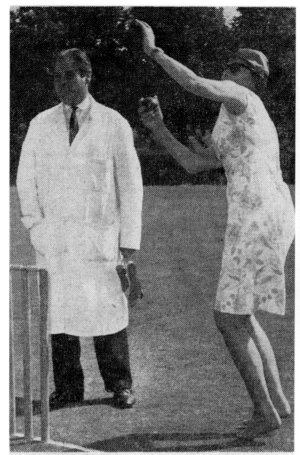

Celia Johnson bowling the first ball during the match between the Sussex Press XI and the Chichester Festival Theatre team in Chichester yesterday. Ald. Charles Newell (umpire) carried Miss Johnson's shoes—a change from the usual sweater that umpires wear round their waists.

9053

Cutting courtesy of *The News*, Portsmouth, 29 August 1966. Evershed-Martin Family archive

Ben Kingsley as First Murderer (left), *Macbeth,* **1966.**

Photo: Zoë Dominic

they paid him £20 a week, and us £5 a week. But then you could have a good meal in The Old Cross for 1/9d.'

Chief Electrician Bill Bray has similar memories: 'I once made the mistake of asking her for a pay rise. "Don't be so bloody ridiculous!" was her response, as the door slammed, shaking the building.'

Sarah Badel remembers the production partly for the cricket – something that was, in the future, to become something of a sub-plot in the history of CFT.

'Celia [Johnson] was a great cricket fan and she used to listen to test-match commentaries backstage, on a tiny radio, during matinees of *The Cherry Orchard*. It used to amaze me that, on cue, she would come on in floods of tears as Madame Ranevskaya – or maybe it was just because England were doing so badly!'

In the CFT-versus-the-Press Cricket Match, held on Monday 29 August, Celia Johnson in fact bowled the first ball. The umpire held her shoes as she ran up to the wicket. Tom Courtenay made 12 and Paul Rogerson was last man out. The press, however, won.

Macbeth, the final play of Clements' opening season, was both a box-office and a critical success. Clements played Macbeth to Margaret Johnson's Lady Macbeth, with Tom Courtenay taking the role of Malcolm. Harold Hobson described it as: 'one of the great Macbeths of our times'.

But the play's reputation for being unlucky held good. The director Michael Benthall was ill throughout, Margaret Johnson broke two ribs, Clements lost his voice. During a rehearsal of the duel scene between Macbeth and Macduff, Clements and McAnally (using bamboo canes in place of swords), got out of step with one another, resulting in McAnally being taken to A&E with a broken nose and two black eyes.

Accidents notwithstanding, the 1966 season ended on a high note. Good takings, excellent reviews, fine performances and a new company of actors who were to return time and again. In *The Miracle Theatre*, Evershed-Martin reported Clements as saying: 'It has been a greater success than I hoped for, even in my wildest dreams.'

CFT went into 1967 with high hopes, good expectations, and a season that promised much. However, things did not to go according to plan.

1967

Clements announced his choices for 1967 early in the year, saying it was scheduled to be 'a season of laughter.' Starting with a good, popular romp, Eden Phillpott's *The Farmer's Wife*, the second play was Farquhar's *The Beaux' Stratagem* – a play in which Clements and his wife, Kay Hammond, had enjoyed spectacular success in 1949. The 1967 season saw the Chichester debuts of Fenella Fielding, Anton Rodgers and Prunella Scales. The third play, Shaw's *Heartbreak House*[1] was to be followed by the flagship production, Danny Kaye in the Goldoni classic, *The Servant of Two Masters*.

So began one of the most notorious and controversial stories in CFT's history. Although an international star of the big screen and the small, Kaye had not appeared on stage for some twenty years and so his commitment to Chichester was a huge media story. Rather than the usual launch of the season, a press conference was instead held at the Waldorf Hotel[2] in London to announce the news.

Kaye, by all accounts, was in good spirits. When asked what salary he would receive, he replied £75 per week, then added he had asked for £76 but: 'that skinflint Clements would not agree'.

'It is a new kind of challenge that will stimulate me as a performer. I may fall down in Chichester. I may be the biggest bomb ever. If I were going to do Hamlet, I'd be a lot more concerned, but this is out-and-out comedy, a Hoakey comedy,

Michael Aldridge, Irene Handl and Bill Fraser at the press launch of *The Farmer's Wife*, 1967.

Photo: Zoë Dominic

and I think I have some kind of acquaintance with that.' (As quoted by Evershed-Martin in *The Miracle Theatre*.)

Later in February, Kaye came down to see the Theatre, then visited the Millstream Hotel in Bosham. Reserving the entire top floor of one of the wings of the hotel – for his entourage and friends who might come to visit during the run – he requested it might be extended and redecorated.

The first signs that the production might run into trouble was the unfortunate timing of the Piccolo Theatre of Milan, guests of the RSC, who brought their acclaimed Commedia dell'Arte production of *The Servant of Two Masters* to the Aldwych in London in the spring, just three months before Kaye was due to open in Chichester.

'Now that we have seen the real thing,' wrote critic Felix Barker in the *Evening Standard*, 'heaven help you… This was not simply laying a theatrical flare-path; it was comic precision bombing… The style of the acting, the beauty of the 18th-century Venetian setting and the brilliant invention of Ferrucio Soleri in your part of the servant Arlecchino, is going to be very, very hard to follow… Well, Danny… we are all longing for you. But oh! You've got something to beat.'

The next piece of unfortunate timing – if something so devastating and serious can pos-

---

[1] This was to be the first production of Shaw's perennial classic at CFT. In 2000, it was directed by Christopher Morahan with Joss Ackland as Shotover. In 2012, it will be directed by Richard Clifford and with Derek Jacobi in the lead role.

[2] In February 1960, the press conference to announce the launch of CFT had been held at the Waldorf.

An Italian Straw Hat, 1967.

Photo: Zoë Dominic

sibly be described so mildly – was the outbreak of The Six Day War between Israel and Egypt. Kaye's support for Israel was well known.

Sarah Badel remembers the moment when the news came through:

'We first knew he wasn't coming when we were sitting on the stage doing the first read-through of *Heartbreak House*, with Irene Worth and Diana Churchill. I was playing Ellie Dunn and was rather intimidated by them. We had just started reading the play. Sir John, who was directing, seemed very on edge indeed. Doreen Dixon came rushing into the Theatre and said: "Sir John, Sir John!"

' "No!" he snapped, "not now. Can't you see we are in the middle of the read-through? For goodness sake!" "But, Sir John, this is important."And Irene, with a sixth sense like a cat, suddenly sang: "I know what it is, Danny isn't coming!"

'Sir John shot her a look. Doreen whispered in his ear and he rose and said "excuse me," and left. That's all he said. And that's what it was. Danny Kaye wasn't coming.

'So, poor Sir John. This was going to be the flagship of the season and he didn't have a play or a star.'

It is difficult, even now with the benefit of hindsight, to decide why Kaye did withdraw. Wanting to do his bit for the troops, fears of the comparisons between the Chichester and the triumphant Aldwych production, or a clash of personalities between him and the director, have all been suggested. Whatever the reasons, Kaye not only reimbursed in full the money spent on the Millstream refurbishment – in the region of £6,000, according to Paul Rogerson – but also covered Chichester's expenses and costs of reprinting tickets and literature. None of this stopped the press attacks, the local newspapers were particularly virulent and it left Clements with an enormous headache.

After attempts to find a suitable star to replace Kaye[1], the decision was made at the last minute, to put on *An Italian Straw Hat* by Labiche and Marc-Michel instead, partly because Peter Coe had directed it before and there was only a couple of weeks to get the production ready.

The whole theatre was roped in to help with costumes, scenery, painting the set, props, as Bill Bray remembers: ' 'Dunkirk Spirit' broke out, important actors were accepting tiny roles, anyone who could hold a paintbrush was involved in painting the set – in fact, the entire back wall of the Theatre was painted white. All balustrades, rails and so on, were painted bright pink.'

Most of the backstage staff worked round the clock to get the show ready on time. Rehearsing, changing sets, doing technical work once the performance was over. Bray remembers being so exhausted after an all-night tech that he fell asleep in the auditorium in his sleeping bag.

---

[1] The play was to have a spectacular new lease of life in 2011 in the form of Richard Bean's magnificent adaptation for the National Theatre, *One Man, Two Guvnors*, staring James Corden in the title role. There, Goldoni's 1746 classic comedy was updated to Brighton in 1963.

He was woken by an usherette tapping him on the shoulder twenty minutes before a matinee was due to begin!

But, all the hard work paid off. The production was a triumph. And I've never forgotten Sarah Badel, beautiful in white silk and tulle, with her high, pip-squeak voice.

Badel, too, remembers it: 'It sold out. People were queuing for returns. Many came two or three times, because it was great fun and done with tremendous flair... Peter Coe did a tremendous job and the audience got into the adversity out of which the show had emerged; spirit of the Blitz and all that. There was a surge of loyalty to the Theatre. I remember it played the last night of the season and it had a tremendous send-off. There was dancing in the aisles, balloons coming down from everywhere.'

Out of adversity, triumph. John Clements had well and truly shaken off the shadow of Sir Laurence Olivier.

1968

The 1968 season saw a new play by Peter Ustinov, *The Unknown Soldier and His Wife* – with Ustinov not only directing, but also playing the role of the Bishop. This was followed by Alec Guinness' first appearance at Chichester, with Eileen Atkins, in a critically acclaimed production of T S Eliot's *The Cocktail Party*. Ralph Koltai designed *The Tempest*, the set and the costumes all in sweeping shades of white, with Clements as Prospero, and a young Simon Ward. The final play of the season was Thornton Wilder's *The Skin of Our Teeth*. Although directed by Peter Coe and starring Millicent Martin, it failed to capture the affection of either audiences or critics. The 1968 season had been less eventful, certainly, than the previous year, but it set a good foundation for the rest of Clements' time at Chichester.

Prunella Scales and Simon Ward in *The Unknown Soldier and His Wife*, 1968.
Photo: John Timbers/ArenaPAL

Alec Guinness and Eileen Atkins in *The Cocktail Party*, 1968.
Photo: John Timbers/ArenaPAL

1969

Clements announced the final season of the decade would be eighteen weeks long, beginning with Brecht's *The Caucasian Chalk Circle* – bringing Topol to the CFT stage – then followed by Pinero's *The Magistrate*. This was to see the debut of an actress destined to become one of Chichester's most popular – and regular – performers, Patricia Routledge:

'The reason I came to Chichester in 1969 really was to play opposite Alastair Sim in *The Magistrate*, which was unforgettably wonderful. That God-given face to start with and then, when it starts to move, it is even more interesting, and then when it moves with the mind and the intention behind it, even more wonderful.'[1] It was also to see the arrival of the much-loved and legendary Janet Edward, who worked at CFT from 1969 until her death in 1996. Starting in the Box Office, she became Front of House Manager and Box Office Manager – holding both posts at the same time for a short period.[2]

Like Badel, Routledge recalls how meticulous was Clements' attention to detail and how he liked to have every move choreographed just right. A revival of Pinero's good-natured farce of a less-than-honest wife (when it comes to her age) and an honest, if confused, older husband, it was a box office hit when it was first performed in 1885.

Topol in *The Caucasian Chalk Circle*, 1969.

Photo: John Timbers/ ArenaPAL

Routledge again: 'I remember rehearsing the end of *The Magistrate*, where all the characters come on and it's quite difficult to stage what one calls the walk-down. He was losing his patience just a little bit, because we couldn't get it sorted out. And he said: "I don't know, I don't know. I designed the end of this with my soldiers last night and it worked." People did admire the way the play looked like a dance, and it's important on that stage.'

Patricia Routledge also played in *The Country Wife*, the third play in the season. Set in the London of 1675, when England is wallowing in the after-effects of two lost wars, the Plague and the Great Fire, the production starred Maggie Smith and also brought a surprising visitor to Chichester – Warren Beatty.

According to Peter Biskind's 2010 biography, Beatty and screenwriter Robert Towne, having seen the play, were debating what the contemporary equivalent of the dandy lothario, Horner, would be. Beatty suggested an actor? Towne disagreed. A hairdresser, he suggested and Beatty agreed.

'Beatty hired Towne to write a script for $25,000. The working title was *Hair*. Later, it would become *Shampoo*.' (*Star: The Life and Wild Times of Warren Beatty*.)

The final play of the season, the final production of a decade that had seen the Theatre built and opened, and the first steps of man upon the moon, was Shakespeare's *Antony and Cleopatra*. John Clements and Margaret Leighton took the title roles[3]. Their intimacy was to prove, for some in Row A, rather too convincing...

According to Evershed-Martin, all four plays were wanted by theatres in London, but since Topol and Maggie Smith had commitments – and the Shakespeare was too expensive to transfer – it was only *The Magistrate* that found a new

---

[1] Possibly an apocryphal tale, but the story goes that Sim was once asked by a younger actor if he knew the best place to stand on the CFT stage to deliver a funny line, he replied: 'Yes, dear boy, I shall be standing on it.'

[2] Her brother, Tim Andrews, also worked there from 1973 – 1975. Another brother, the actor Anthony Andrews, started his theatrical career at CFT as a scene shifter. Known for a range of film and television roles – most famously as Sebastian Flyte in *Brideshead Revisited* - he will play Anthony Eden in the world premiere of *A Marvellous Year for Plums* in the 2012 Festival Season.

[3] In 2012, the roles are to be played by Kim Cattrall and Michael Pennington with the award-winning actress and director, Janet Suzman at the helm.

home. It opened in September at the Cambridge Theatre with Patricia Routledge and Alastair Sim reprising their original roles.

Routledge takes up the story: 'We played to packed houses, with people standing at the back. I learned from [Sim] never to be impatient with a slow audience. He knew he could woo them to their knees, never by playing for laughs.'

This was the perfect end, not only to Clements' fourth season as Artistic Director, but also to the first decade in the life of CFT. The 'head-waggers' had been proved wrong, the critics had been won round or at least had begun to pay attention, to listen, to come, to review, to consider. The National Theatre had begun its life in the green parkland of Sussex. Many of Britain's finest actors and actresses had played upon the stage. Composers and designers and directors had experimented with space and light and sound. But most of all, Powell and Moya's extraordinary building had become part of the Chichester landscape.

'I have lived
To see inherited my very wishes
And the buildings of my fancy.'

Coriolanus
WILLIAM SHAKESPEARE

Maggie Smith in
The Country Wife,
1969.

Photo: John Timbers/
ArenaPAL

**Alastair Sim and
Patricia Routledge
in *The Magistrate*,
1969.**

Photo: John Timbers/
ArenaPAL

**John Clements and
Margaret Leighton
in *Antony and
Cleopatra*, 1969.**

Photo: John Timbers/
ArenaPAL

The 1970s

Artistic Directors
JOHN CLEMENTS (1966 – 1973)
KEITH MICHELL (1974 – 1977)
PETER DEWS (1978 – 1980)

'The firing breaks out again: there is a startling Fusillade quite close at hand. Whilst it is still echoing, the shutters disappear, pulled open from without, and for an instant the rectangle of snowy starlight flashes out with the figure of a man silhouetted in black upon it.'

ARMS AND THE MAN
(Stage directions)
George Bernard Shaw

I f the 1960s was the era of Jean Shrimpton and David Bailey, the 1970s were the days of maxi skirts and platform shoes. Rather than Apollo 11, the Space Hopper and the Ford Cortina and Raleigh Chopper bikes instead. It was to be a decade of the three-day week and strikes – postal workers, miners and dustmen – ending with the 'winter of discontent' in 1979, when ITV went off the air for five months. But even though colour television had entered most sitting rooms – *Top of the Pops* on Thursdays and Jon Pertwee was 'The Doctor' – the appetite for live theatre was as strong as ever.

The decade began cold and dull and damp on Thursday 1 January, the same evening the BBC began broadcasting its landmark television series *The Six Wives of Henry VIII*. Keith Michell, who would take over at CFT as Artistic Director in 1974, played Henry. Two of his wives – Annette Crosbie and Dorothy Tutin – would also come to Chichester.

For now, though, the business of putting together the season was underway. The 1970 Company included Dora Bryan, Eileen Atkins, Robert Selbie and John Standing, as well as younger actors such as Michael Feast and Laurence Harvey. Due to Clements being ill at the beginning of the year, the season was announced a little later than usual but, on paper, it looked

Sarah Miles and Eileen Atkins in *Vivat! Vivat Regina!* 1970.

Photo: John Timbers/ ArenaPAL

John Clements.

a sure-fire success. A perfectly balanced programme of new writing and classic revivals, allegory and historical drama, comedy.

But disaster struck almost immediately. The opening play of 1970 was Ibsen's *Peer Gynt*. In a new version by Christopher Fry, based on a translation by Johann Fillinger, Sarah Badel was cast as Solveig. Christopher Plummer was supposed to star, but he caught pneumonia and was unable to appear. Roy Dotrice took over, but then got laryngitis.

Sarah Badel: 'It should have been wonderful. But Christopher Fry didn't like the changes being made and Peter Coe, who was directing, knew exactly what he wanted so there wasn't much room for manoeuvre. It didn't do well. Empty seats in any theatre are not good, but at Chichester it looks terrible.'

However, the second play of 1970 – Robert Bolt's *Vivat! Vivat Regina!* – is remembered by many as one of the flagship productions at CFT. A world premiere, it sold out within hours of tickets being put on sale to the public after priority booking was over and, again, there were queues from the box office out into the car park. As Evershed-Martin wrote in *The Miracle Theatre*: 'Not since *Othello* did we have such a pleasant headache.'

An epic piece of work, of the kind that so suits the Chichester stage, it is a play carried by the two queens – Elizabeth I [Eileen Atkins] and Mary Queen of Scots [played by Bolt's wife, Sarah Miles] – and, in many respects, a companion piece to Bolt's highly successful *A Man for All Seasons*, written ten years before. An analysis of the nature of realpolitik, about personal morality versus public responsibility, private emotions versus political necessities, it was a *tour de force* of staging, performance, costume, set. The play asks the question at what cost glory? At what cost ambition?

General Manager Paul Rogerson comments: '[Clements] was very shrewd. When he had shows that transferred to London – like *The Magistrate*, *Dandy Dick* or *Vivat!* – he never revealed they were going until the last week of the season, when he was sure everyone down here had bought their tickets.'

So not until September was it announced *Vivat!* was transferring to the Piccadilly Theatre. It opened on Thursday 8 October, ran successfully for a year, then went to Broadway with Claire Bloom taking over the role of Mary. The portrait of Eileen Atkins as Elizabeth still stares down at audiences as they enter through Door 1.

A double bill of Chekhov's *The Proposal* and Shaw's *Arms and the Man* occupied the third slot in the season, but disaster was to strike again during rehearsals for the final play, Ben Jonson's *The Alchemist*, directed by Peter Dews. The Company were working in the Minerva Studios in Eastgate, a ten-minute walk from the Theatre.

Paul Rogerson continues: 'Laurence Harvey broke his leg while prancing around on a four-poster bed with Edward Atienza... It was just ten days from opening. Peter Dews and John Clements decided that the actor James Booth should take on the role of Face. They took him out for a drink and, after a few, he agreed to do it. Dews stepped into Booth's shoes himself and did the first few performances on the book.'

Harvey was already appearing in *Arms and the Man*, so returned to the stage some halfway through the run with a walking stick and limping. Not inappropriate for a play of fleeing cavalry officers and the walking wounded.

1971

The nineteen-week season opened earlier than in Olivier's day with a revival of Sheridan's *The Rivals*. Fine performances and excellent reviews for Carl Toms' design and set, a Gala Performance, in the presence of Princess Margaret, was set for Wednesday 12 May.

Paul Rogerson, General Manager, remembers the evening very well:

'We were ten minutes into the play, when the superintendent, Fred Turner, came up and said nervously: "Paul, I'm afraid I'm going to have to ask you to vacate the Theatre. I've just heard from Lewes [Sussex Police Headquarters] there is a bomb in the Theatre." Doreen Dixon was out front, having a vodka and tonic. So I told her we had to vacate. "Tell Sir John, tell Sir John!" I rushed round to dressing room 5, which was his room. "Right, you get *her* out, and I'll do the rest.'

'So I crept in through Door 2 and across the front and as I got up to [Princess Margaret] in row F on the gangway, Clements appeared on stage in his wig and his dressing gown and made his announcement that people should leave.

'I led 'her' out and we were half way across to the theatre restaurant, when she said: "Don't you think you ought to go and look after all those lovely people?"'

'When I fetched her from the restaurant later, after they discovered there was no bomb, she said: "Are we going to start from the beginning, or from where we left off?"'

The second play in the season was the world premiere of Lucienne Hill's translation of Anouilh's *Dear Antoine*. First performed in Paris in 1969, it is a dazzling piece about actors

ABOVE : Police cars outside the theatre during the bomb search

RIGHT : The Princess hurries out of the theatre

and acting, the interconnections between theatre and life, illusion and reality. The piece echoes themes explored by Pirandello both in *Six Characters in Search of an Author* and in *Tonight We Improvise*.[1]

Directed by Robin Phillips, the great Edith Evans - then 83 years old – was to lead the cast. At the press conference to announce the season, she did not seem enamoured of the CFT stage when she gave interviews to journalists. By all accounts, she disliked the backstage area too. She did only three performances, before she gave up the part and her understudy, Peggy Marshall, stepped successfully into her shoes.

The third play was notable for seeing the first appearance – and the last – of another of

[1] Michell programmed *Tonight We Improvise* as the first play in his opening season in 1974; however *Six Characters* was not performed at Chichester until 2008.

Princess Margaret in bomb scare.

The Argus, Brighton, 13 May 1971/ West Sussex Record Office

the great actors of our times, Sir John Gielgud. George Bernard Shaw's *Caesar and Cleopatra*, a reflection on conquest and clemency, love and politics, was a play with a great deal of history behind it.

Shaw wrote the part of Caesar for the Shakespearean actor Johnson Forbes-Robertson in 1899. The role of Caesar in Pascal's 1945 movie – which starred Vivien Leigh [who was, at the time, married to Olivier] – had been offered to Gielgud, who turned it down. Six years later, Leigh and Olivier had gone on to enjoy great success with the play in London, where it played at the St James Theatre in repertory with Shakespeare's *Antony and Cleopatra*. There was a deal of expectation, therefore, before Gielgud had even taken a single step onto the stage.

An austere white set, punctuated with rocking horses and rubber balls and slides, intended to bring to mind a children's playground, some critics appreciated the subtleties of Clements' interpretation more than others.

But for me, as a wide-eyed nine year old, the famous scene when Cleopatra [Anna Calder-Marshall] is smuggled into Caesar's chamber inside a rolled up carpet was one of the most unexpected, most thrilling, scenes I had ever seen at CFT. Forty years on, it remains a perfect memory, distinct, one which holds within it the echo of so many other times when I sat with my parents in the auditorium looking at the stage – excited, nervous almost, knowing that when the lights went down, anything might happen.

The 1971 season closed with Sherwood's romantic drama, *Reunion in Vienna*. Michael Billington remembers it as the first review he did for *The Guardian*, but also because he points to a very particular Chichester phenomenon he began to notice from the 1970s onwards – that of critics reviewing the audiences, as well as the productions. He quotes a review by Helen Dawson in *Plays and Players*, September 1971: 'Chichester sometimes has a blurring effect on

intention and reality, not so much of what is happening on stage, but because the audience reaction often feels so strong that it appears to be influencing the production more than directors, actors or the author. Sussex audiences like to clap entrances, exits and anything approaching a Tory sentiment... In a way, Chichester is *the* audience participation show.'

Billington goes on to say: 'I thought that said very succinctly something you will find in all the reviews of Chichester, I think, through this period onwards for the next twenty, thirty, years.[1] They seem to review the audience more than the show, talk about the occasion – I have done it myself – to somehow, rather condescendingly, say this is the most conservative, comfortable audience in Britain. There is a grain of truth in this... but it is also unfair, because Chichester has tried constantly to break away from that image.'

[1] This attitude was still, sometimes, in evidence as late as 2011. I was on a panel on BBC Two's *The Review Show* reviewing *Yes, Prime Minister*. The opening comments from a couple of my fellow guests were all about the age of the audience, their clothes, their attitudes rather than the text or the production.

Edith Evans in ***Dear Antoine***, 1971.
Photo: John Timbers/ ArenaPAL

OPPOSITE
John Gielgud in ***Caesar and Cleopatra***, 1971.
Photo: John Timber/ ArenaPAL

Joan Plowright and Robin Phillips in *The Doctor's Dilemma*, 1972.

Photo: John Timbers/ArenaPAL

Over the past fifty years, many long-term supporters of CFT, with a slight shrug and note of resignation, might justifiably point to the fact that – without any significant measure of public subsidy for most of its fifty-year history – how extraordinary an achievement it is for any theatre to sell thousands of seats, year in and year out and, at the same time, offer audiences the chance to see world premieres, British debuts, reinterpretations and classic texts, alongside revivals of old favourites that, yes, might be termed 'Chichester' productions. What matters is the relationship between the auditorium and the stage, the quality of engagement, not the colour of someone's hair or if they happen to be wearing a blazer...

The cover for the 1972 souvenir programme was designed in the form of a Victorian play-bill, all brown and black and red block letters. The season opened on Wednesday 3 May with John Gay's ever-popular satirical musical *The Beggar's Opera*. It was the first full-length musical to be presented at Chichester, something that is now one of the essential component parts of the summer Festival. Directed by Robin Phillips and designed by Daphne Dare, it starred John Neville and Millicent Martin and was a lavish production. With its cast of characters with superbly appropriate names (nominative determinism, to use the fancy term!) the stage was filled with the antics of Mr Peachum and Lockitt, the keeper of the gaol; by Filch the robber captain, Jemmy Twitcher and Crook-Finger'd Jack; by the saucy meanderings of Dolly Trull and Betty Doxy. Charles Dance, in only his second-ever job in theatre, played Wat Dreary.

George Bernard Shaw's *The Doctor's Dilemma* followed, opening on Wednesday 17 May. First staged in 1906, the play considers certain questions of ethics and judgement faced by the medical profession. Unfortunately, in a case of life mirroring art, it was a production plagued by illness. At certain points during the run, there were as many as five understudies on the stage and Evershed-Martin, in *The Miracle Theatre*, recalls how, during one performance, John Clements was in such pain that he was unable to go back on after the interval: 'The audience suddenly found they were confronted with the character Dr Blenkinsop [Eric Dodson] playing the part of Bloomfield Bonington.'

The third play was Jonathan Miller's directorial debut at Chichester with a landmark, if challenging, production of Shakespeare's *The Taming of the Shrew*. Joan Plowright played Katherina to Anthony Hopkins' Petruchio. Notices were,

ABOVE LEFT

Richard Chamberlain and Michael Aldridge in *The Lady's Not For Burning*, 1972.

Photo: John Timbers/ ArenaPAL

ABOVE

Millicent Martin, Maggie Fitzgibbon and Harold Innocent in *The Beggar's Opera*, 1972.

Photo: John Timbers/ ArenaPAL

for the most part, good – though the *Sunday Telegraph* reviewed Hopkins' performance as verging on 'a ferocious, mad fanatic' and found it 'not light enough'.

But it was the final play that was to define Clements' penultimate season. Christopher Fry's powerful 1948 classic, *The Lady's Not For Burning*. Written in 1948, the action is set in an English village during a 14th-century witch hunt. With Fry's characteristic beautiful and lyrical language, the play pits prejudice, bigotry and human stupidity against openness, love and independence of thought. Directed by Robin Phillips, it boasted a tremendous cast – Anna Calder-Marshall, Michael Aldridge, June Jago – with Richard Chamberlain, one of the most sought-after film and television actors of the time, in the lead. As critic Harold Hobson wrote in the *Sunday Times*: 'Its wit glitters like a diamond; and like a diamond, the play is hard and indestructible.'[1]

The 1972 production was a triumphant suc-cess, attracting near capacity audiences and the season closed on Saturday 9 September on a high note.

However, for the first time since opening ten years before, the Theatre did not shut it doors and go into hibernation. Instead, possibly pre-cisely because he was going in to his final year in charge, Clements agreed to stage a Christmas production – *Toad of Toad Hall* – with some of the 1972 Company coming back to CFT for the winter. The production ran for two weeks and gave a clear message that, so long as the qual-ity was high and the production fitted in with the principles and excellence of the summer Festivals, audiences would come.

---

[1] When it was revived at the Minerva in 2002, directed by Sam West, *The Guardian* commented: 'the real sur-prise is that the verse turns out to be such an affable and accessible form and that the language is so exciting.' Christopher Fry – then 95 years old – was in the audi-ence. Fry, who died in June 2005, is one of the writers who made the most significant contribution to CFT.

1973

Topol in *R Loves J*, 1973.

Photo: John Timbers/ ArenaPAL

With perhaps a wry nod to his own position, John Clements opened his final season in May 1973 with another of Anouilh's poignant plays translated by Lucienne Hill, *The Director of the Opera*. The wit of the choice did not go unnoticed by the *Daily Mail*: 'Sir John conquered all early doubts about his policy for Chichester, after the loss of Olivier, and his seasons have brought joy both to the Theatre's faithful audiences and to its accountants alike. Let us hope, therefore, for the gratitude we owe him, that any similarity between his present job and his current work ends with the title.'

A requiem for middle age, the director of the title – a successful and brilliant man in his professional life – is humbled both by his family and by striking workers within the provincial Italian opera house he runs. That irony, too, would not have been lost on the audience, given Britain was in the grip of strikes and the three-day week and power cuts. Clements received outstanding notices for his performance, many of them also taking the chance to review his eight years as Artistic Director of CFT at the same time.

Andy Neal joined as a stage hand in 1973 and, over his thirty years at CFT, was to rise to the position of First Stage Dayman: '[*The Director of the Opera*] was the first set I worked on. It had a backcloth beautifully painted to look like the auditorium of an opera house, with lots of little holes where the lights would be and it was very brightly backlit. It was spectacular.'

The second play was Chekhov's *The Seagull*. Despite Irene Worth and Robert Stephens garnering praise for their performances, the production seems to have been admired, but not loved, by the critics. Their inked enthusiasm was lukewarm.

It was followed by a musical version of Ustinov's play *R Loves J*. The production was directed by Wendy Toye CBE, the first woman ever to direct a play at Chichester. A dancer, film director and actress, Toye had collaborated with directors such as Cocteau and Carol Reed in the past, and was to direct eight productions at Chichester during the 1970s. But although audiences liked Topol as the General, the reviewers were not impressed and thought the Cold War politics at the heart of the play had been overtaken by events. For example, *The Stage* said: 'It is a sluggish drawn out affair with

precious little wit, unmemorable music, and with a rather dated air.'

The fourth play – and last of the Clements' era – was Pinero's *Dandy Dick*. A wonderful, high-jinx farce – bringing Alastair Sim and Patricia Routledge back together on the CFT stage – the stage crew every night earned a round of applause after their major scene change, carried out on the trot to the tune of the 'Post Horn Gallop'.

Andy Neal again: 'For set changing we had as many as twenty-three crew. The number was dictated by the biggest scene change in the season and how many people it would take to do

that... With plays in rep on a Thursday and a Saturday, we would come in and change what was up the previous night – Show A – and put up Show B for the matinee, then we would change it back to Show A. After the evening performance, we would take down Show A and put up what we had of Show C for rehearsal the following day. They were long days, but great fun.'

Certainly, in the 1970s, I was not alone in choosing to remain in the auditorium during the interval to watch the crew doing the scene changes. For me, it's another example of how the open thrust stage at CFT draws the audience in,

John Clements in
The Director of the
***Opera**, 1973.*

Photo: John Timbers/
ArenaPAL

Next parrot, please

(Or the day Sir John got the bird)

What a squawk there was going on at the Chichester Festival Theatre — and all because an audition was being held for the part of the parrot in the Theatre's forthcoming pantomime, Treasure Island.

Sir John Clements, who plays the part of Captain Long John Silver, was given the bird constantly

throughout the day — and he is pictured with Angela, belonging to Mr. J. Vickers.

More pictures and full story — Page 15.

More pictures and full story — Page 15.

as participants in the making of theatre.

After the 1973 season closed in September, *Dandy Dick* transferred to the Garrick Theatre in London and opened in October. In December, another Christmas show – this time an adaptation of *Treasure Island* – and with Clements himself playing Long John Silver. It was the perfect end to his eight years at the helm. Over eight seasons, Clements had staged 32 productions, eight of which had gone into London. He is remembered fondly and with great admiration by all those who worked with him.

Paul Rogerson: 'Clements was a very good director, theatre manager and a fine actor. He was also very good at comedy, though not in real life! He had a car with the number plate FUF – which I christened Fearful Uncle Fred, because he was known by everybody as Fred. He was always Mr Clements, then Sir John.'

It had been announced at the beginning of the 1973 season that Clements' successor was to be Keith Michell. A very different era was about to begin.

Looking back, Michael Billington comments: 'I think in retrospect, one realises now how good Clements was and how much we miss the kind of very elegant, straightforward classic revivals that he produced and supervised.'

ABOVE

Press launch of 1974 season: (left to right) Peter Gilmore, Keith Michell, Diana Dors, Alfred Marks.

Photo: CFT

1974

Keith Michell had, of course, been part of Olivier's first Company and knew the stage well, knew Chichester well. An accomplished painter and illustrator – he taught art in his native Adelaide before making his stage debut there in 1947 – he was also a familiar face on television, as well as stage, and was looking for a new challenge.

Michell remembers the first approach: 'Teddy Smith rang me up and asked me to take over as Artistic Director. I felt it would be foolish not to do it, because maybe being an actor was not enough. [CFT] was now well established and it was established with a star system, which was right for it. It's no good having a lot of actors nobody had heard of, however good they were, this far out of London and hoping people would come. They needed a draw.'

Michell's appointment was covered in the trade press, including *The Stage*, in February 1973: 'The hope, and the belief, is that [Michell] will make his own footsteps, firmly and freshly, so that with his own inspiration and guidance Chichester will get another vital phase of its extraordinary life.'

A few weeks later, Michell moved to Chichester, with his wife (actress Jeanette Sterke) and their two children. He was an immediate favourite with the staff and crew of the Theatre.

Paul Rogerson, General Manager: 'Keith was so different to Clements. For a start, he was a film and television star, as well as a stage actor. He drove a Triumph Stag. When he arrived, he said straightaway: "My name's Keith, my wife is Jenny and that's how we want to be known by everybody." He was a quiet and gentle man, and insisted he was on first-name terms and on an equal footing with everyone. However, there was no getting away from the fact that he was "The Director".'

Michell's opening season was anticipated eagerly. The souvenir programme carried simply the words 'Chichester 74' and his signature. The image was one of his own, distinctive paintings, geometric diamonds like broken glass, gold and orange and brown theatrical players' masks, hinting at the Greek drama that was to be staged. Inside, a short article written by Michell about following in the footsteps of Olivier and Clements: 'Each time I have "viewed" at Chichester, I've felt that same stir of excitement I had the first time I saw it – coming in from the

green and (on a good day) sunshine and looking up at the shadowy structure of crosswork patterns, gantries and lights, or down at the functional thrust of that beautiful stage, I remember Sir Tyrone Guthrie referred to a theatre as a sacred place. It is true of this one. It *is* rather like entering some modern temple. It *is* a place of communication.'

CFT's fortunes notwithstanding, it was not the easiest of times to be taking over running a theatre. Michell takes up the story: 'When I arrived in '74, it was to a backdrop of the three-day week, IRA bombings, two general elections, corruption scandals, miners' strikes and a financial crisis. There were train and petrol strikes as well and I asked Equity [the trades union representing actors] what we should do if audiences could not get to Chichester. They said: "you'll have to close". I said: "I don't think so."

'But of course, getting a season ready each year was a nightmare, even without all those external things going on. Looking back, I had no idea what was involved and I don't think you do until your third or fourth season.'

Everyone interviewed for the book commented on how inclusive Michell's years were, how there was a sense of everyone being treated on an equal level. Also, that although he was quiet and gentle as an Artistic Director, as an actor he had an extraordinary power, a commanding presence the instant he stepped on to the stage.

Keeping to Clements' twenty-two week Festival, Michell's first season had two works in translation – *Tonight We Improvise* and Turgenev's *A Month in the Country* – an adaptation of Sophocles' *Oedipus Tyrannus* and Vanbrugh's 1705 farce, *The Confederacy*, which itself was an adaptation of an older French play.

Rogerson again: 'Keith worked so hard: he directed, acted, designed sets, even the programmes, as well as running the place. But he got some stick from the critics in his first season, especially for *Oedipus* with Diana Dors as Jocasta (and original music by Tangerine Dream) and Pirandello's *Tonight We Improvise*, which begins with a fifteen-minute monologue. When we got all these bad notices, the Board suggested that they cut down on the critics' First Night free bar...'

Michael Billington agrees the season got off to a rocky start: '*Tonight We Improvise*, directed by Peter Coe, totally ramshackle, dreadful reviews... The evening is a blur. Pirandello is very difficult to do, it's all about theatrical games, whether

ANGEL Chicago stars in a new Christmas musical based on the Nativity at Chichester Festival Theatre. The musical, Follow the Star, written by Wally K. Daly runs until January 11. Grabbing plenty of praise are baby snatchers (left to right): King Herod (Lewis Fiander), Assy (Michael Howe), Oxy (Brett Forrest), and Angel Chicago (Tony Robinson).

The Argus, Brighton. 27 December 1974 / West Sussex Record Office

OPPOSITE

***Oedipus Tyrannus*, 1974.**

Photo: Mark Gudgeon

OVERLEAF

Keith Michell preparing for *Cyrano de Bergerac*, 1975.

Photo courtesy of Keith Michell

you are watching theatre or reality, and it takes a highly disciplined form of staging… And then *Oedipus Tyrannus*, with Diana Dors, directed by a young Polish director who was, frankly, cast above his worth.'

Researching for this book, and realising how the production was not considered a success at the time, is fascinating. *Oedipus* remains, for me, an extraordinary piece of theatre, an evening where something changed in my understanding of the possibilities of the stage. It was my first experience of Greek tragedy, that strange mixture of collusion and dread and emotion so raw it seems almost in bad taste to watch. More than thirty years later, I still remember the feeling that I should leap out of my seat and intervene. Stop the catastrophe from unfolding. And Keith Michell, with his gouged eyes blinded and bloodied, defeated by Fate but yet defiant still, standing in the centre of the stage. Then the closing words of the Chorus:

'Look ye, countrymen and Thebans,
this is Oedipus the great,
He who knew the Sphinx's riddle
and was mightiest in our state.
Who of all our townsmen gazed not
on his fame with envious eyes?
Now, in what a sea of troubles
sunk and overwhelmed he lies!

Therefore wait to see life's ending
ere thou count one mortal blest;
Wait till free from pain and sorrow
he has gained his final rest.'

Oedipus Tyrannus
SOPHOCLES

It was left to *A Month in the Country* to end the season on a positive note. Supported by Derek Jacobi and Timothy West, Dorothy Tutin (who had played Anne Boleyn to Michell's Henry in the award-winning 1970s BBC television series, *The Six Wives of Henry VIII*) in particular received superb notices and was awarded Actress of the Year for her portrayal of Natalya at the *Evening Standard* Theatre Awards.

But for many Cicestrians, the defining production of Michell's opening season was the Christmas show. *Follow the Star* was Jim Parker's new musical nativity for children, directed by Wendy Toye. Many of us remember Tony Robinson, as Angel Chicago, choosing children to come down onto the stage. Diane Goodman, CFT Project Administrator – and responsible for all the photographic and illustration research for this book – remembers it as the first production ever she saw at CFT. 'I can still sing every word!' she says.

Like Diane, I have the score, the album (an LP, of course, it being the 1970s) and can remember a shocking number of the lyrics too. It was Robinson's debut at CFT. He was to return the following summer in Ibsen's *An Enemy of the People*, then again as Feste in *Twelfth Night* and the ever-so-'umble accountant, Majorin, in *Monsieur Perrichon's Travels* in 1976.

Follow the Star was a wonderful, magical end to Michell's first season in charge and for many of today's audiences – who now come with their own children to see the wide range of shows for children and young people presented in Chichester – it was their first experience of CFT.

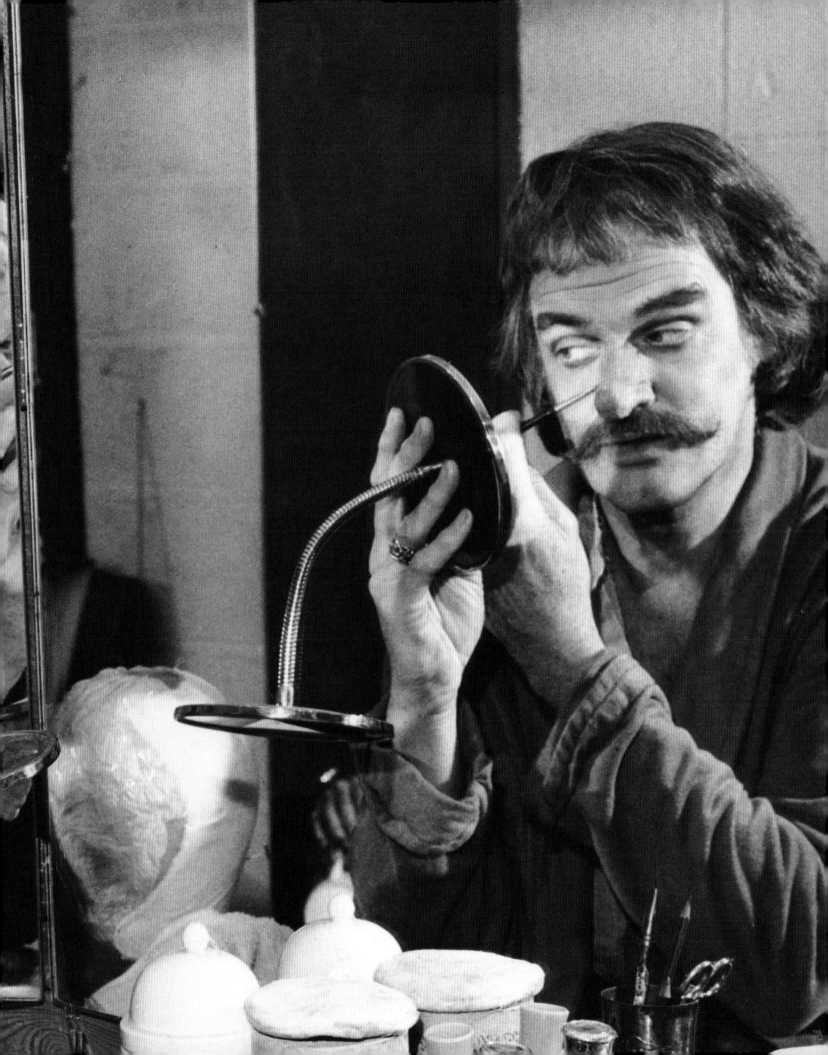

1975

Cyrano de Bergerac, 1975.

Photo: Zöe Dominic

It was a long, dismal winter with strikes and acrimonious industrial relations continuing. Evenings spent waiting for six o'clock, when the electricity went off, and eating supper by candlelight. Harold Wilson's minority Labour Government was in office. In the Hit Parade, Status Quo, Steve Harley & the Cockney Rebel and the Bay City Rollers. On the television, *It Ain't Half Hot Mum* and *Dad's Army*.[1]

In the world at large, the times they were a' changing. In January, Brian Clough took over the ailing football club, Nottingham Forest. In February, Margaret Thatcher defeated Edward Heath for the leadership of the Conservative Party. In March, the National Front organised a march in London against further European integration.

It was against this backdrop of economic misery and instability that Michell opened his second season on Wednesday 14 May with a world premiere of Christopher Fry's translation of Rostand's *Cyrano de Bergerac*.[2]

[1] Another tangential link with CFT. In October 1975 a stage show – based on the series – opened at the Shaftesbury Theatre, London, after a two-week run in County Durham. The revue – *Dad's Army: A Nostalgic Music and Laughter Show of Britain's Finest Hour* – was produced by Roger Redfarn, who was to be responsible for one of Chichester's most successful shows in the 1980s, *Underneath the Arches*.

[2] Five years earlier, the novelist Anthony Burgess had been commissioned to do a new translation and adaptation of the play for CFT's sister theatre, the Tyrone Guthrie Theater, Minneapolis.

Michell played the eponymous hero – skilled duellist, courageous soldier, poet, true friend – with Barbara Jefford as Roxane, the object of his affections, and a young Christopher Cazenove as the tongue tied, beautiful Christian. Neither *The Guardian* nor *The Times*, nor the *Evening Standard* much liked the production, but in the *Daily Telegraph*, John Barber wrote: 'In gallant defiance of our economic blues, Chichester has flung onto the stage a romantic extravaganza of love and war with a huge cast... it is a gesture that this big stage can happily enlarge.'

The second play of the 1975 season was Ibsen's 1882 dark, comic masterpiece, *An Enemy of the People*. This production brought to Chichester a man who was to play a key role in the history and fortunes of CFT over the next thirty years – the actor, writer, poet and essayist, film, television and theatre director, Patrick Garland. It was the first of more than 20 productions he was to direct at Chichester, in both the Main House and the Minerva.[1]

An Enemy of the People lays bare the hypocrisy and corruption of the political system. At the heart of the story is Dr Stockmann, a man of integrity, and his attempts to do the honourable thing, to speak the truth.

Patrick Garland remembers the production well: 'I have done a lot of Ibsen since, but *An Enemy of the People* was the start of it and my first play at Chichester. Donald Sinden, with whom I had worked before, had based Dr Thomas Stockmann on a character he knew who was very eccentric and wore strange clothes. Donald created him as a comedic figure and he got a lot of laughs that the character seldom gets in other productions. I encouraged the eccentricity because I realised that if Donald made Stockmann endearing to the public, and a

comedic figure, when the play turns and [he] is suddenly telling these rather pious, right-minded people truths they don't want to acknowledge, then the audience having taken him into their bosom and found him funny and eccentric, can't suddenly back out of it. They were hooked. They were stuck with him... A great leading man, he took the responsibility, but he was also a great company man, kind and generous, and never

[1] As the fifth (and also eighth!) Artistic Director, it is appropriate that Garland should have been invited to direct the Thanksgiving Service for Sir Laurence Olivier at Westminster Abbey in 1989.

Barbara Jefford and Donald Sinden in *An Enemy of the People,* **1975.**
Photo: John Timbers/ArenaPAL

Joseph Fiennes (centre) in *Cyrano de Bergerac,* **2009.**
Photo: Catherine Ashmore

Hannah Gordon and Topol in *Othello*, 1975.

Photo: John Haynes/
Lebrecht Music & Arts

went in for rows... unlike Rex Harrison!' [1]

Keith Michell remembers the second season as immediately much more successful than his first: '*An Enemy of the People* was Patrick Garland directing at his best, and *Cyrano de Bergerac*. *Othello* – with Topol playing Othello to my Iago – we transferred to Hong Kong. It was always my intention to take Chichester out to the world.'

<hr>

[1] Everyone who sent in their memories of CFT or who worked backstage, or front of house, also spoke warmly of Sinden and how charming and kind he was to everybody, whatever their job. The same was also said about Patrick Garland too. When I arrived in the dark days of 1998, as Administrative Director to work with the new Theatre Director, Andrew Welch, I found a handwritten card waiting for me on my desk from Patrick wishing me the best of luck.

As does Michael Billington: '*An Enemy of the People*... was extremely good, because Donald Sinden reminded us that Ibsen's play about a man versus his community is essentially comic. I thought that was brilliant.'

However, even though the critics were lavish in their praise, the box office was sluggish and sales were slow. A new play by Andrew Sachs, *Made in Heaven*, which opened on Tuesday 15 July did not do well and, for the most part, the critics savaged it. Irving Wardle wrote in *The Times*: 'Chichester bashing is now a popular sport, but this is an unspeakable piece.'

And Jack Tinker in the *Daily Mail*: 'It is an overblown, overwritten, overspoken piece of nonsense so insubstantial one finds it hard to excuse in these times of economic austerity.'

Evershed-Martin admitted he was at first alarmed when he heard Michell had chosen *Othello* for the closing production of the 1975 season, with memories of Olivier's 1964 performance so fresh in audience's minds. However, the director Peter Dews – who would take over as Artistic Director from Michell in 1978 – wisely set the piece in a very different period and setting.

Patricia Routledge, well known and much loved by the CFT audience, was cast in the role of Emilia: 'I took medical advice on my death. Iago [Michell] stabs me, but Emilia's got a lot to say before she dies and it has got to be understood. I asked a doctor:

'"How am I going to do this convincingly?"'

'He asked: "Where are you going to be stabbed?"'

'I said: "He is coming from behind and stabs me in the small of my back."'

'"Ah," he said quietly, "renal failure. He'd get the kidneys, so you can go on for quite a while."'

Her meticulous preparation paid off and she received outstanding notices. For example, this review in *The Stage & Television Today*: 'For some time now a delightful player in comedy and musicals, Patricia Routledge has emerged as an artist of considerable stature with her performance as Emilia... She creates a character of imagination, depth and power and brings to all her scenes, especially at the close of the play, the urgency, passion and significance of authentic tragedy.'

The company reprised its Christmas success with a second outing for *Follow the Star*. I was there and, this time, was successful in being invited on to to the stage by Tony Robinson. I can't remember what we were called upon to do – sing, dance, nod, smile – only that, though a year older, it was as enjoyable and joyous a show as it had been the previous December.

1976

1976 was a year of significance for CFT, as much away from Chichester as within the green folds of Oaklands Park.

In March, the National Theatre on London's South Bank began to unveil its buildings, theatre by theatre. Under the direction of Peter Hall – who had been Artistic Director since taking over from Laurence Olivier in 1973 – the Lyttelton was the first space to open, with a season of plays transferred from the Old Vic. It was followed by the Olivier in October. [1]

The Queen officially opened the National Theatre complex on Tuesday 26 October, twenty-

Hannah Gordon and Patricia Routledge in *Othello*, 1975.

Photo: John Haynes, Lebrecht & Arts

---

[1] The complex had been due to open in 1973, but was delayed because of construction problems. The Cottesloe, the smallest of the three spaces, did not open until March 1977 with *Illuminatus!* – an eight-hour play by Ken Campbell.

four years after she had laid the foundation stone at the site adjacent to the Festival Hall. CFT Founder Leslie-Evershed Martin and his wife, Carol, were in the audience.

Laurence Olivier, the first Artistic Director of both Chichester Festival Theatre and the National Theatre, welcomed the audience with a quote echoing Shakespeare's *Henry V*: 'It is an outsize pearl of British understatement to say that I am happy to welcome you at this moment in this place.'

But back in January, the usual putting together of the season occupied everybody's attention. Keith Michell was at the Hong Kong Festival, with *Othello* and *Cyrano de Bergerac*. In the UK, the dismal winter of strikes and terrorist attacks continued. Twelve IRA bombs were set off in London's West End. The business of casting and employing back stage crew and technicians, the business of printing the brochure and the tickets, dusting down the gels and the lights and ensuring that everything was in good and working order, continued.

The 60-page 1976 souvenir programme – with a psychedelic cover reminiscent of Huxley's *Antic Hay* – lists the directors as Peter Dews, Patrick Garland, Keith Michell and Eric Thompson[1] And with an impressive cast line-up that included Patsy Byrne, Michele Dotrice, Susan Hampshire, Jeanette Sterke, Gordon Jackson, Tony Robinson, Barbara Windsor and Rex Harrison.

The opening production was *Noah*[2], a translation by Arthur Wilmurt of André Obey's 1930 play, followed by Shakespeare's *Twelfth Night* – which

I remember fondly – and Somerset Maugham's *The Circle*. But the defining production of the 1976 season was Patrick Garland's *Monsieur Perrichon's Travels*, starring Rex Harrison.

Patrick Garland remembers[3]: 'It was Rex's first and only appearance at Chichester and he did not get good reviews, but he was not well cast for it. I directed, but I hadn't cast him. I just accepted it because it was Rex. Best comedian there ever was… He did what no actor can do today, the art of underplaying. Rex used to say: "These young actors and comedians think all they need to do is stand centre stage and walk down to the front of the stage and shout. They should learn that comedy is not like that. Comedy is the art of concealing, not revealing." '

However, his reputation for causing trouble off the stage is easily as secure as his abilities on the stage and, as Tim Bouquet says in his note to the interviews, many of the anecdotes he was told concerning arguments, fights and snubs involved Rex Harrison. Garland agrees he could be difficult: 'He was not one for concealing his feelings offstage. You always knew when Rex had arrived at CFT; you could hear him parking. He had, at that time, a rather large American car and he couldn't squeeze it in, there wasn't room. Rex just slammed his car into reverse to try to get into the space. Then he did it again, scraping and shunting until he got it in, making a complete junket of the car that was next to him.'

There was also a rather public rivalry between Olivier, Harrison and Alec Guinness, as Garland remembers: 'Olivier was very jealous of Rex because Rex was a massive Hollywood and Broadway star and he wasn't in the same league as a "movie star". Rex was equally jealous of Olivier, because Olivier was the greatest

---

[1] Remembered fondly as the creator and narrator of the BBC children's television series, *The Magic Roundabout*, Eric Thompson was also an actor. Married to the actress and director Phyllida Law – who several times played at Chichester – their children are the actresses Emma and Sophie Thompson.

[2] A new adaptation of *Noah* by Rachel Barnett is the Chichester Festival Youth Theatre production scheduled for summer 2012.

[3] Garland wrote a memoir about Rex Harrison – *The Incomparable Rex* – which was published in 1999, nine years after the Oscar and Tony award-winning actor's death.

**Rex Harrison and
Tony Robinson
in** *Monsieur
Perrichon's Travels,*
1976.

Photo: Zoë Dominic

stage actor of his generation and he wasn't. He'd always refer to Olivier as "*your* friend Laurence Olivier." However, they were both equally jealous of Alec because he was both a great stage actor and a movie star. And the funny thing is, Alec never gave a fig. He didn't like Rex and would never mention him. Rex loved to stride with his abnormal self-confidence and aura down Madison Avenue [in New York] being pursued by photographers and autograph hunters, while Alec would phone me up and say: "I'm coming into Chichester today and, if you feel like it and can bear it, it would be very nice to have lunch with you." '

During the course of his years at CFT, Keith Michell started New Ventures. Michell explains: 'I was really keen to find new talent at Chichester, which is why we started New Ventures at the Dolphin & Anchor.'[1]

As well as giving opportunities to younger actors, cast in the Festival Season – such as Tony Robinson[2] - many backstage staff and crew also took part in New Ventures. With one-act plays and rehearsed readings, held in the old ballroom (now the upper floor of Waterstones), debut directors also tried out their skills.

Michell's project, which was to develop into The Tent in the 1980s, led ultimately to the building of the Minerva Theatre, which opened in 1989. One of the highlights of the 'fringe company' was the performance of Eliot's Murder in the Cathedral – Michell himself played Becket – in the nave of Chichester Cathedral. A beautiful production of light and shadow, strengthening the twin relationship of the Cathedral with the Theatre.

---

[1] The Dolphin & Anchor Hotel was, in the 1960s and 1970s, the major hotel in Chichester. Dating from 1910, when the two original establishments combined – the Dolphin dates from 1649 and the Anchor from 1768 – the building is opposite the Cathedral in West Street. Wetherspoons and Waterstones now occupy the site.

[2] Robinson was listed in 1977 programme as New Ventures Production Associate.

1977

Ingrid Bergman in *Waters of the Moon*, 1977.

Photo: Zoë Dominic

The Board had made the decision to extend Michell's three-year contract by a year. His final season is seen by many, audiences and critics alike, as his finest. Four plays, the first opening on Tuesday 10 May and the last closing on Saturday 17 September. Each was, by chance perhaps, rather than by design, directed by a CFT Artistic Director – past, present or future. So, John Clements directing *Waters of the Moon*, Keith Michell with *In Order of Appearance*, Peter Dews directing *Julius Caesar* and Patrick Garland's production of George Bernard Shaw's *The Apple Cart*.

N C Hunter's *Waters of the Moon* brought an international film star to Chichester in the shape of Ingrid Bergman. Some critics, Michael Billington in *The Guardian* among them, were not won over by either the play or her performance: 'What on earth is the point of reviving this kind of tepid naturalistic piece in a theatre that cries out for dash and flamboyance?'

Others, such as Herbert Kretzmer in the *Daily Express*, were more generous: 'A play of gentle melancholy, rich in humour, directed with skill by John Clements.'

More than thirty years later, people still remember Ingrid Bergman fondly and talk of how her presence at CFT both brought in new audiences, and a new generation of autograph hunters to stage door.

In Order of Appearance – written by Wally K Daly and Keith Michell, with music by Jim Parker – was a light-hearted, charming look at the progress of history, from Julius Caesar to George VI. Remembered not only for the industrial size washing machine that was needed – the white robes of the senators (though set in the Jacobean period, rather than Rome of 44 BC) were sodden, stained red after every performance – but also for the way we, the audience, became the audience in the senate during Mark Antony's famous speech. I remember twisting round in my seat, listening to the voices of the rabble shouting, in the aisles, from the walkways, an exhilarating moment of pure theatre joining stage to auditorium. As John Barber in the *Daily Telegraph* reviewed how the scene...

'...so often muffed, won a great round of applause. Peter Dews has taken an extremely

bold line with his Julius Caesar. It works well so must be counted one of the Sussex Theatre's greatest successes'.

But again, as so often at CFT, it was one show that was to define the season and also brought Michell's time as Artistic Director to a triumphant conclusion.

George Bernard Shaw's 1928 satirical comedy, *The Apple Cart*, brought another of Chichester's most successful and popular actresses to CFT for the first time. Cast as Orinthia, the King's Mistress, opposite Keith Michell, Penelope Keith was already well known as Margo in the BBC hit sitcom, *The Good Life*.[1]

Garland remembers working with Penelope Keith for the first time: 'Keith [Michell] cast Penny, but from the start I genuinely thought

she was someone special, a very witty girl and often just wonderfully funny.'

Penelope Keith herself partly took the job at Chichester as a way of having a relaxing summer: 'I was rehearsing *The Good Life* during the day, and playing in *Donkey's Years* at the Globe – directed by Michael Rudman[2] – in the evenings, then recording *TGL* on the Sunday. I was also doing other things, like *Private Lives*, for television and it was Jubilee year, so there were galas on Sundays, *and* I was recording books. I knew I was running myself into the ground. So when I was phoned up by my then-agent asking if I would do *The Apple Cart* at Chichester – I had never read the play, few people had – I thought if I went to Chichester, that would be

Keith Michell and Penelope Keith in *The Apple Cart*, 1977.

Photo: John Timbers/ ArenaPAL

---

[1] Written originally for Richard Briers, who played Tom Good, it also starred Felicity Kendal as Barbara and Paul Eddington as Jerry. All four principals have had great success at CFT.

[2] Michael Rudman was to be Artistic Director at CFT in 1990. It was an unhappy experience. But his time is remembered fondly by many staff who were there. He was the only surviving AD who did not wish to be interviewed for the book.

good because then it would mean I couldn't do anything else.'

Penelope Keith continues with her first impressions of the stage: 'It [the stage] was terrifying... I learned very soon that it is very difficult to hear what you can't see, if you can't see somebody's face, especially in something as wordy as Shaw. Now having played it an awful lot, I love it. I go home after appearing on that stage feeling terribly free, but initially it's very frightening.'[1]

Straight away, it was clear Garland had a hit on his hands and, in a tremendous cast that included Jeanette Sterke, Dandy Nicholls, June Jago and Nigel Stock, the on-stage chemistry between the two principals was clear.

Garland once more: 'He [Michell] had this extraordinary quality, which I think is very rare and rather neglected. He had the quality of grace.'

Looking back, Penelope Keith remembers her first season at CFT for two reasons. First, working with Michell: 'Acting with Keith was wonderful fun, very wicked. Twinkle in his eye. I think a lot of joy has gone from the work now, but then it was just fun. *The Apple Cart* is terribly wordy, it's longer than *Hamlet*, and in the middle

of a long speech one performance, Keith forgot a phrase or two and, being a musician, began to hum until he remembered where he was. I don't think the audience noticed at all.'

But second, because it was Jubilee year, Michell put together a Gala on Sunday 12 June in the presence of Princess Alexandra.

'Chichester asked me to do a skit in its Gala... The world and his wife were there. It was lovely and Princess Alexandra was the Royal visitor. It was the height of the IRA bombing campaign and so there was a very heavy police presence. I came down the steps from my dressing room, bumped into this policeman and thought: "Oh, he looks dishy", then went on stage and did Fanny Burney – "How to Behave at the Court of Queen Charlotte". But I don't remember much about it because I had just met my future husband [Rodney Timpson]. We got married the next year.'

1977 is also notable for being the first year that CFT received significant sponsorship from a commercial organisation, something that of course was to become more and more essential in the years ahead.

General Manager, Paul Rogerson: 'We'd lost the Arts Council's guarantee against loss and we had to do something. So [Michell] brought in Tony Chardet to do sponsorship. He invited Martini & Rossi down to see *Murder in the Cathedral*.

---

[1] She was voted Showbusiness Personality of the Year by the Variety Club of Great Britain and awarded the Society of West End Theatres Award for Best Comedy Performance 1977.

Murder in the Cathedral, 1977.

Photo: Unknown/West Sussex Record Office

They thought it was wonderful and gave us 600 advertising sites on the London underground for the whole of the Festival – think what that must have been worth. And I had a safe full of Martini in my office!'

So it was, against the continuing backdrop of strikes and discontent, of economic gloom and shaky political leadership in Westminster, Michell's directorship came to an end.

Michael Billington: 'He was an honourable man and a very good actor, but I'm not sure how I could define the Michell years. Where Olivier's gave us glamour and excitement and a buzz, and the Clements years gave us very good revivals of central classics, I'm not sure how I could define the Keith Michell years other than stars... That was one thing he excelled in.'

But, alongside the programming, the importance of both New Ventures and partnership with a major sponsor should not be underestimated. It is also a hallmark of Michell's years in charge, that it is a time remembered by all those who worked at CFT as very happy days, an equal and balanced relationship between creative teams, actors, backstage staff, front of house and audiences. Two plays of his closing season played to audiences of 97 per cent – with the average overall for 1977 standing at 88 per cent. *The Apple Cart* transferred to the Phoenix Theatre, London, and during Michell's time CFT productions had gone to Hong Kong, Brussels, Luxembourg and Australia, fulfilling Michell's aim to 'take Chichester out to the world'.

1978

Clive Francis, Geraldine McEwan and Fenella Fielding in *Look After Lulu*, 1978.

Photo: John Timbers/ ArenaPAL

Peter Dews' appointment as Michell's successor was announced in November 1977. But shortly before he took over, he suffered a minor stroke. Concerned about his health, the Board therefore asked Patrick Garland to act as an Associate Director to support Peter Dews in his first season.

Sadly, his tenure was plagued by difficulties. Michael Billington: 'He was a man for whom I had an enormous admiration, but he only had a few seasons and one year he had people constantly falling ill, so was always having to recast things at the last moment – it was a patchy three years.'

Although the full season was understandably announced later than usual, the 1978 Company was strong and the first play, Oscar Wilde's *A Woman of No Importance*, opened in May to fair reviews. For example, this in the *Daily Mail*: 'It has assembled on its vast octagonal arena some of the most superb women of importance the English stage can boast. Directed by Patrick Garland, there are Sian Phillips, Margaretta Scott, Barbara

Murray, Gayle Hunnicutt and Rosie Kerslake… an elegant evening.'

The Inconstant Couple was neither a runaway hit nor a disappointment. The third play, an adaptation of Henry James' *The Aspern Papers*, received excellent notices – especially the performance of 90 year old Cathleen Nesbitt. As the great J C Trewin wrote in the *Birmingham Post* about Nesbitt's first appearance on stage in her wheelchair: 'For a moment it seemed that every light in the theatre blazed.'

The final play of the season, *Look After Lulu*, was to boast an impressive cast that included Peter Bowles, Fenella Fielding, Geraldine McEwan and Clive Francis. However, Sheridan Morley, writing in *Punch* in July 1978, wrote a hard-hitting, if wry, assessment of Chichester's character under its fourth Artistic Director:

'We are now three-quarters of our way through the first Peter Dews season at Chichester and already it's possible to reach certain conclusions about the new regime. The main aim seems to be a series of field trials for the Haymarket.[1] We've had a star-studded Oscar Wilde, an elegant Marivaux and now the Michael Redgrave *The Aspern Papers* (with a Coward/Feydeau farce still to come), all of which would have looked better behind a London proscenium arch…

'Through his long and very successful management John Clements did almost nothing there that had not been done better somewhere else. He turned Chichester from an exciting new theatre into a gracious revival house and that, alas, is what its audience has now come to expect.'

[1] These debates about the pros and cons of transferring shows from Chichester to London – whether it reduces a local audience or extends it; whether it dilutes CFT's individuality or, rather 'takes Chichester out to the world' – have been had ever since the association with the National Theatre in 1964 and 1965. The discussions were to become particularly heated during 1980s and the 1990s. In 2012, with seven CFT shows either playing in the West End – or having done so and now touring – it is seen a source of pride and artistic success.

1979

As 1978 gave way to 1979, the circumstances were not propitious for live theatre of any kind. The Winter of Discontent[2] – as the winter of 1978/79 was to become known – was characterised by widespread strikes, battles between the unions and government and rampant inflation. Political instability, a breakdown in industrial relations. Most of Britain was at a standstill.

Callaghan's Government was in disarray. Jeremy Thorpe – who had resigned as leader of the Liberal Party in 1976 following allegations over his private life – was due to go on trial for incitement to murder later in the year. Margaret Thatcher was now leader of the Conservative Party. And in the early weeks of 1979, the weather turned bitter. Blizzards and deep snow, roads impassable.

Difficult times to programme a summer Festival, difficult times to be adventurous, perhaps. The critics, certainly, saw it as a 'safe' season and renewed their allegations that Chichester was becoming, merely, a place to trial shows in before they transferred. Critic Jack Tinker in the *Daily Mail* again: 'When Chichester first established its annual Festival, its greatest successes were the plays that utilised the new theatre's great octagonal arena to its fullest extent. Inevitably they were diminished when they transferred to the confines of West End stages. Now, sadly, they seem simply designed for the fast trip to London.'

The season opened with George Bernard Shaw's *The Devil's Disciple*. A swashbuckling, all-guns-blazing sort of a production, John Clements played General Burgoyne, once again therefore

[2] The opening lines of Shakespeare's *Richard III* – 'Now is the winter of our discontent' – were quoted in a report. The phrase was then deployed in a speech by Labour Prime Minister, Jim Callaghan, and subsequently picked up by much of the press. And it stuck.

Cast including John Clements, Christine McKenna, Ian Ogilvy and Brian Blessed in *The Devil's Disciple*, 1979.

Photo: John Timbers/ ArenaPAL

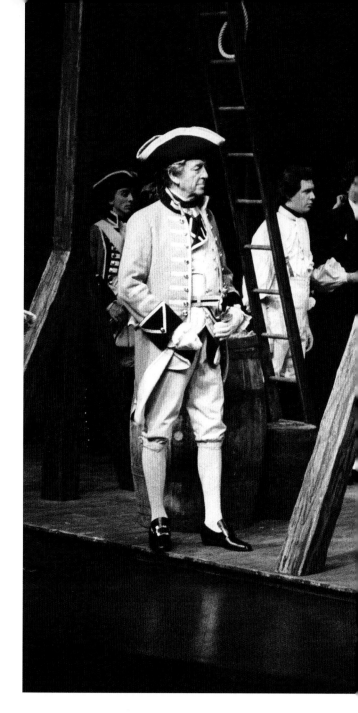

following in the footsteps of Laurence Olivier who played the role in the 1959 film adaptation. Ian Ogilvy – heartthrob star of the television series *Return of the Saint* – was very popular and there were always a fair number of front of house staff being 'helpful' around stage door when he was due in. *The Eagle Has Two Heads* by Jean Cocteau, although marked by several outstanding performances, is best remembered for the exorbitant amount of money spent, most particularly the cost of the elaborate staircase, the centre piece of the set.

My father Richard Mosse, Company Secretary, remembers the figures being brought to the Board's attention: 'A shudder went around the table. There were several raised eyebrows.'

The third play, *The Importance of Being Earnest*, starred Googie Withers as Lady Bracknell, playing alongside Hayley Mills and Millicent Martin. Dews himself directed the production. Looking through the cuttings, the impression given is that it was considered a good, rather than a great, production. The *Daily Telegraph*: 'Everyone looks the part, elegantly so, but the Wildean wit lacks bite and edge.'

The final play, Hart & Kaufman's *The Man Who Came to Dinner* saw Charles Gray as Sheridan Whiteside.[1]

The 1980s were about to begin, a decade of power dressing and big hair and Duran Duran. Margaret Thatcher's first period of Government, the first (and, to date, only) female Prime Minister. Looking back now, it's clear that the winter of 1979, going into the spring of 1980, were very difficult times for CFT.

For me, though, they were golden months. That summer was my first experience of being part of the working life of the Theatre, my first proper wage packet. Front of house selling programmes

and ice creams, the weeks of revision in May and exams in June, then glorious hot months of July and August and September. In those days, the usherettes wore long, ankle-length pinafore dresses (brown) with shirts with a bow at the neck (a kind of gold brown). By the end of the evening, having made many journeys up and down the stairs, across the carpet in the foyer, the artificial fibres in our uniforms were charged with electric static. We, literally, gave off sparks. Many of those thanked at the beginning of the book – Sharon Meier, Karl Meier, Janet Bakose, Paul Rogerson, Andy Neal, Bill Green, Colin Hedgecock, Bill Bray – were also

[1] As it happens, Andrew Welch was to programme both these plays in the 1999 Main House season. Then, the part of Whiteside was taken by Richard Griffiths. Patricia Routledge played Lady Bracknell, to outstanding reviews.

there then. This loyalty to CFT – and, when need be, defence of it – seems to me a wonderful (and particular) Chichester phenomenon.

There is a particular kind of atmosphere that settles on the foyer and the backstage areas when the audience is inside the auditorium and the house lights are down. Conversations conducted in whispers, tiptoeing up the stairs of Doors 5 or 6 to catch the end of the play, always obliged to leave during the curtain call to be ready to open the doors and see the audience safely home. A sense of purpose and a job well done, of being part of something that matters, and will continue

to matter, long after the last cars have left the car park. As David Hare writes:

'The theatre is the best way of showing the gap between what is said and what is seen to be done, and that is why, ragged and gap-toothed as it is, it has still a far healthier potential than some poorer, abandoned arts.'

'The Playwright as Historian'
Sunday Times Magazine,

November 1978
DAVID HARE

The 1980s

Artistic Directors
PETER DEWS (1978 – 1980)
PATRICK GARLAND (1981 – 1984)
JOHN GALE (1985 – 1989)

'Had we lived, I should have had a tale to tell of the hardihood, endurance and courage of my companions which would have stirred the heart of every Englishman. These rough notes and our dead bodies must tell the tale. It seems a pity, but I do not think I can write more. (Pause) Last entry. For God's sake look after our people.'

TERRA NOVA
Ted Tally, 1977

This was the era of big hair and shoulder pads, lavish sets, wigs and costumes. Casts with whiskers, casts on roller skates. It was a period of free-market economics and seismic shifts in attitudes to subsidy and the purpose of live theatre – was it for art, for entertainment, for social good, for social change? Proponents of each took up positions in opposite corners of the ring, with their fists (metaphorically speaking) raised.

Some critics and commentators would also say that, after the tumultuous changes, developments, successes of the 1960s and the 1970s, the 1980s was a decade where British Theatre – with few notable exceptions (feminist and black theatre companies, most notably) – went backwards rather than forwards in terms of its ambitions. Increasingly ill-tempered debates about reliance on subsidy rather than box office (for theatres other than CFT!). Also, charges of a lack of politically or artistically challenging work. In a state-of-the-nation article in *The Stage*, Michael Billington wrote:

'This was the decade of *Cats, The Phantom of The Opera* and *Les Misérables*; and if anyone objects that the last-named stimulates revolutionary fervour, I'd say that it actually makes poverty picturesque.'

Joan Collins in
***The Last of Mrs Cheyney*, 1980.**
Photo: John Timbers/
ArenaPAL

Stage crew in the dock, *Terra Nova*, 1980.

Photo: Andy Neal

Others say that the growing gulf between subsidised and commercial theatre was damaging to both sectors and that funding bodies – the Arts Council key among them – did not pay enough attention to the need to balance the books.

Whatever the situation in general terms, for CFT, the 1980s started badly. By February, and with Peter Dews still battling ill health, the season was not finalised let alone on sale. The Productions Board, anxious and ham-strung, asked various people to help, Duncan Weldon among them.

Theatre Director from 1995 – 1997, Weldon had first come to CFT as a young photographer on a photo shoot for *Vogue*. Thirty years later, he was a successful West End producer, involved in many of the transfers of CFT productions to London and lease holder of the Haymarket Theatre in London. Weldon had worked with Peter Dews in Canada.

Weldon takes up the story: 'Although he was perfectly all right, he had lost a lot of his energy and Teddy Smith [Chairman of the Board] said: "Would you unofficially help him, he is having a rough time?" I threw some ideas his way – such as Joan Collins in *The Last of Mrs Cheyney*, which was Joan's return to the English stage.'

Although RADA-trained, Joan Collins was Hollywood royalty, the sultry star of films such as *The Stud* and *The Bitch*. It was a coup to have her in Chichester and she was perfectly cast in Lonsdale's romantic comedy about a jewel thief who passes herself off as a society lady.

When the play first opened at the St James' Theatre, London in 1925, critics were charmed. It ran for more than 500 performances. Then, the *Sunday Times* had said: 'It is not a good sort of play, but it is a very good play of its sort.'

The same newspaper in 1980, was less inclined to be generous: 'This play moves from one melodrama to another... these are just for the proverbial tired businessman and that only if he is very tired and business is unusually bad.'

Reviews notwithstanding, it did very well at the box office and got the season off to a much better start than might have been expected.

But for many of us who worked at CFT that season, 1980 will always be associated with Ted Tally's epic *Terra Nova*. Directed by Peter Dews, the play tells the tragic story of Scott's last expedition to the Antarctic. Drawn from the journals and letters found on the frozen body of Captain Scott, the play blends scenes from his attempts to beat his Norwegian rival, Amundsen, to the South Pole. Never previously performed in Europe, *Terra Nova* won an Obie Award in Tally's native America.[1]

---

[1]A screenwriter as well as a playwright, Tally was to go on to win an Oscar in 1991 for Best Adapted Screenplay for *The Silence of the Lambs*, as well as the WGA Screen Award, Chicago Film Critics Award and an Edgar.

Hywel Bennett, star of the popular television series *Shelley*, played Scott, with Benjamin Whitrow as Amundsen.

Andy Neal, First Stage Dayman, remembers the production vividly: 'It was the most astonishing play I ever worked on; all the crew felt the same way. Pamela Howard's set was stark, dramatic but simple, made of folds of white cloth to look like snow and ice drifts, and the actors would just appear from behind them pulling sleds. The Scott Polar Institute was very involved in the production and we had the watercolours that Henry Bowers had painted on the expedition hanging in the foyer. The sleds were three-quar-

ter-size mock-ups of originals, made as much as possible from the same materials, and the clothing was just like the originals too. It was a really hot summer, but people were sitting there shivering: that's how good it was. A brilliant piece. Hywel Bennett was remarkable and, uniquely in my experience, the stage crew wore white.'

Paul Rogerson also remembers it, though for slightly different reasons: 'During the run, Brian, the Night Watchman – and a former SAS man – came to me and said: "Paul, I'm very concerned. I keep finding tubes of KY Jelly in the top dressing rooms and I think there is something going on." He was a very devout Catholic, old Downside

Peter Birch, Benjamin Whitrow, Hywel Bennett, Christopher Neame, (seated) David Wood and Martin Sadler in *Terra Nova*, **1980.**
Photo: Zoë Dominic

boy; he used to go to Mass every day. I reassured him we were not turning the place into a brothel. The cast covered themselves in the stuff to make it look like perspiration on stage.'

It was, however, something of a disaster at the box office, playing to one of the lowest average houses in a play in any Festival season. Leslie Evershed-Martin, writing in 1987, thought that it was a reflection of how audiences in such difficult economic times wanted escapism not tragedy.

The charges of escapism might well be true, but I wonder if the play was simply ahead of its time. That it was too soon for British audiences to accept a revisionist history of Scott. Times are different now, in these days of 'warts-and-all' biographies and denigrating of those considered 'heroes', but this was not the case thirty years ago. Or perhaps the Antarctic and white waste-lands of ice and snow simply didn't appeal to a summer Festival audience. But, either way, as I write this in January 2012 – one hundred years after Scott's fated final voyage – the beauty of the closing words printed at the head of this chapter echo, still, in my mind.

The second half of the season, Shakespeare's *Much Ado About Nothing* and Boucicault's 1844 light melodrama *Old Heads and Young Hearts*. Adapted by and starring Peter Sallis, it is remembered for wonderful individual comedic performances, although again the critics were lukewarm.

At the beginning of the 1980 season, the Board had announced that Patrick Garland would be taking over from Peter Dews as Artistic Director. The news had been greeted both with enthusiasm and a sense of expectation.

Janet Bakose, came to CFT in 1978 for a summer job in the box office prior to going on to work for the BBC. She enjoyed it so much, she decided to stay, becoming Box Office Manager, then working for Paul Rogerson and becoming Theatre Manager & Licensee when Rogerson retired. She

remembers the sense of excitement:

'Patrick was an unusual character in that he saw no divide between the actors and those who worked here, and that is what set him apart from all other Artistic Directors. When a show opened, he would be around to see what you thought and he would take it on board and listen, and give everybody the time of day. Every season, he invited the entire staff to Sunday lunch at his house. He loved the Theatre and I think the people of Chichester loved him.'

But however popular the appointment was to be, the pressure on Garland's first season was significant: 'As Artistic Director, I found the biggest problem was the dilemma of how to cater for an audience whose taste was never really bent to the experimental and adventurous, whereas the Theatre lent itself to precisely that sort of production. One had to work out some sort of compromise solution.'

Critic Michael Billington feels Garland got the balance right: 'What he [Garland] did, it's the secret of Chichester I suspect, is to balance crowd pleasers with work that is of actual interest. *Feasting with Panthers*, the play about Oscar Wilde with Tom Baker, was a good piece of work, so Patrick put his marker down quickly. If you look at those opening seasons, they are actually quite adventurous.'

The 1981 company was an eclectic one – Claire Bloom, Tom Baker, Patricia Hodge, Christopher Timothy, Joss Ackland and a young television star, Jonathon Morris, as well as leading stars of music hall and revue, Chesney Allen and Roy Hudd.

The Cherry Orchard, which opened on Wednesday 6 May, booked well, as did *Feasting*

with Panthers. Devised by Peter Coe about Oscar Wilde's trials in the 1890s. Tom Baker, a very popular television actor starring in *Doctor Who* at the time, played Wilde and the production was much admired, popular. *The Mitford Girls* was the perfect summer musical, star casting and glamour and sequins – and Oz Clarke[1] providing the male love interest. It did very well in Chichester, but failed to find its audience when it transferred to the Globe Theatre in London in October 1981. The Duke of Richmond, who

---

[1]Robert 'Oz' Clarke, was to become best known as the wine expert on the popular BBC series *Food and Drink*. He started his career, however, as an actor, working at Northampton, the RSC, the National, the Old Vic and Chichester, before making the shift from theatre to television.

had been involved in CFT from the earliest days and was, for many years, a Trustee, particularly remembers the show:

'I loved *The Mitford Girls* which was marvellous; not everybody liked it but coming from one aristocratic family, one is always interested in what they got up to in another!'

But the barn-storming, bells and whistles hit of the 1981 season was *Underneath the Arches*. Written by Garland, Brian Glanville and Roy Hudd – and directed by Rodger Redfarn – it was a musical revue about Bud Flanagan, Chesney Allen and the Crazy Gang. It starred Christopher Timothy, Roy Hudd and Allen himself, then 87 years old.

Janet Bakose: 'It was one of those extraordinary pieces in that advance bookings were a dis-

aster. Nobody was coming. The things that had booked well were *The Cherry Orchard*, because it had Claire Bloom in it – although it wasn't a great production – and *Feasting with Panthers* with Tom Baker as Oscar Wilde.'

Garland remembers how the Crazy Gang were fearless on the massive thrust stage that had been the undoing of so many classically trained actors: 'They were absolutely brilliant and they knew how to work that stage from all the front cloth and pantomime work they had done. They had no fear of it at all… People like the Crazy Gang treated the stage with a kind of contempt; they would walk right out to the front of it without a trace of nerves.'

Billington also remembers the production as being a breakthrough: 'People said you couldn't

do that sort of show at Chichester and [Garland] proved that you could. I remember seeing it on the day of the Royal Wedding;[1] I thought it was quite wonderful.'

Thirty years later, many of the longest serving staff and management still remember the atmosphere backstage, as well as front of house, when that company was there.

Bakose says it was one of the happiest groups of performers CFT ever played host to: 'They were such an extraordinary company and so different to theatre people... Every night the show got a standing ovation, especially when Chesney Allen came on. There was a scene with a revolve and it started out with Christopher Timothy, who played the young Chesney, singing "Strolling", standing by a bench and a lamp post. As the revolve turned you didn't notice that seamlessly Allen stepped on and replaced Timothy, so when it came back to the front he started singing in his extraordinary voice and the entire audience would dissolve in tears. Every night, the staff would want to sneak in and stand at the back. And the last night, everybody was in there and it was the most amazingly emotional moment.' When the show transferred to the Prince of Wales Theatre in 1982, Garland hired coaches and took the Theatre staff up to London to see it.

However, despite this, the 1981 season was not a financial success. Evershed-Martin records in *The Miracle Theatre* that CFT lost all its reserve funds. John McKerchar, a professional accountant who had joined the Board in 1964, took control of the budgets and helped get things back on track. He was to play a key role in the difficult times ahead. The issue was, as it was to be in the decades to come, the problem of spiralling costs – the expense not only of mounting productions, but the day-to-day running costs of supporting the building and the staff who cared for it.

TOP

Christopher Timothy and Roy Hudd in *Underneath the Arches*, 1981.

Photo: Reg Wilson/ Rex Features

The Crazy Gang and Chesney Allen.

West Sussex Gazette, July 1981. West Sussex Record Office

---

[1] Wednesday 29 July 1981, the wedding of Lady Diana Spencer to Charles, the Prince of Wales.

1982

Financial worries notwithstanding, CFT went into the 1982 season with high hopes. It opened with Shaw's *On the Rocks*, *Valmouth*, then Keith Baxter's *Cavell* (with Dulcie Gray and Joan Plowright) as the third play and *Goodbye, Mr Chips* (with John Mills) at the end of the season. It was a strong company that included Alexandra Bastedo, who was married to Garland,

Jean Marsh, Judy Campbell, the great Robert Helpmann CBE[2], John Mills and Keith Michell.

But much of the excitement concerned performances off the stage, rather than on. The American actress, singer and revue artiste, Bertice Reading, came to Chichester to play in *Valmouth*, which opened on Wednesday 19 May,

---

[2] Principal with the Sadler's Wells and the Royal Ballet Company, the Australia dancer, director and actor was also well known to British audiences as the sinister Child Catcher in the 1968 film *Chitty Chitty Bang Bang*.

Joan Plowright and Dulcie Gray in *Cavell*, **1982.**

Photo: Reg Wilson/
Rex Features

RIGHT
Bertice Reading in *Valmouth*, **1982.**

Photo: Zoë Dominic

with Fenella Fielding. The Company was invited up to the House of Lords by Lord Bessborough, President of the Theatre Trust and long term-member of the CFT Productions Board.

Paul Rogerson explains what happened: 'She [Bertice Reading] struck up a relationship with Sir Richard Thomas Valentine Blake, who was 17th Baronet Black of Galway. He as also a second-hand car salesman and liked a drink (aka "Shakey Blakey".) They got married in a registry office, had a blessing in the Cathedral, then they all went to what was then the Victoria pub in St Pancras, which was pretty riotous.'

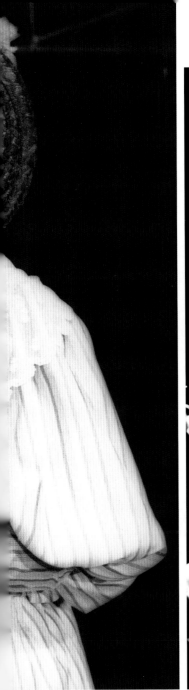

Colette Gleeson and John Mills in *Goodbye, Mr Chips*, 1982.
Photo: Reg Wilson/ Rex Features

John Mills and Nigel Stock in *Goodbye, Mr Chips*, 1982.
Photo: Reg Wilson/ Rex Features

1983

Michael G Jones, Jonathon Morris, Lucy Fleming and Patricia Hodge in *As You Like It*, 1983.

Photo: Reg Wilson/ Rex Features

The 1982 season had been artistically successful, but the Theatre once again made a loss. Times were changing. Live theatre was ever more expensive and, with no subsidy, takings at the box office could not cover the costs incurred. Even when all seats were sold, the overheads meant that the theatre was struggling.

In February 1983, it was announced that West End impresario, John Gale, would join Garland as Executive Producer to help ensure shows ran to budget and to bring in more transfer income. Gale's target – as he put it in an interview with critic and biographer Felix Barker in 1989 – was to put CFT £500,000 in credit in three years. Garland was to have a 51 per cent say in play

choice, Gale 49 per cent; on financial decisions, the percentages were reversed.

John Gale explains why he accepted Garland's invitation: 'What attracted me to Chichester was that I had made a reputation in the West End for putting on lightweight comedies and had some huge commercial successes – like *Boeing, Boeing*, which ran for 2000 performances. Then there was *No Sex Please, We're British*, which ran for sixteen years in London. I had done some serious plays too, but I had got to the point where I thought I don't want to arrive at the pearly gates to be asked by Saint Peter what I had done – and have to say I'd put on *No Sex Please, We're British*.'

Eyebrows were raised and suggestions made that Garland might resent such a partnership. Gale remembers finding it amusing, not least because the initial invitation had, in fact, come from Garland.

Garland expands: 'I had done *Shut Your Eyes and Think of England*, with Donald Sinden – very similar to *No Sex Please* – and that's when I first met John. We became very good friends. He was an excellent commercial producer. We're very different people, but that is what worked. He was good at a lot of things that I am not good at. I knew the Theatre needed someone with a strong profile to keep the budget in order, which he really did. He was very good with costume designers, who were always spending money, as were set designers, and he kept all those things together.'

In the same interview with Felix Barker 1989, when Gale was stepping down as Theatre Director, Gale is clear about where he considers the problems lie. Namely, that even with sold-out houses every night, the figures only add up if the budgets are 100 per cent adhered to and there is additional income to provide a cushion for those shows – some of great artistic merit, some just that fail to capture the audience imagination – that do not perform at the box office.

Gale remembers conversations of the time with the Arts Council: 'The finances of the Theatre really needed stabilising, because there was no one to pay the losses... I remember, in 1983, Leslie [Evershed-Martin] and I going to see Lord Rees-Mogg, who was Chairman of the Arts Council at the time, and I said to him:

' "Quite honestly, it's a disgrace that the Arts Council doesn't support Chichester Festival Theatre.

'He said: "What did you lose last year?"

'I replied: "We didn't lose anything, we made a small surplus."

'So he said: "There you are, you don't need Arts Council money."

'I regarded the Arts Council then as being there to subsidise failure.'

Eyebrows were raised even higher, though,

Omar Sharif and Debbie Arnold in *The Sleeping Prince*, 1983.

Photo: Reg Wilson/ Rex Features

when the 1983 season was announced. Three of the plays were what Chichester expected and enjoyed – Priestley's *Time and the Conways*, Shakespeare's *As You Like It* and Rattigan's *The Sleeping Prince* (with Omar Sharif and Debbie Arnold taking the roles made famous by Olivier and Vivien Leigh). It was another excellent Company of players of distinction, one that included familiar faces such as Alexandra Bastedo, Patricia Hodge, Jonathon Morris, Googie Withers and Simon Williams as well as international stars in the shape of Sharif and Arnold.

But the shock was the play Garland and Gale chose to open the 1983 season, John Osborne's *A Patriot for Me*. Starring Alan Bates in the lead, based on the true story of the Austro-Hungarian officer Alfred Redl in the 1890s, the play is about homosexuality, blackmail, and lays bare in explicit detail the anti-Semitism and homophobia of the pre-First World War years.

With a huge cast and a Drag Ball, the play was notorious for having been refused a licence for 'public exhibition' in 1965. Because Osborne refused to agree to the savaging of the text suggested by the censor, the play was only able to be seen at the Royal Court in London when the theatre turned itself into a private club for the duration. *Patriot* had not been done since. Now,

twenty years later and in Chichester, here were Garland and Gale deciding the play deserved a revival – and in its uncut form.

By 1983, the Lord Chamberlain had gone, but the whiff of scandal surrounding the play remained. Leslie Evershed-Martin and Lord Bessborough were unhappy about the play being scheduled. David Evershed-Martin remembers the family discussions.

'I disagreed entirely with my father. It domi-nated conversation at home. I thought it was wrong he made up his mind without seeing it and when they refused to budge, I think it was wrong he didn't go and see it...[1] I thought it was an excellent play. Nothing offensive about it.'

The newspapers whipped up a storm, with critic Nicholas de Jongh writing in _The Guardian_: 'A whiff of scandal is drifting through the prim cathedral city of Chichester. After years of liv-ing in the deep, safe recesses of the past dressing itself up in annual star-invested revivals of old favourites, Chichester Festival Theatre is about to meet up with the theatrical present.'

My father, Richard Mosse, remembers being rung up by Lord Bessborough, who was hoping to find a way of persuading Garland and Gale not to go ahead: 'I had a phone call from Eric one evening. He said: "Richard, I've got half the cabinet here at Stansted House[2] and this play is wall-to-wall buggery. You've got to do something to get it off."'

Garland remembers it as a make-or-break moment: 'I got to the point where I either had to stick to my guns or abandon doing it, which would have been horrible for me... [Evershed-Martin] just didn't really understand why John [Gale] and I thought it was a modern classic, but it was a huge success, particularly culturally... beautifully done by Ronald [Eyre], a stunning performance by Alan [Bates] and people liked it and admired it.'

John Gale takes up the story: 'Patrick phoned me and said: "I have told the Board if I can't do the play, I shall resign." I said: "That's wonder-ful, Patrick because if you resign, I'll have to resign. This is the shortest job I have ever had in my life!"'

---

[1] In _The Miracle Theatre_, Evershed-Martin gives a detailed account of his views in the chapter entitled 'Controversies'. _A Patriot for Me_ was the only play in CFT's history that he did not see.

[2] Bessborough's country estate in Sussex.

Bill Bray, Chief Electrician, and Andy Neal both cite *A Patriot for Me* as being one of the highlights of their time at CFT. Members of the stage crew were extras in the Drag Ball!

Duncan Weldon transferred the production to London, and then to America: '… where audiences were not so good. Nothing to do with the homosexuality, they found the anti-Semitism of some of the characters too much. On the first night in Los Angeles, a member of the audience came down to the front of the stalls and started shouting at the actors… then half the audience walked out. We played the full run, but the bookings stopped and the headlines appeared.'

The 1983 season sticks in the collective consciousness for another reason too, namely the arrival of a huge yellow and white marquee on the ground opposite the Festival Theatre. Donated by Henny Gestetner, it was to be the successful – much-loved (and missed!) – halfway house between Michell's New Ventures and the new studio theatre which was would open in 1989, the Minerva.

John Gale explains: 'Keith Michell had started New Ventures and it was initially a huge success. But by the time I got to Chichester, it was failing because nobody ever knew where they were going to be. They were scattered all over the City. I decided that if we put up a marquee next to the Theatre, then everybody would see it and know where it was.'

The opportunity was not only to attract young audiences, but also to offer young actors and actresses who had small roles, or ensemble parts in the Main House, the chance to take leading roles in The Tent[1].

---

[1] The spirit of The Tent is being revived in 2012 with a new structure built on Oaklands Park and funded by community support. Called 'Theatre on the Fly', it will offer a base to three young directors, producing plays, play readings, films, revues and cabaret.

CFT Tent will provide a variety of shows

IN addition to the Chichester Festival Theatre season many of the stars are involved in the C.F.T. Tent entertainment, which is providing a variety of shows at lunchtimes and late night as well as evening performances.

They begin on August 22 with Falkland Sound, the first half of which is drawn from a message from the Falklands — David Tinker's letters gathered by his father Hugh Tinker.

The second half is based on verbatim transcripts of interviews made during May and June 1983 by the original Royal Court Company of Falkland Sound.

A celebration of the horse in music, poetry, and drama gets its first airing on August 27; while Aubrey Woods presides over a special general meeting of Roughover Golf Club 1936. The first of four performances is on August 24.

There will be four lunchtime performances of Aurora Leigh, dramatised by Michelene Wandor from the verse novel by Elizabeth Barrett Browning. The first is on August 31.

A double bill brings together Yes and No by Graham Greene and Say Something Happened by Alan Bennett. The former is a delightful comedy dialogue between an inexperienced actor and a formidable director, while Alan Bennett's work is an ironic view of a retired couple and the girl from the social services.

Edward Kemp, who lives in Chichester, recently won the Texaco/N.Y.T. Young Playwright competition with his first play — The Iron and the Oak. It will be staged five times and deals with a kidnapping drama set in Germany, in which a group of terrorists take a civil servant hostage.

Ballboys by David Edgar is a comic melodrama in which two ballboys plot the downfall of a brilliant Swedish tennis star.

The entire company is involved in The Late Night Revue, while on September 4 and 11 there are two poetry evenings.

In addition Bash's Backstage Boogie Band (C.F.T.'s own rock revival) has two late night gigs.

Further details of all these events are available from the Chichester Festival Theatre.

Picture shows some of those involved in the C.F.T. Tent productions.

Bognor Regis Post, 13 August 1983. West Sussex Record Office

Jonathon Morris directs *The Final Furlong* in rehearsal in The Tent, 1983.

Photo: Diane Goodman

1984

After hitting the headlines for all the wrong reasons (some would say the *right* reasons), 1984 should have been something of a quieter affair. As it turned out, the quality of the Company – including Annette Crosbie, Paul Eddington, Matthew Francis[1], Alec Guinness, Joanna McCallum, Joan Plowright, Maggie Smith, Gareth Valentine, David Yelland and newcomer Stephen Fry – and the balance between box-office success and critical acclaim for two of the four productions made it one of the most significant of the Garland/Gale seasons.

[1] An actor and director, Francis was the first Artistic Director of The Tent. He subsequently went on to become Artistic Director of Greenwich Theatre.

The 1984 Season, opened on Wednesday 2 May with Alan Bennett's *Forty Years On*. Paul Eddington played the Headmaster, with John Fortune as Franklin and a 26 year old Stephen Fry as Tempest, his first professional part.

Patrick Garland: 'Alan [Bennett] is very strict about casting… and he is usually right, he has a very good judgement and he approved Stephen completely. I had always hoped to do *Forty Years On* one more time at CFT, with Stephen as the Headmaster, because now he would be the right age, but my health got the better of me.'

Oh, Kay! – a musical by Ira and George Gershwin – was followed by Shakespeare's *The Merchant of Venice*. Alec Guinness played Shylock as a suave, self-possessed man of the world. It was an extraordinary, mesmerising per-

formance, as Garland recalls: 'In the courtroom scene, he was very chilling with his "pound of flesh". He had this tiny knife, which he was constantly sharpening on a piece of leather. It was a domestic, down-to-earth kitchen knife – typical of him, it wasn't a scimitar – and the scene was building and building and Antonio [Richard Warwick] was getting more and more frightened – as indeed he does, just before the trial scene and Portia [Joanna McCallum] does her "mercy" speech. Alec was on a little stool, just sharpening the knife, then he stopped and, holding it in his left hand, rose, walked over to Antonio – who was sitting there bound – pulled his brace apart and bent down and listened to his heart. It was incredibly terrifying, a beautifully placed bit of theatrical business.'

Congreve's _The Way of the World_, with Joan Plowright, closed the 1984 season.[1] As the play transferred to London, and CFT prepared for a Christmas show and concerts and the gentle addition of more weeks to the schedule, it was also the end of Garland's first period as Artistic Director of CFT. Financial concerns notwithstanding, it is remembered by those who worked there as a very happy time.

---

[1] In 2012, as part of the fiftieth anniversary season, Penelope Keith will play Lady Wishfort.

Sarah Badel: 'Patrick likes actors, sympathises with them, he enjoys the storytelling. Some directors think actors are pieces to be moved around and rather tiresome, but Patrick encourages you to offer things.'

And Keith Michell adds: 'If it had been humanly possible, I would have had Patrick direct everything.'

Michael Billington makes the point that the programming was more challenging than Garland is given credit for: 'I think, looking back now on Patrick's programme, one realises how adventurous it was.'

However, despite Gale's success in putting the theatre on an even keel, nonetheless there was consternation in some quarters when John Gale was appointed Theatre Director in his own right after Garland left.

Michael Billington again: 'Three actors created the venue, then we have directors Peter Dews and Patrick, then a producer comes in to run it. John Gale is an admirable producer in many ways but my impression was he didn't have quite that appetite for adventure that Patrick did and was very reliant on safe stars, which is not to say there weren't some good productions – for example, _The Scarlet Pimpernel_ in 1985, which Nicholas Hytner did with Donald Sinden.'

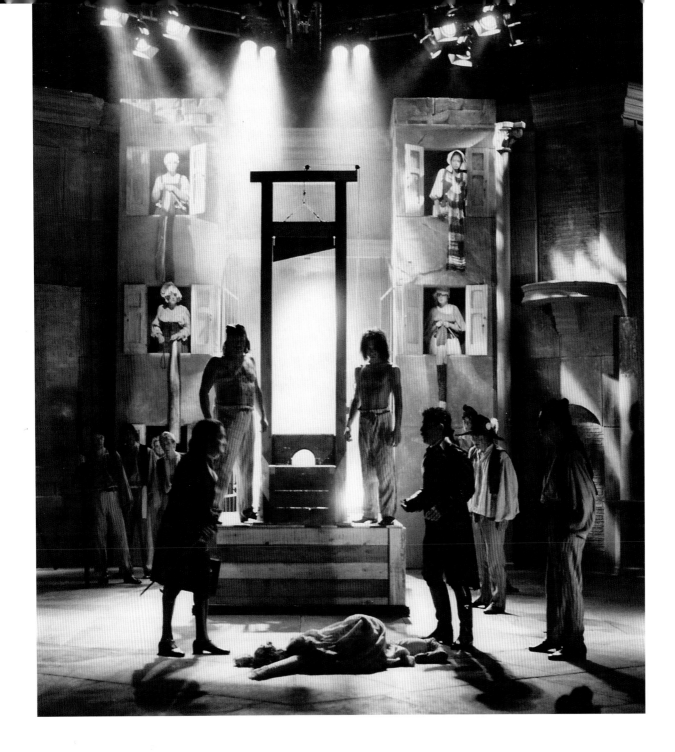

1985

Max Davies – who had joined the Board in the mid 1980s and was to replace Kenneth Fleet as Chairman in 1994 – remembers the first Gale season fondly: 'John was a very commercially successful Theatre Director. "Gale Force" was not always easy to control, but he did the Theatre proud. When he left, he left £1 million in the bank... He was very brave. The first play he put on was *Cavalcade*, which I thought was a very clever thing to do. It's not much of a play, but it involved hundreds of local people.'

Noel Coward's *Cavalcade* tells the story of three decades in the life of the Marryotts, a quintessential British family of the time, and their servants. Beginning at the dawn of the 20th century, it ends on New Year's Eve, 1920. The play premiered in London in 1931 at the Theatre Royal, Drury Lane, and was a box office hit, running for nearly a year. Made into a film in 1933, it won an Oscar for Best Picture. But, because of its huge cast, it is rarely staged.

The Scarlet Pimpernel, 1985.

Photo: Reg Wilson/
Rex Features

Cavalcade, 1985.

Photo: John Haynes/
Lebrecht Music & Arts

**Simon Chandler and
Joanna McCallum
in *Cavalcade*, with
Alastair Brett, son
of Lucy Brett, Head
of Development,
1985.**

Photo: John Haynes/
Lebrecht Music & Arts

The CFT version involved some 200 local amateurs working with professional actors in one of the most elaborate productions Chichester had ever seen.

John Gale: 'I felt that the Theatre and the city should be better integrated. I had done a lot of Coward in London and it had been an ambition of mine to put on *Cavalcade*.'

It is one of the two productions Gale is most proud of – the other being *A Patriot for Me* – and rightly so. Twenty-seven years later, Cicestrians still boast about having been 'Cavalcaders'.

The 1985 Company included Desmond Barritt, Edward Fox, Denis Quilley, Celia Imrie, Donald Sinden (and his son Jeremy), Diana Rigg, and an up-and-coming young actor, Alex Jennings. But, looking down the lists of Company and crew for that year, for me it is the directors that most stand out. First, actor/director Philip Franks who, as well as continuing to appear on the CFT stage, has directed a play in every season since 2006 as well as the ever-popular CFT Christmas Concerts; Michael Grandage, one of the leading directors of his generation, who went on to be Artistic Director of Sheffield Theatre, then highly acclaimed Artistic Director at the Donmar Warehouse from 2002-2012; finally, a young director then known for opera, Nicholas Hytner. He was to direct the closing play of the 1985 season, a version of Orczy's classic 1903 play (the novel followed in 1905), *The Scarlet Pimpernel*.

Set during the Reign of Terror, the early years of the French Revolution, it also had a substantial cast.

John Gale: 'It was the most stunning production, the visual impact of it. It opened and the stage was empty, then suddenly you heard a murmur and then the dock doors opened at the back and there was a lot of smoke coming out. And slowly, through these doors, a huge guillotine – you didn't realise it was a guillotine at first – rumbled forward. As it got through the dock doors, the shutters on either side of the stage came down and you saw all these women with their huge pieces of knitting about ten feet long. And as they watched, this massive thing trundled to the front. There was a body lying on it and a huge blade swished down and the head dropped into a basket. It was the simplest trick but I'd have never seen anything like it.'

Andy Neal also remembers the guillotine: 'We built it out in the theatre car park at the back. It arrived built, but it didn't work, so we took it apart and put it back together. The scene dock was so small then that sets had to be brought in pieces and, once in, everything had to be laid on its side, because you didn't have the height to stand it up. And then you had that eighteen-inch step up onto the stage.'

Gale continues: 'In the opening of the second act, the revolutionaries with their pikes came onto the stage... We used the extras from *Cavalcade* to do the shouting, so the noise was unbelievable and the whole stage was draped with the Tricolore and suddenly they went off, dragging this flag off the stage, and there on an English village green was Percy Blakeney (Donald Sinden) playing bowls with his cohorts and the Prince of Wales (Rowland Davies). Donald thought Hytner was brilliant.'

And the crew thought Donald was brilliant too. Andy Neal again: 'He loved Chichester and we loved him. He was from that school of actors that knows that theatre is a team game. Don loved

Donald Sinden and Joanna McCallum in *The Scarlet Pimpernel*, 1985.
Photo: Reg Wilson/ Rex Features

a joke and so did we. In *Pimpernel*, there was a scene when Desmond Barritt – playing Brogart – got thrown down the trap and the crew would be down there with mattresses helping him to land safely. About thirty seconds later, Donald would arrive on stage and start looking for him. Eventually, he would look down the trap and so we would wave and say hello and he'd make a face at us. Then we got ambitious. One day, he looked down and we had brought the Martini tables in from outside and we were all sitting around having cocktails. We'd do a different thing every day. He really looked forward to it. We never got him to crack, but it was close.'

1985 also saw the launch of the Youth Theatre, which would play such a key role in CFT's success in years to come. Growing out of Saturday morning storytelling sessions for children, ads were placed in local schools and the *Chichester Observer*. The first CFYT production, *Shades of Grey* was an improvised piece based on the lives of refugees and evacuees. The budget for the show was £25.[1]

---

[1] An early member of CFYT was Honeysuckle Weeks, who in 2010 would play Eliza Doolittle in *Pygmalion*. Rupert Everett was Henry Higgins.

CFYT's *Peter Pan*, 2006. Millie Eden, grand-daughter of Keith Michell, seated far left.

Photo: Mike Eddowes

ABOVE

CFYT performing *Ragged Streets*, 1985.

Photo: Unknown

RIGHT

Celia Imrie and Edward Fox in *The Philanthropist*, 1985.

Photo: Reg Wilson/
Rex Features

John Gale was clear about why he wanted things to change: 'I thought we should end this story-reading crèche and start a youth theatre instead, because if you can get people interested in theatre from an early age, they are liable to become theatregoers for the rest of their lives. At the end of my time at Chichester [1989], I never imagined there would be 280 members of CFYT and a similar number waiting to get in.'[1]

[1] In 2012, CFYT is acknowledged as one of the finest youth theatres in the country. There are 621 members in Chichester and four satellite sites – Bognor Regis, Leigh Park, Littlehampton and Midhurst – with another 513 on the waiting list. Additional permanent groups are the Youth Dance Group, the Youth Theatre for young people with disabilities (called CFYT Friday) and the Technical Youth Theatre.

1986

There was more community involvement in 1986 in *The Spershott Version*, which went out onto the streets to tell part of Chichester's history at the time of the Great Plague. Gale himself played the Mayor and his wife Lisel played Mrs Spershott.

For the first time, five productions rather than four were to play in the Festival Season. It opened earlier than usual – the First Night was Wednesday 16 April – with *Annie Get Your Gun* (starring the 1970s pop icon, Suzi Quatro), followed by Bagnold's *The Chalk Garden*, Vanbrugh's *The Relapse*, Peter Coe's adaptation of *Jane Eyre* with Jenny Seagrove and Keith Michell and, finally, *A Funny Thing Happened on the Way to the Forum* with Frankie Howerd.

Richard Briers in
The Relapse, **1986.**

Photo: Reg Wilson/
Rex Features

ABOVE RIGHT

**And 25 years
later, Lucy Briers
(standing)
with Catherine
McCormack in**
Top Girls, **2010.**

Photo: John Haynes/
Lebrecht Music & Arts

RIGHT

**Keith Michell and
Jenny Seagrove
in** *Jane Eyre* **1986.**

Photo: Reg Wilson/
Rex Features

The Company also included Dorothy Tutin, Richard Briers, Paola Dionisotti, John Sessions and Googie Withers.

The season was very successful at the box office, though reviewers were often critical of Gale's choices. It was a clear illustration of the perennial problem of programming a large theatre – the quality of work versus the need to sell as many tickets as possible, and how to reconcile the two. Max Davies remembers a conversation along these lines: 'John and I are good friends, but I remember criticising him once, which is a dangerous thing to do. He was banging on about artistic merit and I said: "John, I didn't think there was much artistic merit in *A Funny Thing Happened on the Way to the Forum*." I wish I hadn't said it. He just went for me.

'"Sold 95 per cent!" he shouted at me.

'I said, "I thought we were talking about artistic merit."'

1987

The 1987 glossy souvenir brochure has David Goodman's original Minerva head design silver embossed on a royal blue background. As well as information about the four shows to be presented in the Festival – *Robert and Elizabeth*, Wilde's *An Ideal Husband*, Bolt's *A Man for All Seasons*, starring Tony Britton and an adaptation of Goldoni's *Miranda* – there are detailed plans about a major building project to mark CFT's Silver Jubilee year.

John Gale explains his ambition: 'Chichester was probably the only major theatre in the country not to have a permanent studio theatre. The Theatre was making surpluses and we had considerable reserves. Leslie was terribly enthusiastic and the Theatre Society, which had 17,000 members, was mad keen because they were going to get a Club Room. At a meeting of the Trust, a month before the start of the 1987 season, the Theatre Society contributed an initial £150,000 towards an estimated £1.5 million building cost.'

The Theatre Society, which had been formed in 1960 and played so crucial a role in raising the funds to see CFT built in the first instance, was one of the largest supporters' organisations of its kind in the country. Many local people had been members since its foundation, former Board member Tony French among them, who joined in November 1960 having attended the first public meeting about the launch of the Theatre.[1]

Sadly, it is beyond the scope of this book to

[1] A former (and, in 2012, current) Mayor of Chichester, French was to be a key member of Chichester District Council and CFT Board member and played an essential part in saving the Theatre from closure in 1997.

cover the history and leading players of the Theatre Society in any detail. Keith Michell and Lord Olivier were joint Patrons, Leslie Evershed-Martin as the President, and the roll of honour of the countless others who gave their time to the Society over the years includes John and Sue Hyland, Ruth Wrigley, Norman Siviter, Maureen Davis-Poynter, Barbara Blay, Geoffrey Marwood, David Goodman and Gillian Wintle.

Not all members of the Board were as enthusiastic as the Theatre Society about the idea of building a second theatre, however Gale raised the money and the project went ahead. In addition to the Theatre Society's contribution, the Theatre Trust put in £250,000 and the Productions Company £300,000.

John Gale again: 'Kenneth Fleet, who had become Chairman of the Productions Company Board in 1983 was very bright[1]. At a Trust meeting in April 1988, he announced he had persuaded Worthing-based Nissan UK to give us a £500,000 covenant towards the Minerva, which enabled us to start the building.[2] And I got the restaurant, which was leased out to Town & Country, to pay £250,000 to build the kitchens.'

1987 also saw the beginning of the career of another young director, Sam Mendes. He remembers his first sight of CFT: 'I had gone through the British Theatre Directory and written letters saying, "I want to come and be an assistant director at your theatre, please will you have me: I don't need any money." I got only two replies – one from the National Theatre Studio saying "no thanks" and another one from

Chichester saying that John Gale would like to meet you, but it is too early, come and look us up again in the summer.'

Having lost, then found the letter once more, Mendes took Gale at his word:

'After my finals finished I went down by train and walked through this very conservative look-ing town and across that rather unappealing car park – you have to remember I was just down from Cambridge, where I had directed all the 'Bs', Brecht, Berkoff, Bond and Beckett – and I saw that blue hexagonal sign as you drive into the theatre: *Robert and Elizabeth*, *An Ideal Husband* and *A Man for All Seasons* and I thought: "Oh, no. No way can I work here; this is not what I want to be doing at all." So I went into the interview with John Gale kind of feeling I had nothing to lose.

'Then about half way through John said: "There is also The Tent."

'I said: "What is The Tent?"

'He said: "It is a studio theatre in a marquee, which is going up in two weeks."

'Immediately my spirits lifted. John had this huge faith in me with nothing much to go on. He gave me this huge chance in my career.'

Twenty-five years on, both Gale and Mendes admit that the decision was not made entirely on his potential as a director.

Mendes continues the story:

'At first, [Gale] wasn't completely sold. I think he was never completely comfortable with Oxbridge boys and intellectuals, it wasn't his world. He thought we should all go to the RSC.

'Then he said: "What are your other inter-ests?" in a slightly suspicious way, as if we were all hothouse flowers brought up to do theatre and study. "Actually," I said, "I'm a cricketer."

'Immediately his entire demeanour changed. "How good?"

"I played for England Schoolboys, then I played a lot for the university." His entire face lit up.

Joanna Lumley and June Whitfield in *An Ideal Husband*, 1987.

Photo: Reg Wilson/ Rex Features

---

[1] Fleet had been city editor of the *Daily Telegraph* and *Sunday Telegraph*, as well working for *The Times* and the Express Group.

[2] Fleet was a personal friend of Octav Botnar, Chairman of Nissan UK, a noted philanthropist who gave away millions. In 1991, he fled the UK rather than face arrest for tax fraud. No one at CFT was aware of this at the time he made his contribution to the Minerva.

"Every year we have a grudge match against the RSC and we've lost for the last few years."

'After that the interview went extremely well. And so I came to Chichester and I felt the weight of John's expectations more on the cricket field than I did in The Tent.' [1]

Mendes moved down to Chichester for the summer: 'I arrived in 1987 and I was on £49.50 a week, cash in hand (probably not strictly legal). I had a room in a house opposite the Theatre at the non-car park end in that little modern estate. The first two people I met who were also starting in the Tent on the same day were Vicki Mortimer [2] – who has subsequently become one of the best theatre designers in England – and a young lad, incredibly shy with a huge quiff and a King Kurt [3] t-shirt whose name turned out to be Toby Stephens. He was on the stage crew, pretty shy. It wasn't until somebody told me that he was Maggie Smith and Robert Stephens' son that I knew who he was.'

Bill Bray, Chief Electrician, also remembers Stephens as a quiet and hard-working member of the backstage team.

To start with, however, Mendes wasn't sure what he was supposed to be doing: 'John [Gale] was magnificently gung-ho but had this slightly slapdash style of management which was to throw everybody into the same pot and say: "Make your own way, you'll find your feet." So nobody formally introduced me to anybody; I was just around. A couple of weeks later they told me that my main job was to be Assistant Director to Alison Sutcliffe, so that's what I did, assisted her. I was a terrible assistant direc-

---

[1] CFT won that year's match!

[2] Mortimer, post-Tent, was to design four shows in The Minerva. *The Triumph of Love, Cloud Nine, The Purity Game* (all 1989) and *Thérèse Raquin* (1990).

[3] King Kurt was a British psychobilly rock band best known for their hit single *'Destination Zululand'* (1980).

tor and I have felt guilty about that ever since. I don't think I was any support whatsoever. I sat there thinking: "I wouldn't do *A Midsummer Night's Dream* like this; I'd do it that way." I am sure that I was horribly insufferable, but anyway I had a lovely time and I got to know the cast and watched and learned and spent time in a professional rehearsal room which, however much I thought I was the bee's knees, I had never done before.'

Diane Goodman, Project Administrator and stalwart of this book, also started her career, in 1983, in The Tent, in the role of Assistant Stage Manager.

Mendes continues the story: 'Then at the end of my first season, John gave me a late-night one-night show. I used some of the actors from *A Midsummer Night's Dream* and did a double bill of two Chekhov plays, *The Bear* and *The Proposal*. It was my first ever professional production and I did them as vaudeville. I took Chekhov at his word and I played them extremely broadly; they were funny, but in the way that one-night performances can be, because you know it is never going to happen again, there is a social event quality to them that can elevate something that is perhaps not entirely special to 'legendary' status! Vicki Mortimer designed it. We had zero money so she used the back of some giant flats from the Main House and painted on them the titles of the plays in black. We used furniture from stock and that was my first show.'

John Gale thought the one-night double-bill was fantastic, so offered Mendes the chance to direct a full show the following year. Then, the person running The Tent decided not to stay and, to his amazement, Mendes was offered the job: 'So that's how I ended up, in my second year, running The Tent with having ever only done a one-night performance and having never done a professional show other than that. It was a tremendous leap of faith from John.'

CFT Cricket team,
1985.

Photo: Courtesy of
Jeannie Brook Barnett

LEFT

**Sam Mendes
(front right), Bill
Bray, Patrick
'Paddy' Mirams at
CFT cricket match,
1988.**

Photo: Amanda Mirams

1988

Keith Michell, Jeanette Sterke and Gerald Harper in *The Royal Baccarat Scandal*, 1988.

Photo: Reg Wilson/ Rex Features

Despite the continuing 'drizzle of complaint' (to use Stoppard's phrase) from critics about 'Chichester-on-Sea' and blazers, the 1988 season was to be one of Gale's most critically acclaimed: Coward's *Hay Fever* as the opening show; Donald Sinden and Anna Carteret in Shaw's *Major Barbara*, directed by Christopher Morahan; *The Royal Baccarat Scandal*; and Christopher Fry's *Ring Round the Moon* with Googie Withers, June Whitfield and Holly Aird, bringing the season

to a close on Saturday 1 October.

Across the road from the Festival Theatre, building work was well underway. The yellow and white tent – set between the scaffolding, concrete and hexagonal glass domes of the Minerva and the white wooden restaurant building – welcomed visitors to the ever-expanding theatre site.

Mendes assisted Christopher Morahan on *Major Barbara* and Elijah Moshinsky on *Ring Round the Moon*, and directed Brian Friel's *Translations* in The Tent, among other shows. Then Gale took another leap of faith by offer-

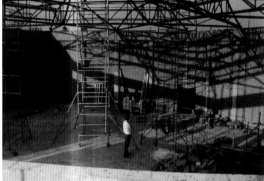

ing Mendes the job as the first Artistic Director of the Minerva when it opened in 1989.

Gale remembers the arguments about his decision: 'Sam's appointment was almost over the Board's dead body because they didn't want anybody so young. I insisted that I had the right to appoint who I wanted and that this was who we were going to have.'

And, of course, as significant as successes on stage were CFT's triumphs on the cricket pitch. This second year running, Mendes scored 100 and, in his interview with Tim Bouquet, joked he felt in that, at least, he had 'fulfilled

his promise' to John Gale.

Chief Electrician and then Head of Lighting, Bill Bray – who was also part of the team that included Stage Manager Patrick Mirams[1] – remembers the pressures of the match and Gale's contribution to their victory: 'John Gale was their secret weapon. Sitting on the boundary, MCC tie and umbrella, roaring instructions'.

---

[1] In another family link, Patrick and Amanda Miram's daughter, Holly, is interviewed as one of the inaugural members of Technical Youth Theatre some twenty years later (see page 225).

Googie Withers and Ruth Hudson in *Hayfever*, 1988.

Photo: Reg Wilson/ Rex Features

Minerva Theatre being built, 1988.

Photo: Amanda Mirams

The Tent repositioned behind the administration block, 1988.

Photo: Amanda Mirams

1989

Gale's final season as Theatre Director, 1989, was a tumultuous year.

The Minerva was opened on Saturday 22 April 1989 by Lavinia, Duchess of Norfolk, on budget and on time. Many of the actors of the 1989 Company were there to toast the new space, as were members of the Theatre Society, the Board and those with strong connections with CFT.

Although there was a great deal of excitement, not everyone was unreservedly enthusiastic. Some felt that the addition of a second theatre might, in the long run, turn out to be problematic. Duncan Weldon, who was to be Theatre Director from 1995 – 1997: 'I told John Gale that by opening the Minerva he had scored a huge success and made a big mistake at the same time; that the theatres would compete. When it first opened, the Minerva was a drain on the Main House. And the other problem has always been that actors want to play the Minerva, they don't want to be in the Main House.'

While Gale was programming the Festival in the Main House, Mendes was putting together the inaugural Minerva season. The first production was *Summerfolk*. Written by Maxim Gorky in 1903, it was in part based on an imagining of Chekhov's life.[1] The cast included Tom Hollander, Lesley Sharp, Angela Thorne and Peter McEnery. *Love's Labour's Lost* followed, then Caryl Churchill's *Cloud Nine*, directed by David Leveaux.

Sam Mendes: 'We had new plays – Shirley Gee's *Warrior* – and we did a musical. And none of them had very many performances... everything on a Tent-style budget. I had a full company of eight – the Minerva Company – and we

---

[1] The British premiere of the play had been given by the Royal Shakespeare Company in 1974, directed by David Jones.

***Summerfolk* company including Tom Hollander (fourth from left) 1989.**

Photo: Amanda Mirams

LEFT
Sam Graham in *Love's Labour's Lost*, 1989.

Photo: Paul Carter

OPPOSITE
Tom Hollander in *Cloud Nine*, 1989.

Photo: Paul Carter

A Little Night Music, 1989.

Photo: Michael Le Poer Trench

OPPOSITE
James Bolam in Victory! 1989.

Photo: Reg Wilson/ Rex Features

supplemented them with actors from the Main House.'

With hindsight, Mendes feels that although that opening season in the Minerva did attract a new and younger audience, some of the supporters of The Tent were lost: 'There is a freedom you get from an invented space that you can't get in a building that's purpose-built. You have to put more money into productions, it becomes more institutional and more establishment. I felt that first season we had maybe fallen in between two stools; not done anything mainstream enough to get the Main House audience in, but at the same time not youthful or experimental enough to please those who used to come to The Tent. It is achieving that balance that is the challenge in the Minerva.'

Across the road, the Main House Festival season opened triumphantly with another community production. Gale was closing his time as Theatre Director as he had started it with

Victory!, an adaptation by Patrick Garland of Thomas Hardy's *The Dynasts*. The first half of the play is the Battle of Trafalgar, the second half the Battle of Waterloo.

Michael Billington remembers coming to review it: 'One of the greatest Chichester productions which has not been much heralded or celebrated. I remember it started in the street – it was a community project with professional actors obviously. We assembled down by the Cathedral, by the Cross and it began with bands and short scenes. Then we moved through the streets of Chichester and gradually moved into the Theatre for this play about the Napoleonic Wars with James Bolam as Napoleon. Now it's very fashionable to do big community work everywhere but here was a theatre tapping into the local community in 1989, before it was the popular thing to do – it gave pizzazz and an excitement to Chichester.'

Victory! was to be followed by *The Heiress*,

then *London Assurance* with Paul Eddington directed by Robin Phillips – who was tipped to be the next CFT Artistic Director – then Sondheim's *A Little Light Music* as the final production.

However, things did not go according to plan. Behind the scenes, there were problems with *London Assurance*. Mendes remembers being called into John Gale's office – Phillips was there too – and being asked if he would take over directing the play:

'I'd skimmed it a bit when it was announced as part of the season but that was all.

'I said: "But, I've never read the play, I know the gist of it, but I haven't designed or cast it."

'And Robin looked up at me and said: "You can do this. You'll be fine. I saw *Summerfolk*. You can do this."

'John was clearly angry but he was trying to avert a crisis; make the best of it. John could be bullying, he was loud, he was enthusiastic, but I don't think I have ever met anybody who loved a theatre as much as he loved Chichester. And he fought for that play and he was so cross that the play he was so excited about with Paul Eddington and Angela Thorne was in jeopardy.'

Shell-shocked, Mendes went home and tried to prepare for meeting the cast the next day. Unfortunately, a combination of nerves and repeated late nights, meant he fell asleep at the kitchen table. The result? He went to CFT the next day still having not read the play and feeling completely unprepared.

Mendes takes up the story:

'Not good for the nerves. Before I went in Paul Eddington came up to me and said: "I went to see a remarkable, remarkable production last night."

'I thought, why is he telling me this?

'He continued: "It was a production of *Summerfolk*. I thought it was absolutely extraordinary and I also thought the person who directed it has it in him to direct a fantastic production

of *London Assurance*. I want you to know that you have my total support."

'Paul was the most enchanting man, one of the greatest gentlemen I have ever met, and a superlative actor, incredibly funny, just a wonderful man.'

Mendes remembers that Eddington said much the same to the cast. He gave them his word he would do his best and, on the Monday morning, work began in earnest. They only had three weeks of rehearsal before press night, but it was the success of 1989. Duncan Weldon transferred it to the Haymarket in London, both Eddington and Thorne received outstanding notices and it's one of those productions that brings a smile to the faces of the long-term CFT staff when it's mentioned. Another example of the 'Blitz' spirit, of everyone pulling together. Of the best work coming out of the least auspicious circumstances.

Even though, in terms of the books, John Gale's last season was actually his least successful financially – averaging 75 per cent financial capacity – CFT passed the £1million mark in advance bookings before the Season opened. Gale relinquished the reins as Artistic Director leaving £1million in the bank.

The final word goes to Sam Mendes: 'He barrelled on, John, he just bulldozed through. Even if money was tight he'd say; "We're doing it. If you build it, they will come." And I took some of that energy and spirit to the Donmar when I started there. I think that John Gale is one of the unsung heroes of Chichester Festival Theatre. He was always looked down upon by the subsidised sector, then and now, but the truth is that he created something that would have been impossible if he had played it by the book. If he had behaved in a way deemed appropriate by the funding bodies he would never have got anywhere.'

The end of another season, another decade. In theatre generally, the 1980s had been years of transformation, in bad ways as well as good. The West End had changed, some said, into a tourist industry. It was a decade that had seen, with a few honourable exceptions, the focus on 'bums on seats' driving out new writing from the centre of theatrical activity. The question was what might lie ahead in the 1990s?

'We need new forms of expression.
We need new forms, and if we can't
have them we had better have nothing.'

The Seagull
ANTON CHEKHOV

The 1990s

Artistic Directors
MICHAEL RUDMAN (1990)
PATRICK GARLAND (1991 – 1994)
DUNCAN C WELDON (Theatre Director) and **DEREK JACOBI** (Associate Director) (1995 – 1996)
DUNCAN C WELDON (Theatre Director, 1997)
ANDREW WELCH (1998 – 2002)

'It was the best of times, it was the worst of times, it was the age of wisdom, it was the age of foolishness, it was the epoch of belief, it was the epoch of incredulity, it was the season of Light, it was the season of Darkness, it was the spring of hope, it was the winter of despair, we had everything before us, we had nothing before us, we were all going direct to heaven, we were all going direct the other way …'

A TALE OF TWO CITIES
Charles Dickens

The 1990s were destined to be the toughest decade in CFT's history. Five different Artistic/Theatre Directors, three of whom – Rudman, Garland and Welch – came as theatrical White Knights, as it were, into already difficult situations. On two occasions, CFT nearly closed its doors for good. And as the decade progressed and CFT's troubles seemed to intensify rather than diminish, Chichester itself began to lose patience. The once amicable relationship between the City and Oaklands Park was under threat.

So, the worst of times. But looking back, although there's no doubt mistakes were made, it is important to remember that some of the problems faced at Chichester were shared by theatres everywhere else. It is beyond the scope of this book to analyse the wider situation in any depth, but for those who would like the context within which CFT was operat-

Born Again, 1990.
Poster, copyright and courtesy of Gerald Scarfe

Simon Ward and Hilary Drake in *Rumours*, 1990.

Photo: John Haynes/ Lebrecht Music & Arts

ing, Michael Billington's excellent *State of the Nation*[1] lays out in engaging and authoritative detail the history of British Theatre from 1945 to the present.

It is also important to remember that, financial troubles and governance problems notwithstanding, at CFT they were also some of the best of times on the stage. Audiences in the Main House and the Minerva saw some of the most imaginative, challenging, thrilling productions, as well as others that didn't deliver what had been hoped. That, after all, is the nature of novel writing and playwriting, painting and sculpture and music, dance and design and directing. Beside my computer on

---

[1] *State of the Nation: British Theatre Since 1945*, Faber & Faber, 2007

my desk, I have scribbled words from Samuel Beckett pinned up on a postcard: 'Try again. Fail again. Fail better.' Risk is an essential part of the creative process. And as with every decade before, in the 1990s careers were started at CFT, new directors and designers and writers cut their teeth. So, with apologies to Mr Dickens, if not the very best of times, then pretty exciting times nonetheless.

The winter of 1989/1990 was – appropriately enough – one of the stormiest on record. And the 1990s, in Chichester as elsewhere, was to be a decade of forging new relationships, a recalibrating of the relationship between audience and artist, private sponsorship and corporate support especially for theatres, such as CFT, that had no significant public subsidy.

There was a plethora of new 'entertainment possibilities', as the ad boys and girls might put it: mobile phones and personal stereos, the internet; multi-million-dollar movies such as *Pretty Woman* and *Home Alone* and on the small screen *Keeping Up Appearances* and *Friends*; the race between BSB and Sky to launch new satellite and cable television channels. Everyone chasing the leisure pound, leisure time, competing for audiences.

This is the backdrop against which Michael Rudman arrived to take up his position as Artistic Director. It had been a late appointment – taken by the Board after Robin Phillips had left both the production of *London Assurance* and the Theatre as a whole – but looked to be an excellent decision.

Rudman had begun his career at the Nottingham Playhouse in 1964, before running the Traverse Theatre in Edinburgh from 1970 – 1973, then becoming Artistic Director at Hampstead Theatre until 1978. From 1979 – 1982, he was Director of the Lyttelton Theatre at the National, under Peter Hall, and continued there as an Associate until 1988.

CFT was always comfortable with a director

at the helm and Rudman intended to direct several shows in the Season himself. Two in the Main House – Shakespeare's *The Merry Wives of Windsor*, with Penelope Keith, Phyllida Law and Bill Maynard to open and Neil Simon's *Rumours* as the fourth production (with a cast including Polly Adams, Una Stubbs and Simon Ward) – as well as Peter Meyer's translation of Anouilh's *Eurydice* in the Minerva.

The most eagerly anticipated piece of programming was the final show in the Main House, a world premiere directed by Peter Hall, Rudman's former colleague at the National Theatre. *Born Again* was a musical based on Ionesco's play *Rhinoceros*, with music by Jason Carr, a libretto by Julian Barry and Peter Hall and with set and costume designs by Gerald Scarfe. With Broadway star Mandy Patinkin in the lead, it was scheduled to run for three weeks.

Theatre Manager Janet Bakose: 'It was a massive set and they actually had a full-size glass

TOP

Phyllida Law, Bill Maynard and Penelope Keith in *The Merry Wives of Windsor*, 1990.

Photo: John Haynes/ Lebrecht Music & Arts

LEFT

Penny Downie and Alan Howard in *Scenes from a Marriage*, 1990.

Photo: Paul Carter

lift that came through the stage and actors in full-size rhino costumes in the lift smashing the glass every night. It was extraordinary, all those costumes designed by Gerald Scarfe, but they weighed so much. Actors were sweating, passing out and falling over in them. It was an extraordinary piece, but I suppose the most extraordi-

Mandy Patinkin in
***Born Again,* 1990.**

Photo: John Haynes/
Lebrecht Music & Arts

nary thing was that it actually didn't take off. The show was only playing to 400 a performance.'

The critics liked the piece, the public didn't. Max Davies, then Chairman of the Productions Board: 'People go on about *Born Again*, but my wife and I thought it was jolly good. Yes, the show lost money, but Peter Hall did bring in £100,000 from elsewhere, so our losses were very limited. And we thought that to get Peter Hall to put something on at CFT was a bit of a coup.'

Paul Rogerson, then General Manager & Licensee, agrees: 'It was very exciting having such a strong personality as Peter Hall working here and a great production to do. Rudman took Hall out to lunch with two or three of us,

somewhere on South Street. After lunch, we walked up to the Theatre and I remember Hall saying – because the stage was completely clear – that this was the most magical, most exciting place to work in. Hall had a special caravan behind the restaurant: known as Peter Hall's headquarters.'

Janet Bakose looks back on the 1990 Season: 'I remember every single show in the Minerva in Michael's year being fantastic and powerful and everybody wanted to see them. But that caused problems in the Main House, where tickets didn't sell. The only show that sold was the British premiere of *Rumours*, that was the big hit. That did sell out.'

1991

The 1990 season suffered losses estimated in the region of £500,000 – £200,000 attributable to *Born Again* – and when it was discovered that Rudman hadn't got directors or actors confirmed by the time priority booking for the 1991 season was due to go out, he was asked to leave.

Max Davies again: 'Michael is a delightful chap and a fine director, but as Artistic Director, he couldn't cope... he had to go.'

Paul Rogerson agrees that things were difficult, although he thinks that a clash of personality between Rudman and Leslie Evershed-Martin, then Chairman of the Trust[1], also contributed: 'Michael is a great director, a real Texan gentleman, and I think it is very sad he was given the heave-ho so mercilessly. We had a meeting in London, which I was at, and Leslie was appalled that Michael was presenting the shows to the Board without any artists,

[1] Leslie Evershed-Martin was Chairman of the Trust Company, which had responsibility for buildings and the site, as opposed to the Productions Company which was responsible for overseeing the creative side of things.

no mention of any stars, he hadn't even really started casting. He'd had a year of turmoil ... and then Michael completely overstepped the mark with Leslie.'

All visitors to CFT, past and present, know that one of the distinguishing features of the foyer is the collection of the black and white (and now also colour) photographs of past performances, actors, actresses – Olivier and Plowright, Guinness and Jacobi, Maggie Smith, Patricia Routledge and Penelope Keith – a visual history of those actors and actresses who have helped make CFT the theatre it is.

Paul Rogerson continues: 'One day, Michael said to me: "Captain" – which is what he always called me – "Captain, get those pictures down." He wanted them replaced by pictures either side of each doorway of the production that was playing at the time. I took all the old ones down, including those of the Royal Family. Then Leslie came to me, clearly very upset, and said: "Who authorised this?" That was his [Rudman's] undoing with Evershed-Martin. As far as he was concerned, that foyer was sacrosanct.'

Janet Bakose remembers hearing the news: 'Suddenly it was announced that Michael

Tony Britton and Keith Michell in *Henry VIII*, **1991.**

Photo: Robert Workman

Rudman was going and that Patrick Garland was coming back!'

Garland was touring with Rex Harrison in America with *My Fair Lady* when he received the call. He had achieved a huge amount since stepping down from CFT: he had directed *Hair* in Israel, *Billy* with Michael Crawford and *The Tempest* at the Open Air Theatre in Regent's Park. He had taught English at Bishop Otter College (now the University of Chichester), as well as publishing a novel about his father's life in World War I and a highly-acclaimed biography of Rex Harrison.

Garland admits he had no intention of going back to CFT: 'When Leslie told me that they had no programme, I hadn't a thought in my head. But I felt I had no choice but do to what I could.'

The Productions Company was virtually bankrupt, so Garland brought in Peter Stevens as Administrator to turn round the finances. Stevens had commissioned and opened the Nottingham

Playhouse and was its first Administrator, working with directors John Neville, Peter Ustinov and Frank Dunlop. He went on to become Programme Producer at Granada TV, Personal Assistant to Peter Hall at the National, then General Administrator at the National Theatre. He had also had a spell as Executive Director at the Shakespeare Festival Theatre in Stratford, Ontario.

Peter Stevens takes up the story: 'Historically they had done very well, but now CFT was in disarray. It was more about controlling costs than improving income, although under Rudman that had taken a huge dip. We set about putting the place back together and re-presenting it.'

In February, staff were called to a meeting in the Minerva. Most of those admit they were certain they were going to be told that CFT was closing.

Stevens continues: 'I told them: "You know the circumstances, but we are going to go ahead and it will be all right." Patrick [Garland] and I wanted them to feel safe with us. We had inher-

ited a terrific staff [1] and I am a believer in letting people get on with what they are good at. Chris Bush-Bailey[2] was a terrific Production Manager and was just tremendous in getting the sets built and keeping everything together. I think it is also significant in our success that most of the key jobs – publicity, promotions, box office, general management – were done by women. They get things done.'

While Peter Stevens set about computerising the box office and organising new uniforms for the front-of-house staff, Garland had a matter of weeks to get a whole season together for two theatres. The only show programmed for the Main House was Kesselring's *Arsenic and Old Lace*, which Garland kept as the first play of the

season. The second show was Ian Judge's modernist version of *Henry VIII*, with Keith Michell as Henry, Dorothy Tutin as Katherine of Aragon and Tony Britton[3] as Wolsey.

To give himself time to concentrate on the Main House, Garland appointed Caroline Sharman – who now runs the New Theatre Royal, Portsmouth – as Artistic Director for the Minerva. She directed the premiere of Louise Page's *Adam Was a Gardener* with Sharon Maughan. The season also included a new musical, *Valentine's Day*, with a young singer called Ruthie Henshall. Another young Minerva director, who also assisted in the Main House, was Edward Hall.[4]

Garland programmed Pinero's *Preserving Mr Panmure* as the last show of the Main House season, with Michael Denison in the lead. It was a marvellous production and fondly remembered. But it was the third show that was destined to be

ABOVE LEFT
Robert Hands, Gemma Lowy, Fiona Fullerton and Judy Parfitt in *Valentine's Day*, **1991.**

Photo: John Haynes/ Lebrecht Music & Arts

RIGHT
***Preserving Mr Panmure*, 1991.**

Photo: John Haynes/ Lebrecht Music & Arts

---

[1] These scenes were to be repeated in December 1997, when the Theatre was hours away from shutting its doors for good. Then, only a last minute intervention from Chichester District Council – and the agreement that the both the Productions Board and Trust Board should resign – prevented the receivers being called in.

[2] Known as CBB, Chris was the very popular Production Manager from 1990–2000, taking over from the equally popular and well-respected Bill Green. Chris was an enormous support during my time as Administrative Director. He died suddenly from a heart attack in 2000. At his funeral in St George's Church, Whyke, with standing room only, the theme music to his beloved *The Archers* was played!

---

[3] Britton also directed *The Sisterhood* in the Minerva.

[4] Hall – who took over as Artistic Director of the Hampstead Theatre in 2010 and runs the all-male Shakespeare company, Propeller – directed *Chambers of Glass* by Graeme Fife as a late night show in the 1991 season, returned in 1992 with *Cain*, then in 2001 with Sondheim's *Putting it Together* as part of the main Minerva season.

the smash hit, and which allowed CFT to survive to fight another day.

Tovarich is a musical play in two acts based on the comedy by Jacques Deval, in which aristocratic, but destitute, Russian émigrés are forced to go into domestic service to earn a living. Based on Deval's 1935 play, it opened on Broadway in 1963 with Vivien Leigh playing the Grand Duchess. Garland cast prima ballerina Natalia Makarova as Tatiana Petrovna Romanov and Robert Powell as the Prince. The flashy, nouveau-riche couple – the Duponts – for whom they worked were played by Rowland Davies and Sarah Badel.

Garland explains his decision to invite Makarova to Chichester: 'I cast her because I knew her, but I took a great chance with her. She didn't really speak English. She used to insist: "I do speak English, Patrick. I speak English very good." I said: "You don't, Natalia, you talk English, but you don't speak it." But she was exquisite in the part, she really was delightful.'

Sarah Badel also recalls her distinctive accent and idiosyncratic way of speaking: 'I remember the night when Boris Yeltsin prevented the coup against Gorbachev[1] and everybody had been watching their televisions or listening to their radios all day. At the end of the performance, after we had all taken our bows, the lights went up in the auditorium. "I go to speak to the people," [Makarova] said. She went to the edge of the stage. "Dear people of Chychester, tonight is great night for history of my people." And she gave this wonderful speech about how democracy and freedom had been fought for and won in her beloved Russia, and the whole audience got to its feet and cheered her to the rafters... Lovely woman.'

The final word goes to Patrick Garland: 'In the original, the man sits at the piano and she sings. Makarova wasn't much of a singer, but having this prima ballerina was too good a chance to miss, so I changed it around and she did this lovely, simple little dance, to one of Chopin's mazurkas, and she choreographed it. On the first night, one of the good ladies of the Theatre Society turned to her friend and said: "You can

---

[1] The attempted coup against Mikhail Gorbachev's reforms took place over three days in August 1991. News channels were broadcasting pictures of events as they unfolded, the military and protesters in Red Square, Moscow, and Boris Yelstin defying the 'Gang of Eight'.

say what you like, my dear, but *that* girl has had dancing lessons!'"

After it closed in Chichester, *Tovarich* toured, then transferred to Her Majesty's Theatre in the West End.

Looking back on Garland's second period in charge, critic Michael Billington says he thinks Garland got the balance just right between pleasing the crowd and challenging the audience: 'Again, looking at all Patrick's seasons there's always enterprising things *Preserving Mr Panmure* with Michael Denison – which was a play that had never been heard of, let alone seen. *Henry VIII* not an easy or conventional choice. Garland's back exploring the possibilities of what the theatre can do and should do.'

Garland himself pays tribute to the dedication and hard work of everybody at CFT during that difficult year. He, too, raises the point that Chichester is too big an auditorium to fill without well-known names: 'Michael [Rudman] had done a season without stars, and it fell flat on its face. The Theatre has always needed stars to succeed. You can't just put a bunch of good actors nobody has heard of and hope they and the play will win an audience. But I think that is true of theatre audiences generally, not just Chichester.'

This question of star casting – the pros and cons – was to dominate discussion for much of the 1990s and the early years of the next century as well, as was debate about balancing safe programming in box-office terms and presenting more adventurous work. The country itself was still in the iron grasp of a deep and entrenched recession. And, despite *Tovarich*, the Theatre's finances were still in a fragile state.

Peter Stevens: 'From a deficit of £750,000, we managed to make a small surplus of £70,000, which we did every year. Our great platform for income stability was the Theatre Society, which had 20,000 members; at the time, the Royal Opera House only had 12,000 in their support group. We had to reconnect with them. They had priority booking and such was their loyalty that by the time each season opened, all tickets were forty per cent sold. Given we were aiming to break even at sixty-five per cent, there was not much further to go. I also put the rent up for the Productions company, so the Trust got another £25,000 and it stopped their reserves, which were very depleted, sliding down further.'

Natalia Makarova and Robert Powell in *Tovarich*, 1991.
Photo: John Haynes/
Lebrecht Music & Arts

Natalia Makarova in *Tovarich*, 1991.
Photo: John Haynes/
Lebrecht Music & Arts

1992

Richard Briers
and Judi Dench in
Coriolanus, 1992.

Photo: Richard H Smith

One of the strengths of CFT has always been the affection, connection and loyalty those who work there feel for the place. A sense of ownership that extends from those involved in the fundraising, the building, the establishing, the growing reputation, most of all the productions. However, on occasion, this can also be unhelpful when incoming managements want to make changes or move the Theatre forward... as Peter Stevens was to discover when he suggested the name of the Theatre should be on the building. The Founder, Leslie Evershed-Martin, objected strongly.

Stevens continues: 'He [Evershed-Martin] said: "Everybody knows it's a theatre." My view

was that not everybody did know. He was totally resistant to it and in the end the Board had to vote on it. He was in a minority of one... So I got on to the Civic Trust and they designed a good sign. David Goodman did the lettering. We also put the Minerva sign up and we floodlit the Main House.'

Meanwhile, Patrick Garland was looking at an ambitious season with a tremendous company of actors, including Richard Briers, Alexandra Bastedo, Judi Dench, Donald Sinden, Jean Boht, Denis Quilley, Kate O'Mara, Christopher Timothy, Jenny Seagrove and Tom Hollander.

The Main House season opened with Tim Supple's production of *Coriolanus*, starring Kenneth Branagh, Richard Briers and Judi Dench. Dench and Branagh had worked together in 1988,

Kenneth Branagh in *Coriolanus*, 1992.

Photo: Richard H Smith

when Branagh's Renaissance Theatre Company partnered with the Birmingham Rep on a touring season of plays – *Renaissance Shakespeare on the Road*. Dench had directed *Much Ado About Nothing* and, in 1989, she directed Branagh as Jimmy Porter in Osborne's *Look Back in Anger*.

The Season – performances, productions, the marriage of new work and familiar, the box office – was very successful.

Garland was delighted with *Coriolanus*: 'It was a tremendous cast and a success, though I think a grudging success, because doing the "minor" Shakespeares is always a problem. Chichester is more *Hamlet*[1] and the Scottish Play.'

And the critics were delighted too. Michael Billington: 'Again, the community was involved because the problem with *Coriolanus* is what do you do about the crowd, do you have five or six equity members shuffling around trying to look like a crowd? What director Tim Supple did was get in the community so there was a size-able crowd of fifty people on that stage, which gave Branagh something to play off and it was just exciting. Branagh was in the early years of his fame as a Shakespeare actor so again a very, very good choice.'

The second play in the Main House was *Venus Observed* by Christopher Fry with Donald Sinden as the 50-year-old Duke attempting to settle down with one of his three mistresses.

[1] Although as it happens, and despite a plethora of new Hamlets recently (Jude Law, David Tennant, Rory Kinnear among them), *Hamlet* has never – yet - been produced at Chichester.

Eileen Atkins and Penelope Wilton in *Vita and Virginia*, **1995.**

Photo: John Timbers/ArenaPAL

CENTRE

Tom Hollander and Jonathon Morris in *Me and My Friend*, **1992.**

Photo: John Timbers/ArenaPAL

The play had been a commission from Laurence Olivier in 1950, to mark his taking over the management of the St James' Theatre. The CFT cast included Kate O'Mara, Jean Boht and Susannah Harker. Billington again: 'I think that's something to Chichester's credit that it has stayed very loyal to Fry who was obviously local and a passionate supporter of the Theatre. I felt it honoured him and the best way to honour a writer is to put their plays on – *The Lady's Not for Burning* they had done, but not *Venus Observed*, which people had forgotten about.'

The premiere of a new play by Melvyn Bragg followed. *King Lear in New York* was directed by Patrick Garland and tells the tale of Robert [John Stride], a leading actor who, having worked for the past ten years in films and struggling with a drink problem, is about to make his theatri-

cal comeback in an off-Broadway theatre. The production was reviewed cautiously well – with individual performances being praised – but it struggled to fill the Main House auditorium.

In the Minerva, the season opened with Gillian Plowman's powerful black comedy, *Me and My Friend*. The play had won the Verity Bargate Award in 1988 and tells the story of four vulnerable people – Bunny, Oz, Julia and Robin – who have recently been released from a psychiatric hospital into the 'Care in the Community' scheme, an early-release programme for mental-health patients. Housed by social welfare in two small Council flats, they are encouraged to find jobs and take their place in the world, despite having been judged mentally unfit by the court. Also in the Season were Deborah Moggach's *Double Take* and Eileen Atkins star-

ring in her own play, *Vita and Virginia*, with Penelope Wilton. Adapted from correspondence between Sackville-West and Woolf, the two-hander transferred to the Ambassador's Theatre in London. There were Sunday performances, late night shows and one-offs too. In the list of players for the 1992 Minerva season, as well as Eileen Atkins and Judi Dench, other actors and actresses included Philip Franks, Tom Hollander, Alan Rickman, Juliet Stevenson and Samuel West, son of Prunella Scales and Timothy West.

The closing show in the Main House was Oliver Goldsmith's popular comedy of manners, *She Stoops to Conquer*, which was first performed in London in 1773. Iain Glen played Marlow, with Susannah Harker as Kate Hardcastle. Denis Quilley and Jean Boht played the older genera-

tion. Directed by Peter Wood, the critics loved it. Alastair Macaulay, reviewing in the *Financial Times*: 'Chichester's exuberant new staging of *She Stoops To Conquer* had the audience responding with wave upon wave of laughter and rounds of applause after several strong exit lines.'

Charles Spencer[1], writing in the *Daily Telegraph*, felt the same: 'Chichester Festival Theatre has a real hit with which to end the season.'

And when the Main House shut its doors on Saturday 3 October, there was a palpable sense that CFT was on its way up once more.

---

[1] Spencer began his career at the *Surrey Advertiser*. He then worked for the *Evening Standard*, *The Stage*, and the London *Daily News*, before joining the staff of the *Daily Telegraph* in 1988 as a sub-editor on the arts pages. After a couple of years as deputy theatre critic, he was appointed lead theatre critic in 1991.

TOP RIGHT

King Lear in New York, 1992. Melvyn Bragg meets the cast and director, (L-R) Melvyn Bragg, Jenny Seagrove, Maria Miles, John Stride, Kate O'Mara and Patrick Garland.

Photo: John Timbers/ArenaPAL

BELOW

The cast of *She Stoops to Conquer* raise a toast to Her Majesty on CFT's thirtieth anniversary, 1992.

Photo: Louise Adams/ *Chichester Observer*

1993

The following season was one of hits and near-misses (financially speaking). A strong opening in the Main House – Shaw's *Getting Married* with Tony Britton and Dorothy Tutin – followed by Susan Hampshire in Tim Luscombe's production of Coward's *Relative Values* (which transferred to The Savoy Theatre) and Thornton Wilder's *The Matchmaker* to close the season. In the Minerva, the same successful formula of short plays – Patrick Hamilton's *Rope*, which transferred to the Theatre Royal, Windsor – and

late-night extras, with a dazzling (and large!) company of players including Joanna Lumley in *Forces Sweetheart*, Prunella Scales and Timothy West in *Behind Our Scenes* and Alec Guinness in *A Commonplace Book*. The company also included Anthony Head, Katy Secombe, Judi Dench, Michael Williams, John Barrowman and 1980s pop sensation, Toyah Wilcox.

But in audience terms, the hit of the 1993 season was the musical *Pickwick*. Starring Harry Secombe and Roy Castle – and based on

ABOVE
Anthony Head and John Barrowman in *Rope*, 1993.
Photo: John Timbers/ArenaPAL

RIGHT
Toyah Wilcox in *Carrington*, 1993.
Photo: Paul Carter

Dickens' *Posthumous Papers of the Pickwick Club* – it had a sizeable cast that included Ruth Madoc, Alexandra Bastedo and David Cardy. A delightful production, much loved by members of staff who worked the show, it transferred to Sadler's Wells in London. But problems with juggling costs and returns, not to mention co-production income not coming in as promised, meant financially *Pickwick* was not a success.

Max Davies, then Chairman of the Productions Board, explains: 'It was a very expensive musical, with Harry Secombe and a big cast and scenery that cost a fortune. We couldn't really afford to put it on. It did really well at CFT, but Birmingham Rep had agreed to put up half the cost and offered us guarantees. Then it went bust, when the Birmingham Corporation pulled the plug, and we didn't get paid. We were left carrying the can. We lost something like £100,000 on that.'

The cast of *Pickwick*, 1993.

Photo: John Timbers/ArenaPAL

1994

Peter McEnery and Sharon Maughan in *A Doll's House*, 1994.

Photo: John Timbers/ ArenaPAL

business. The sudden death of Labour Leader John Smith, leading to the infamous dinner between Tony Blair and Smith's heir apparent, Gordon Brown, at a restaurant in north London, was to set in train a sequence of events that would change the direction of Britain for the next fifteen years.

In theatre, too, there were green shoots of a renewed celebration of new writing – the third of David Hare's ground-breaking trilogy, *The Absence of War*[1] , had premiered at the National Theatre 1993, under Artistic Director Richard Eyre. As had Tom Stoppard's dazzling, award-winning *Arcadia*.

In Chichester, Garland went into his last season keeping to the formula that had worked so well, namely a combination of high-quality revivals of classic plays with outstanding casts: in the Minerva, Chekhov's *Three Sisters*, J B Priestley's *Dangerous Corner* and Ibsen's *A Doll's House* with Sharon Maughan and Peter McEnery. Set design was by Simon Higlett[2] . The main fare was washed down with a mixture of revue shows, late-night one-off productions. In short, a programme any studio theatre would be proud to present.

In the Main House, a distinguished company of actors – including Dulcie Gray, Michael Denison, Patricia Routledge and Guy Henry – presented Bernard Shaw's *Pygmalion*, with Peter Bowles

In the country as a whole, however, indications were that better things might lie ahead. There were signs of economic recovery after the catastrophic events of September 1992 and 'Black Wednesday' two years before, when the Conservative Government had been forced to get out of the Exchange Rate Mechanism. Against a backdrop of calls for closer European integration – strongly resisted by many in the Conservative party, challenging John Major's leadership – 1994 would see the Channel Tunnel finally open for

[1] Hare's trilogy of plays about contemporary Britain – *Racing Demon* (1990), *Murmuring Judges* (1991) and *The Absence of War* (1993) – was revived at the Birmingham Rep in 2003, directed by Rachel Kavanaugh and Jonathan Church.

[2] Since 1990, Simon Higlett has been responsible for over 30 productions at Chichester. Recipient of two TMA Best Design Awards – and with a worldwide reputation for design for theatre and opera – productions at CFT include *King Lear*, *The Life and Adventures of Nicholas Nickleby*, *The Barchester Chronicles*, *Yes, Prime Minister* and *Singin' in the Rain*, as well as CFYT shows such as *A Christmas Carol* and *The Snow Queen*.

Peter Greenwell,
Liz Robertson,
David Kernan, Pat
Kirkwood, Robin
Ray and Louise
Gold in *Noël: Cole
Let's Do It!*, 1994.

Photo: John Timbers/
ArenaPAL

LEFT
**Rupert Everett
and Honeysuckle
Weeks in
Pygmalion, 2010.**

Photo: Manuel Harlon

FAR LEFT
**Peter Bowles and
Fiona Fullerton in
Pygmalion, 1994.**

Photo: John Timbers/
ArenaPAL

as Higgins and Fiona Fullerton as Eliza, as well as Arthur W Pinero's *The School Mistress* and a celebration of the works of Noël Coward and Cole Porter. *Noël/Cole: Let's Do It!*, compiled by David Kernan, had already enjoyed a successful tour – including the Arts Festival in Memphis – and Louise Gold in particular was very well received by Chichester audiences. It was also the first play reviewed by Phil Hewitt – the author, critic and popular Arts Editor for the *Chichester Observer* – in July 1994, thereby beginning his long relationship with CFT. As Gold herself said in the interview: 'It's a little bit of history on the stage.'

But, as so often at CFT, one show was to define the season. For 1994, that show was Richard Brinsley Sheridan's *The Rivals*, starring Patricia Routledge as Mrs Malaprop and Timothy West as Sir Anthony Absolute.

Patricia Routledge remembers the production fondly: 'Oh, glorious! That was a lovely production. I play Mrs Malaprop once every twenty years, it seems to me. I did it years and years ago, at the old Guildford Rep, a rather young Mrs Malaprop! Then I was in the opening production at the Royal Exchange Theatre, Manchester [1976]. And then at CFT, directed by Richard Cottrell. I will never forget his directorial talk before the read-through. It was wonderful, the whole background to the play, the social and political background, it was inspiring. I've never known a directorial talk like it. It is really a superb piece and we had a very good time with it. I hope it was my best Mrs Malaprop.'

When the 1994 season closed on Saturday 1 October, Garland could place the keys to his office on the desk in the certain knowledge that he left CFT in a far stronger position than when he'd come galloping back in the spring of 1991, a theatrical *chevalier* to take on a second term as Artistic Director. Chairman of the Productions Board in 1994, Max Davies: 'Overall, Patrick [Garland] and Peter [Stevens] had put the theatre back on an even keel.'

ALL A-BOARD!

Chichester Festival Theatre
Executive cast
In order of appearance

Leslie . . . . . L E Evershed-Martin OBE
(Founder and Vice Chairman)

Teddy . . . . . A T Smith (Chairman)

Eric . . . . . . The Earl of Bessborough

Victor . . . . . V W J Behrens

Richard . . . R H Mosse (Hon Secretary)

Cyril . . . . . Dr C W W Read HSC

Geoffrey . . . G W Marwood

Henny . . . . Mrs H Gestetner OBE

1995

Cartoon of the board, 1974. (L-R) L E Evershed-Martin, A T Smith, the Earl of Bessborough, V W J Behrens, Mrs H Gestetner, G W Marwood, Dr C W W Read and R H Mosse

Artist: P Cole. Courtesy of Barbara Mosse

In the world of theatre, things were different. It was the beginning of a new, robust period of writing. Two of the most important of the so-called 'In Yer Face' writers – Sarah Kane and Mark Ravenhill – were to have premieres of their work during the course of 1995. There were signs that theatre was shifting, moving, changing its shape. Angrier, concentrating on the dirtier side of life, more political and socially aware, it seemed a new day was beginning (and all a far cry from *Cats*.)

In Chichester, the Productions Board[1] made the decision that rather than appointing another director or actor to the post of Artistic Director, instead it would approach a producer, Duncan Weldon.

By 1995, Weldon had been responsible for some 200 productions in the West End, the first being *When We Were Married* in 1970, at the Strand Theatre. As well as many profitable North American and Broadway transfers, he had been responsible for the artistic policy of

[1] The Productions Board included many of those who had been involved in CFT since the earliest days, in one capacity or another, including Victor Behrens, David Evershed-Martin, Anthony Field, Brian Fieldhouse, John Hyland and John McKerchar. The Chairman of the Trust Company was Leslie Evershed-Martin, with Lady Olivier as President and Lord Cudlipp and Henny Gestetner as Vice-Presidents. My father, Richard Mosse, continued as Secretary to both Boards and there was also a significant number of Trustees – Harry Axton, Carol Evershed-Martin, Michael Marshall, Barry Evershed-Martin, David Shalit, Lord Young of Graffham, Clifford Hodgetts, Tony French, David Goodman, John Gale, Christopher Doman, Ruth Wrigley, John Rank, the Duke of Richmond and Geoffrey Marwood among them.

the Theatre Royal, Haymarket, London, since acquiring the lease in the early 1970s. More to the point, Weldon had a long and successful history with CFT.

Weldon explains: 'When Max Davies [Chairman of the Board] asked me to become Theatre Director, I had already co-produced more than thirty plays at Chichester, going back to *Arms and the Man* in 1970 for John Clements. I then got much more involved under Keith Michell... I knew all the Artistic Directors here because I had worked with them all.'

Weldon invited Derek Jacobi to join him as Associate Director. Weldon again: 'Derek is a close friend. I wanted him to come and do some plays here, but he wanted something more meaningful than just being an actor in a company, so I thought that was the best way to get him here, to help me shape the content of the season.'

Jacobi's association with CFT was, of course, also very well established from the Olivier days. He remembers the circumstances that made him accept Weldon's invitation: 'Duncan was a friend of mine and at the time I wanted to be more than an actor and to be involved in running a theatre. In reality I rode on Duncan's coat-tails. He did the work and I was more of a figurehead. It helped that I had audience recognition and could help bring in other actors but, all in all, the experience taught me two things: one I wasn't very good at it and two, I really just wanted to be an actor after all.'

Although Garland and Stevens had done a grand job in difficult circumstances to stabilise the Theatre's finances, the relative contributions from the Main House and the Minerva in the form of ticket receipts did not sufficiently guard against the inherent risks in the business.

Weldon remembers being asked by the Board, what his policy would be. His answer? 'Fill every seat, which this theatre had done quite successfully! My main aim was always to try and put on what the public wants to see and to get them

TOP
Derek Jacobi in *Playing the Wife*, 1995.

Photo: Alastair Muir

LEFT
Lois Harvey, Keith Michell and Penelope Keith in *Monsieur Amilicar*, 1995.

Photo: John Timbers/ ArenaPAL

all in. The Minerva setting up in opposition to the Main House did not make life easy. I started every season making a list of actors who I would like to come to Chichester. There's no point in picking a list of plays and hoping actors will do them.'

Certainly, the 1995 season announced by Weldon was an extraordinary one. True to his word to bring stars to Chichester, the company included some of the finest stage and television actors – Joss Ackland and Alan Bates, Honor Blackman, Dora Bryan and Ian Carmichael, Dinsdale Landen, Celia Imrie, Penelope Keith, Lesley Josephs, Nichola McAuliffe, Leo McKern, Prunella Scales, Keith Michell, John Nettles, Gawn Grainger, Patrick Garland, Geraldine McEwan and Maggie Smith. It also included the international Hollywood star, Lauren Bacall.

Weldon remembers Bacall struggling to adapt to life in Chichester: 'She came to do *The Visit*, which ran from the end of September through October, and played to eighty per cent. I had worked with her a lot and I like her a lot, but she's a star of the serious old type. She was a star

when Hollywood was at its biggest. As long as you treated her the right way, she was fine. She stayed at the Dolphin & Anchor Hotel opposite the cathedral. On Sunday morning, when the bells started ringing, she sent for the manager and demanded that he "stop that bloody noise. I'm trying to sleep!" He said: "Miss Bacall, they have been ringing bells on a Sunday morning for a thousand years." She said: "I don't give a damn how long it's been going on, stop them!" That was one occasion she didn't get her way!'

As well as a wonderful company of actors, there was an impressive cadre of writer/directors too – Alan Ayckbourn directing *A Word from Our Sponsors* and Harold Pinter directing Ronald Harwood's *Taking Sides*, starring Daniel Massey and Michael Pennington[1], both in the Minerva. Pinter also appeared as Roote in his own play, *The Hothouse*, which had not been revived since

---

[1] Michael Pennington, who played Major Arnold in 1995, returned in 2008 for a new production of *Taking Sides*, this time playing the role of Furtwängler. The 2008 revival played as a double bill with the world premiere of Harwood's companion piece, *Collaboration*.

its first performance in 1980. It was also the first time he acted in England for thirty years under the name Harold Pinter, rather than his stage name, David Baron.

In the Main House, both *The Visit* and the play Weldon chose to open the 1995 season – *Hadrian VII* – were directed by Terry Hands, who had been joint Artistic Director with Trevor Nunn and the Royal Shakespeare Company from 1978 and its Chief Executive from 1986.[1]

---

[1] Hands took over as Director of Clwyd Theatr Cymru in 1997.

Starring Derek Jacobi as George Arthur Rose, *Hadrian VII* was a triumphant start to the season. Based on Frederick Rolfe's semi-autobiographical novel of 1904, it tells the story of a devout, chain-smoking Englishman who, having found himself elected Pope (this is a work that blends fact and fantasy), set about a series of reforms that put him in direct opposition with the hierarchy of the Catholic church.

Phil Hewitt reviewed *Hadrian VII* for the *Chichester Observer*: 'It was so striking, a clerical drama very much in three colours, just red, black and white. You looked at it and it was so thrilling, there was something so brilliant about it.' After CFT, the production played at the Lyceum and Sheffield. That 1995 season also included Brighouse's *Hobson's Choice*, with Leo McKern and Nichola McAuliffe, which transferred to the Lyric, and Ranjit Bolt's new version of Molière's *The Miser*, with Ian Richardson.

Ian Richardson in
***The Miser*, 1995.**

Photo: Ivan Kyncl/
ArenaPAL

LEFT
Nichola McAuliffe
and Leo McKern
in *Hobson's*
***Choice*, 1995.**

Photo: John Timbers/
ArenaPAL

OPPOSITE
Derek Jacobi in
***Hadrian VII*, 1995.**

Photo: Ivan Kyncl/
ArenaPAL

**Dawn French,
in *When We Are
Married*, 1996.**

Photo: Robbie Jack/Corbis

1996

In the Main House, there were five productions, including Congreve's *Love for Love*. Derek Jacobi remembers the production for the worst of reasons: 'I got a bad stomach ache during *Love for Love* and was rushed into hospital to have my appendix removed. The CFT hospital curse had struck me again and this time there was no Dame Sybil [see page 35] to come round and read me poetry.'

It was followed by a dramatisation by Willis Hall of Jane Austen's *Mansfield Park*, then Peter Ustinov starring in his own play, *Beethoven's Tenth*. The production, though warmly talked about by those who were working at CFT at the time, was not as successful at the box office as had been hoped. It highlighted, perhaps, the changing times, as Max Davies, then Chairman of

the Productions Board, explains: 'Getting Peter Ustinov to put on *Beethoven's Tenth* was a coup. I absolutely loved it. You'd think with Ustinov and John Neville you'd pack the theatre but we only sold about sixty-five per cent. When the marketing girls talked to people on the street, they found a generational problem. Younger people had never heard of Peter Ustinov.'

The triumph of the 1996 Main House Season was J B Priestley's *When We Are Married.* Starring Dawn French, it was directed by Jude Kelly[1], and boasted a glittering cast that included Chris Larkin, Annette Badland, Alison Steadman, Leo

McKern, Gary Waldhorn and Roger Lloyd Pack (French's fellow cast members from the BBC series *The Vicar of Dibley*).

Set in the rolling Yorkshire heartlands, Priestley's 1938 comedy is set running when a southerner, the chapel organist, turns up on the silver wedding anniversary of three couples with the bombshell that the vicar who married them way back when was not, in fact, authorised to perform weddings.

As Ian Shuttleworth wrote in the *Financial Times*: 'All-star productions seldom equal the sum of their parts, but *When We Are Married* strikes a keen balance between delineating individuals and providing strong ensemble scenes, and in particular Kelly orchestrates the free-for-all arguments in the play extremely well. As the big-name centrepiece of Duncan Weldon and

[1] Jude Kelly, director and producer, was Artistic Director of the Battersea Arts Centre from 1980 – 1985, before becoming the founding Director of the West Yorkshire Playhouse from 1990 – 2002. Kelly is currently Artistic Director of SouthBank Centre in London.

Peter Ustinov and John Neville in *Beethoven's Tenth*, 1996.
Photo: John Timbers/ ArenaPAL

CENTRE
(L-R) (Seated) Dawn French, Alison Steadman, Annette Badland, Paul Copley, Gary Waldhorn and Roger Lloyd Pack in *When We Are Married*, 1996.
Photo: Robbie Jack

Derek Jacobi's 1996 Chichester Main House season, it delivers the goods and no mistake.'

Max Davies remembers the scenes: 'You couldn't get tickets, they were queuing right the way around the Theatre. I've never seen anything like it, for any show. It's a great play, she [Dawn French] was on the telly. Duncan struck gold, no doubt about it.'

After a sell-out run, the play transferred to the Savoy Theatre in London.

The 1996 Minerva season was no less impressive. The most highly anticipated production was

Uncle Vanya with Jacobi in the lead, taking the role made so famous by Michael Redgrave some thirty years previously.

Weldon takes up the story: 'Derek really wanted to do it and I managed to get a fantastic cast for it, as Olivier had – Trevor Eve, Una Stubbs, Frances Barber, Peggy Mount, Constance Cummings, Alec McCowen, Richard Johnson. It was a huge success. It went to the Albery[1], where it played to a twelve-week sell-out.'

As well as Alan Bennett's *Talking Heads* and Simon Gray's *Simply Disconnected* and *Beatrix* – adapted by Patrick Garland and Judy Taylor from the writings of Beatrix Potter and starring Patricia Routledge – there was also Helen Cooper's much admired adaptation of

---

[1] Now called the Coward Theatre.

FAR LEFT
Harriet Walter in
Hedda Gabler,
1996.

Photo: Ivan Kyncl/
ArenaPAL

LEFT
Frank Finlay in
The Handyman,
1996.

Photo: John Timbers/
ArenaPAL

Edward Kemp.

Photo: Clare Park

Ibsen's *Hedda Gabler*. Starring Harriet Walter and David Threlfall, the cast included Phyllida Law, Nicholas Le Prevost and Jenny Quale. It also transferred to London, to the Richmond Theatre. Alan Bates played in *Fortune's Fool* and Frank Finlay, another CFT favourite, appeared in *The Handyman*.

In the autumn, outside of the Festival Season, the Minerva also welcomed co-productions from other theatres. For two weeks at the beginning of November, for example, the Salisbury Playhouse production of Willy Russell's *Educating Rita* played in repertoire with Mamet's *Oleanna*. The director was Jonathan Church, destined ten years later, to take over as Artistic Director.

Another important development during 1996 was the expansion of the Youth Theatre and Education department. Kate Vaughan, the first CFYT director had been succeeded by Clare Rankin, who chose scripted pieces for the burgeoning Youth Theatre to perform including, in 1987, *The Recruiting Party*, written and directed by Edward Kemp.[2]

[2] Writer and director, Kemp was Associate Dramaturg at CFT 2003 – 2005 and would go on to write or adapt several landmark productions at CFT during that period, including *Nathan the Wise* and Bulgakov's *The Master & Margarita*. Currently the Artistic Director of RADA, Kemp is another with strong family connections to CFT. His mother, Pat Kemp, is one of the longest-serving – and most lovely – front-of-house ladies.

In 1990, Abigail Morris was interim CFYT Director. In 1991, Anthea Dobry took over. CFYT was back performing at the National Theatre, as they had done the previous year – as part of the Lloyds Bank Youth Theatre Challenge[1]- and a young playwrights competition with the *Chichester Observer*.

In 1996, after three years with Kate Vaughan returning to lead the Youth Theatre, it was clear that the scope for expanding the department and activities even further was there. Andy Brereton was appointed Education Director. Dale Rooks, who arrived midway through that season, was one of two Assistant YT directors. She was later

appointed Youth Theatre Director in 2002 and is now the longest serving Director of CFYT.

Brereton remembers arriving in 1996: 'I inherited a large, but unfocussed, Youth Theatre and some education work linked to the Festival productions. Sitting on my own in the ex-Catering Manager's office on the corner of Gunter's[2], it all seemed a little overwhelming.'

The Education Department and the Youth Theatre received some support from West Sussex County Council, South East Arts and the Festival Theatre Society. Given a boost in 1996 – and

---

[1] Later to become BT National Connections, now National Connections.

[2] The site where the Steven Pimlott Education and Rehearsal Building now stands, the area is still often referred to as 'Gunter's' after the catering company, Payne & Gunter, who ran the restaurant there before the Minerva was built.

Alan Bates and Rachel Pickup in *Fortune's Fool*, 1996.

Photo: Ivan Kyncll/ ArenaPAL

acknowledged in all the advertising, brochures, programmes – it enabled Brereton to mount an ambitious, properly budgeted production of *Nicholas Nickleby*, the longest and largest ever Youth Theatre production. Directed by Brereton, Rooks was Assistant Director and Amy Jackson[1] the designer of the show.

Programmes of 1996 also acknowledge the Minerva as receiving 'substantial financial support' from the Society, as well as from South East Arts. There were a number of individual and corporate sponsors – listed in the programmes

as Gold Star Patrons and Patrons of the Year – who supported CFT's work, but the Main House received no subsidy at all. The Main House had been designed for a nine-week summer season. Now, it was open for much of the year with all the attendant costs and overheads that went with that. And although the figures show that 1996 was an outstanding year in the Minerva, both for tickets sold and capacity achieved, the ratio of costs to returns in the Main House was less comfortable.

As Weldon says: 'The biggest challenge to all theatres is the cost of putting on plays. I did *When We Are Married* as my first play in London in 1970 and it cost me £15,000 to put on. When I did it here with Dawn, just to transfer it cost £250,000.'

---

[1] Amy Jackson, then only 17 and a member of CFYT, was to go on to design many shows for CFYT including *A Christmas Carol* (2009), *The Snow Queen* (2010) and *The Lion, the Witch & the Wardrobe* (2011). Jackson was also the first recipient of the John Hyland Award.

1997

RIGHT
Kathleen Turner, Leslie Caron, Twiggy and Maureen Lipman at 1997 Festival season launch.
Photo: Ivan Kyncl/ArenaPAL /Duncan Weldon collection

The press conference to announce the 1997 season was a starry affair. Weldon's last season was a wonderful showcase for many fine actresses – Zoe Wanamaker, Dorothy Tutin, Kathleen Turner, Maureen Lipman, Leslie Caron, Julie Christie and Twiggy.

Duncan Weldon: 'I would have wanted more of them in the Main House, but they all wanted to play the Minerva.'

In a programme of classics and revivals, the riskiest venture – on paper at least – looked to be *Electra* in the Minerva with Zoe Wanamaker.

Weldon again: 'I took Zoe and David Leveaux [the director] out for lunch and I thought we were going to do *Summer and Smoke* by Tennessee Williams in the Main House. I thought it was just a matter of meeting and agreeing, but all of a sudden David said: "I think I've got a better idea. I think we should do *Electra*."

'I said: "*Electra* at Chichester? We'd empty the bloody theatre. They're not going to come and see Greek tragedy in the Main House. Keith Michell did *Oedipus Tyrannus* back in 1974 and it was empty, even with Keith in it, who was big at the time, and Diana Dors. If we do *Electra*, it has to be in the Minerva. There it might get an audience."'

A co-production with the Donmar Warehouse[1], it received outstanding reviews, both in Chichester and in London, and transferred to Broadway. Wanamaker won a Tony for her performance.

But while the Minerva was successfully playing host to some excellent productions and performances and audiences were coming, in the Main House the box office was not as strong as it had been hoped. And with six productions, rather than five, the burden of cost on the Main House was higher than ever.

The first play was Michael Rudman directing Michael Denison, Barbara Jefford and Ian McShane in *The Admirable Crichton*, followed by Googie Withers and Stephanie Beacham in *Lady Windermere's Fan*. Later in the season was Sandy Wilson's musical *Divorce Me, Darling!* – with Ruthie Henshall, Marti Webb and Weldon's wife, Ann Sidney – and Somerset Maugham's *Our Betters*, also directed by Michael Rudman, with Rula Lenska, Barbara Jefford and Kathleen Turner. Finally, *The Magistrate* with

---

[1] Sam Mendes was Artistic Director of the Donmar Warehouse at the time, with Caro Newling as Executive Director. A Sussex resident, Newling joined the new Productions Company Board after the crisis of 1997. Co-founder and Director, with Mendes, of Neal Street Productions, Newling was appointed Chair of Paines Plough Theatre Company in February 2011.

Ian Richardson in the role previously taken at CFT in 1969 by Alastair Sim.

All the same, there was a great deal of pressure on the third production in the Main House to deliver the same sort of success enjoyed the previous year by *When We Are Married*. Coward's *Blithe Spirit* was to be directed by Tim Luscombe with an all-star cast – Maureen Lipman as Madame Arcati, Twiggy as Elvira and Belinda Lang as Ruth Condomine. Lipman was a popular choice, not least because of her biographical shows based on the life of Joyce Grenfell. However, in the last week of rehearsals, disaster struck. Lipman was diagnosed as seriously ill and was unable to continue. Dora Bryan gamely stepped in, but the production struggled to find its feet.

Weldon again: 'At the point at which Maureen pulled out, the advance bookings for *Blithe Spirit* were as good as what we'd had for Dawn French in *When We Are Married*. We would have done the same business and probably made £200,000 profit. So we had no choice but to use some of the reserve to underwrite that loss.'

This sent alarm bells ringing with the Board. The costs were higher than could be sustained by the income coming in through the box office and sponsorship. And, as Weldon points out, CFT was now running almost a year-round programme, which substantially added to the overheads too: 'The only reason to keep CFT open in the winter is as an amenity for the town, but if that amenity is going to cost you £1million a year – which was what the winter was costing us out of the summer season revenue – then the local authority should support it.'

Chartered accountant John McKerchar, who had been a member of the Board and a Trustee for some time, remembers the events of the summer of 1997 vividly. He realised a few weeks into the Season that the money coming in – through the box office and private and corporate sponsorship – was simply not enough.

McKerchar explains: 'The Board used me as a quasi Finance Director over some years, although I had no power over the Theatre's finances. In May 1997, I said: "This company is going to be bankrupt and not able to continue trading solvently by 13 August." I could see the way the audiences were shrinking and the costs were escalating by an enormous factor, out of all reason. All they could say was: "Oh John, you are

always the prophet of doom." I said: "I am not. I'm simply telling you the truth."

Then, on Sunday 31 August, Princess Diana was killed in a car accident in Paris. Weldon remembers how immediately, everything changed: 'It affected every theatre; it stopped people going out. In the Main House we were doing a musical, *Divorce Me, Darling!*, which had terrific bookings and reviews. Diana died on a Sunday, but nobody read the review sections. Business stopped next day.'

Weldon and Chairman Max Davies were forced to look at a range of options, some radical. For example, to use the Main House only for special occasions during the summer Festival and, instead, building a new 900-seater non-galleried proscenium arch theatre that could operate year round. A space that would be more suitable for the majority of touring shows that played awkwardly on CFT's open-thrust stage.

Weldon once more: 'I felt that the Theatre had lost its identity because you drifted into the winter and nobody knew what the difference was. I wanted to reinstate that gap so there was a feeling of a Season, not just round the clock like a regular touring theatre that happened to

do a season of its own in the middle. All the plays that came in the winter were designed for pros arches so some of them were really bad; you couldn't see them.'

Current Chairman of the Productions Board, Lord Young of Graffham[1], remembers listening to the presentation: 'It was only by the end of 1996, beginning of '97, that I began to hear stories that the Theatre was in trouble. At one Trustees meeting, they showed us an incredible development plan that would have then cost £14 million-plus, which would have built a third theatre. It was lunacy. The Theatre was already in trouble and the last thing we needed was capacity. In my view – and in the view of many Trustees – they had already made a mistake in building the Minerva because it was just too small. Almost every time we run a play there we lose money even if we sell every ticket.'

---

[1] David Young had been a Trustee for some time. He was Director of the Centre for Policy Studies in 1979, then was to become a key figure in Margaret Thatcher's government. He was Chairman of the Manpower Services Commission, in 1985 was appointed Secretary of State for Employment and served as Secretary of State for Trade & Industry from 1987–1989. From 1990–1995, he was Executive Chairman of Cable & Wireless.

Ruthie Henshall, Ann Sidney and Samantha George in *Divorce Me Darling!*, 1997.

Photo: Ivan Kyncl/ArenaPAL

Dorothy Tutin in *After October*, 1997.

Photo: John Timbers/ArenaPAL

As the long season drew to a close, John McKerchar called a meeting of the Trust in the Minerva and showed the Trustees a PowerPoint presentation showing them, as he puts it: 'the economic facts of life, how the money was ebbing away, but they just couldn't or wouldn't see it'.

The bald situation was that – despite playing to some 200,000 people during the course of 1997 – once box offices losses were taken into account and once the £1 million outlay required for the installation of a new sound system was added into the mix, CFT was in serious financial trouble.

John McKerchar again: 'In 1997 alone, we lost £478,000 and the net cost of the Main House had gone up by £129,000 in three years.'

Max Davies thinks other factors also contributed to the crisis: 'There were a number of reasons, but one of them was that audiences were dropping off. I know that it is a political answer, but I genuinely believe that to be true. We had reserves of about £600,000 and we were on course to lose £500,000. There is no doubt that people liked the plays and Duncan got some wonderful actors.'

However, David Young was not aware of the true extent of the difficulties until he was telephoned by Sir Michael Marshall a few weeks later[1], asking if he might meet with him and with John Gale to discuss where things stood.

In November 1997, the situation went – as the tattered old cliché would have it – from bad to worse. It is well beyond the scope of this book to go into the events that led to Duncan Weldon and his administrator leaving CFT or the complicated sequence of meetings that happened over the next four weeks. Suffice to say the telephone wires, the fax wires, were pressed into service as urgent conversations took place between London and Chichester, Arundel and Graffham, not to mention various other villages in between.

The sky turned blue, white, brown with letters and faxes – printed in the *The Times*, in *The Stage*, notes to and from lawyers and auditors, minutes taken and resolutions proposed, documents hand delivered to Oaklands Park and East Pallant, North Street and Great Peter Street, votes lost and won in council chambers and offices, promises made, assurances given.

The inescapable fact was that CFT was within 48 hours of going into liquidation[2] when Chairman of the District Council, Tony French, brought the matter before the Council.

As well as Lord Young, the late Sir Michael Marshall, Clifford Hodgetts, Harry Axton and Neville Lacey, Tony French was one of the heroes of the crisis hour. So, too, many others – too many to mention individually – who were determined not to allow CFT to shut its doors for good, including the Chief Executive of Chichester District Council, John Marsden, and the Members of CDC who voted in favour of the request for urgent financial assistance taken under the provisions of Standing Order 16 (1). Also, others who dug deep in their pockets, either putting up personal assurances or

---

[1] Sir Michael Marshall, who died in 2006, was an author, businessman, cricketer as well as a politician. He was MP for Arundel from 1974 until 1997, when electoral boundaries were changed. A member of the Trust, he played a key role in setting CFT back on track.

[2] Max Davies commented that advance booking revenues for the Christmas Show – a touring show of *Mother Goose* with Britt Ekland and Sherrie Hewson – were put into a separate bank account in case the money had to be refunded.

The cast of *Mother Goose*, Christmas 1997.

Photo: *Chichester Observer*

helping to access grants or loans from charities and trusts.

For example, Christopher Doman, who was to take over as Company Secretary from my father: 'It was very hairy. I am a Trustee of a grant-making charitable trust, called the Bassil Shippam and Alsford Trust. Michael Marshall made a presentation to us and we lent them £250,000 on a short-term loan, which tied them over and they got through the crisis.' [1]

At the meeting on Tuesday 16 December, after a presentation by Tony French as Chairman of the Council, the decision was taken that Chichester District Council would offer up £300,000 subject to certain conditions, not least of all that CDC (and City Council) should have a representative on the Board. There was also to be a completely new team – both in executive and non-executive terms – to take CFT forward. This meant the existing Boards of both the Productions Company and the Trust Company were required to stand down, something which caused a good deal of distress in many quarters and was seen as unfair by many.

Lord Young comments: 'Looking back, I think it was a bit harsh getting the entire old Board to go, because I think it was the system that was really at fault.'

Clifford Hodgetts agrees: 'Some of the old Board members rightly were upset. John McKerchar was a good friend of mine. He had been warning of disaster for some time and I reassured him it was not his fault. But there had to be a clean sweep.'

Christmas Day came and went, Boxing Day too. On stage, Demoness Vanity, Fairy Modesty, Priscilla the Goose and the Gold Power Ranger continued to entertain in gold and sparkle and feathers. Backstage, in the Director's office, the outgoing Boards – with dignity and with a commitment to put the good of CFT above their own feelings in the matter – handed over to their successors.

David Young was appointed Chairman of the Productions Board, Michael Marshall Chairman of the Trust Company, with Clifford Hodgetts as Deputy Chairman. They were joined by David Shalit and Neville Lacey – senior partner at the accountants Jones Avens – as Deputy Chairman of the Productions Board, by Geoffrey Marwood and by Harry Axton, who already had been instrumental behind the scenes, as Acting Chief Executive until a new Director could be appointed.

Lord Young continues: 'Harry [Axton] started working like a Trojan, rebuilding the books from scratch and getting everything going. We spent most of the Christmas holidays working on this. We faced a future with no Director, no set of accounts, few adequate contracts of employment for staff who worked at the Theatre. The books were not in a good condition, we had a season to get together.' [2]

---

[1] Clifford Hodgetts notes that the Trust later donated this sum to the Theatre. Also, that all Trustees who loaned were repaid in full.

[2] In the event, Axton – who died in 2002 – stayed on until CFT was getting back on its feet again. A Chartered Accountant and Chairman of one of the biggest property companies in the county. One time President of the British Property Federation, and Deputy Chairman of the Audit Commission, he was also Chairman of Chichester Festivities from 1989 and Deputy Organist at St Mary's Church, Lavant. Axton was another of the great unsung heroes of CFT's survival.

1998

After the dramatic events of December 1997, it is tempting to imagine that Thursday 1 January 1998 was a day that dawned with quiet relief. In the words of Samuel Beckett's *Murphy*: 'The sun shone, having no alternative, on the nothing new.'

In the event, it was not like that. *Mother Goose* was still playing on the CFT Main Stage and, between Christmas and New Year, the Board was considering who might take on the role of Artistic Director. No one in the business could be unaware of CFT's problems, lack of finance, lack of time, reputation in ribbons and with staff morale at an all-time low.

Andrew Welch had been running the Theatre of Comedy in London, which owned the Shaftesbury Theatre and had the lease on the Churchill Theatre, Bromley. He had turned the Theatre Royal Plymouth around, which had a deficit when he arrived.

Welch remembers the first conversations: 'I had been doing a revival of *Brief Lives* at the Duchess Theatre with Patrick Garland, and in those idle moments that you have as director and producer, we used to chat about Chichester, so I knew there were problems. But I was somewhat surprised to be approached in late December

1997 by Rupert Rimes, who was the Chief Executive of the Society of London Theatres, and a good friend of Michael Marshall. I came down and met David Young, Michael and Harry Axton. They gave me the job in January 1998.'

In an ideal situation, the brochure for the season should be on the point of going to press in

Issy van Randwyck in *Song of Singapore*, 1997.

Photo: Nigel Norrington/ArenaPAL

ABOVE LEFT

Andrew Welch.

Chichester Observer

*Saturday, Sunday...
and Monday,* 1998.

Photo: Clive Barda/
ArenaPAL

RIGHT
**Simon Callow
in *Chimes at
Midnight,* 1998.**

Photo: Clive Barda/
ArenaPAL

January or February at the latest. After CFT's turbulent few months, there were no plays and no players. Welch continues: 'The brief they gave me? Just to get through the next season, or even the next week! They [Young, Marshall, Axton] were absolutely straightforward and honest about the Theatre's situation. They didn't have a clear view of what the solutions were, none of us did. But the Theatre's reputation had been badly damaged. We had to show actors and directors that Chichester was still a viable proposition.'

The critics also needed persuading. Michael Billington: 'The Theatre was virtually bankrupt when [Welch] arrived. He had a tough job to do.'

And Charles Spencer: 'When Andrew came to CFT it had sunk to the point with some critics that they thought it wasn't worth bothering about any more.'

With only a matter of weeks to programme a summer Festival Season for two theatres, Welch got out his contacts book. As Paul Rogerson pointed out, much as Olivier and Clements had done in the 1960s. He appointed David Suchet, as an unpaid Artistic Associate to advise on programming and, against all odds, started to pull a season together. As Clifford Hodgetts remembers: 'That Andrew got a season together at all was remarkable. A lot of actors would not commit because they had heard the rumours of the Theatre being on the verge of going dark.'

Welch appointed Jude Kelly to direct Eduardo de Filippo's *Saturday, Sunday... and Monday* with David Suchet, and Patrick Garland, to write and adapt *Chimes at Midnight* – starring Simon Callow and CFT favourite, Sarah Badel. But the two critical hits of the season were David Hare's *Racing Demon* – the first ever production of a Hare play at Chichester, starring Dinsdale Landen and Denis Quilley – and the world premiere of William Nicholson's *Katherine Howard*.

A beautiful and lyrical play dramatising the brief marriage of Henry VIII to the fifth of his six wives, the role of Henry was taken by Richard Griffiths. Emilia Fox was the young, naïve Katherine and Julian Rhind-Tutt played Culpepper. The production, directed by Robin Lefèvre and designed by Liz Ashcroft, received outstanding reviews.

I was offered the job as Administrative Director in April 1998 and took up the post in July. A former publisher and an author, rather than a theatre professional, I nonetheless had experience in arts fundraising and sponsorship and in industrial relations. It was perhaps also hoped my local links to Chichester might play a part in helping to restore better relations between the city and the Theatre.

Having programmed the Main House in whirlwind time, Welch turned his attention to the problem of what to do in the smaller house: 'We just didn't have enough money to put anything on in the Minerva, but then friends, bless them,

Denis Quilley, Mark Kingston, Paul Venables and John Harding in *Racing Demon*, 1998.

Photo: Clive Barda/ ArenaPAL

came up with enough money for us to do something. We did Orton's *Loot*, which went into the West End, and the musical *Song of Singapore*.'

One of my fondest memories of working at CFT during that time was being invited by Roger Redfarn to watch the dress rehearsal of *Song of Singapore*. A late summer's afternoon, golden slats of light and green shadows in Oaklands Park. In the Minerva, the gaudy red of a seedy nightclub in 1940s Singapore, exotic flowers and black Chinese silks and Issy van Randwyck, Elio Pace and Simon Slater.

Andrew Welch continues: 'It was very charming and funny and it sold out. In the show, Issy would ask a man from the front row to dance with her. There was some competition from men of a certain age for whose knee she would sit on.'

Christopher Doman, who had been part of the local amateur dramatic society, the Chichester Players, remembers: 'I didn't realise it was part of the show until Issy came over to me, held out

Denis Quilley and Richard Griffiths in rehearsals for *Katherine Howard*, **1998.**

Photo: *The News*, Portsmouth

Richard Griffiths in *Katherine Howard*, **1998.**

Photo: Clive Barda/ ArenaPAL

her hand, and said: "Would you like to dance?" I said: "I most certainly would!" I guess that was the actor in me coming out.'

Welch also brought back another CFT tradition – the cricket team: 'A number of our actors and crew were cricketers, so we revived the team and played three or four matches a season. Jonathan Coy [Cranmer in *Katherine Howard*] was a wonderful batsman. In fact, a pretty good all rounder!'

In an interview with Charles Spencer in the *Daily Telegraph* in May 2002, Welch was quoted as saying: 'It was a bumpy first season. Audiences weren't big enough overall and although we just about managed to scrape through, it was very scary. There were times when I was really worried that we faced closure.'

But, thanks to the hard work of everyone involved – volunteers, production and administrative staff, the commitment of actors, directors, designers and creative teams – not least of all the long serving members of staff who had seen the Theatre through other tough times, CFT survived to see another day.

The end of season figures were boosted by an unexpected – and timely – repayment of VAT. Welch explains: 'Neville Lacey, who was then Treasurer – and a very good one – noticed something called the London Zoo Case, which ruled that VAT had wrongly been levied on a charitable organisation. Neville helped us put our case and we got a rebate of about £400,000 on overpaid VAT. That saved us in my first year, but I knew we would have to seek Arts Council support.'

Neville Lacey, for his work then and subsequently, is without doubt another of the modest superstars of the CFT story.

My memory of those years at the tail-end of the 1990s is of endless, endless meetings. Meetings with MPs, with Ministers at the DCMS, with quangos and committees and local groups. Walking up and down North Street, West Street, to the Chichester City Council, Chichester District Council, West Sussex County Council. South East Arts and Arts Council England in London. Looking at everything, from contracts to catering

arrangements, from the signs in the car park to the seats in the Main House auditorium.

Little by little, a funding package involving all the local councils, then South East Arts and then the Arts Council itself, through its stablisation fund, was put together. Now, in 2012, relations between CFT and funding bodies are excellent. Back in 1998, it was different.

Andrew Welch: 'We went to the Arts Council and asked them to increase the amount they supported us. I admit I don't have warm memories of the Arts Council or South East Arts either. We really had to battle. They always gave the impression that we were not artistic or edgy enough to justify the money.'

Emilia Fox and Julian Rhind-Tutt in rehearsals for *Katherine Howard*, 1998.

Photo: *The News*, Portsmouth

LEFT
Tracy-Ann Oberman in *Loot*, 1998.

Photo: Tristram Kenton/ Lebrecht Music & Arts

1999

As the work behind the scenes to get the Theatre back on an even keel continued, the 1999 season was coming together. Welch invited back Richard Griffiths, Issy van Randwyck, William Buckhurst and Christopher Morahan, as well as those with a long association with CFT such as James Bolam, Christopher Luscombe, Anna Carteret and Patricia Routledge. She was to play Lady Bracknell in the opening production in the Main House, *The Importance of Being Earnest*.

A farce in which the protagonists take false identifies in order to escape their social obligations, Wilde's play was first performed at the St James' Theatre in London in February 1895. Routledge explains why, finally, she accepted the invitation: 'I had turned down Lady Bracknell for twenty years, because there was the memory of Edith Evans going on and on and on.[1] The fact that Christopher Morahan was going to direct

it, changed my mind. I knew he would have a sense of period and style, and that he would honour the text (which he did), and that he would serve the play (which also he did). He stripped the play back to what it had been, removing all the veneers that had built up from other productions. He made it fresh again... It gave me tremendous joy, having said no for twenty years, that it was successful.'

It was a triumphant start to the 1999 season and, when it finished its run at CFT, it went to the Theatre Royal Haymarket. The first performance was Wednesday 4 August, in the presence of the Queen Mother who was celebrating her 99th birthday.

Patricia Routledge admits: 'I knew she was coming before, but the rest of the cast were not told until the last minute. We were frightened enough of the First Night, let alone a royal visit. But we survived! And we received some wonderful notices.'

The second play in the Main House was *Semi-Detached*. David Turner's comedy of social manners opened at the Belgrade Theatre, Coventry, in 1962, with Leonard Rossiter in the lead role. When it transferred to London, Olivier replaced

---

[1] Edith Evans appeared as Lady Bracknell in 1939 – a part she reprised in the 1952 film. She was synonymous with the role.

James Bolam and Anna Carteret in *Semi-Detached*, **1999.**

Photo: Clive Barda/ ArenaPAL

OPPOSITE

Patricia Routledge in *The Importance of Being Earnest*, **1999.**

Photo: Clive Barda/ ArenaPAL

Rossiter as Fred Midway and James Bolam played his son. At CFT in 1999, Bolam played Midway, with Anna Carteret as his wife.

The third play, opening in Coward's centenary year, was *Easy Virtue*. Written in 1924, it was directed by Maria Aitken. Greta Scacchi played the American divorcée, Larita, with Wendy Craig and Michael Jayston as Colonel and Mrs Whittaker. The production received excellent reviews, though it never quite caught alight at the box office.

In the Minerva, Welch built on the success of his first season and commissioned new works as a way of attracting a new, younger audience to CFT[1].

In addition to established directors such as Roger Redfarn with *Nymph Errant* and Christopher Morahan with Whelan's *The School of Night,* starring Jack Shepherd, Welch also brought in young directors at the beginning of their careers, just as Gale and Garland had done in the early days of the Minerva.

'The first commission was *The King of Prussia,* a Nick Darke play about Cornwall. I think it opened the eyes of our audience. Directed

[1] In the same interview in the *Daily Telegraph* in May 2002, Charles Spencer estimates that during Welch's time, audience members in the Minerva under the age of 25 quadrupled.

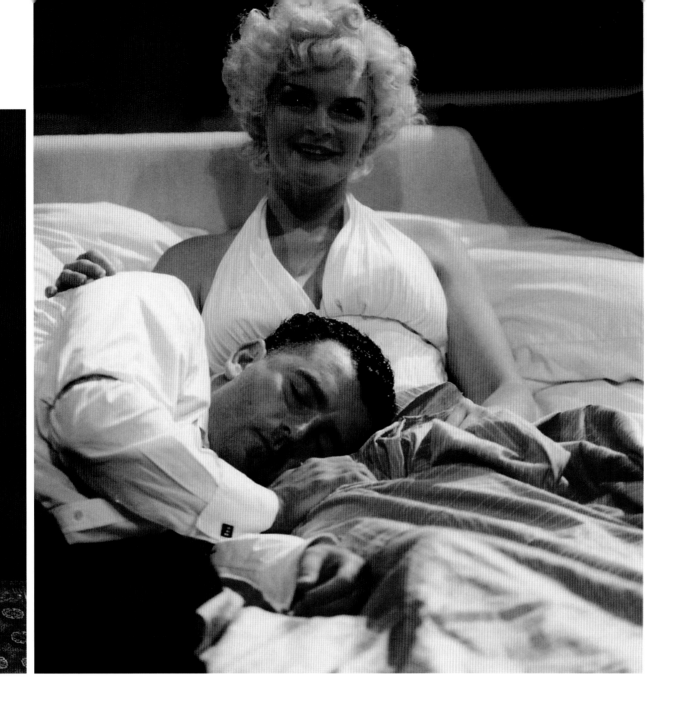

Sharon Small and Martin Marquez in *Insignificance*, 1999.

Photo: Tristram Kenton/ Lebrecht Music & Arts

by Sean Holmes[1], it didn't have huge attendance, probably only playing to 45 per cent, but it was a start.'

Loveday Ingram, another of Welch's Associate Directors, directed Terry Johnson's *Insignificance*. As well as a full programme of late night revue, talks, short plays and concerts – including Summer Sundays, which was a series of concerts by soloists from the London Philharmonic Orchestra – the Minerva season was rounded off by another world premiere, William Nicholson's *The Retreat from Moscow*, which starred the extraordinary Janet Suzman.[2]

Across the road, the final production of the 1999 season in the Main House was *The Man Who Came to Dinner*. Last presented at CFT in 1979, this time Richard Griffiths took the role of Sheridan Whiteside, the house guest from hell. With Issy van Randwyck as the predatory actress Lorraine Sheldon and Christopher Luscombe

---

[1] Having directed a number of award-winning productions, Holmes was also Associate Director of the Oxford Stage Company (2001–2006) and became Artistic Director of the Lyric, Hammersmith, in 2009.

[2] Janet Suzman will be returning to CFT in 2012 to direct *Antony and Cleopatra* starring Kim Cattrall and Michael Pennington as part of the fiftieth anniversary Main House season.

Janet Suzman and Edward Hardwicke in *The Retreat from Moscow*, 1999.

Photo: Tristram Kenton/ Lebrecht Music & Arts

OPPOSITE

Joss Ackland in Heartbreak House, 1999.

Photo: Clive Barda/ ArenaPAL

as the urbane English writer, whose turn at the piano bore more than a passing reference to Noël Coward, it was a charming production that saw the 1999 season out in style.

One of the most important changes had been the growth in the Development and Sponsorship departments, headed by Lucy Brett and joined by Sarah Mansell as a Consultant. With the quality and variety of work on offer during the season, they had coaxed local firms – and some further afield – to start supporting CFT. Whatever did or did not happen with public funding, there was no doubt the role played by individual and corporate sponsors was going to become even more crucial in the decade ahead.

Lord Young remembers drawing a sigh of relief as the season closed on Saturday 9 October on such a high note: 'While 1998 was a good year, 1999 was really a remarkable year. At that time our subsidy from the Arts Council was only

£20,000, and that was for Education. The 1999 accounts show we ended the season without any subsidy before that £20,000 and we lost the same again. The productions might not have been what the Arts Council wanted us to do, but we had to sell tickets. I began to think we were back on an even keel.'

So as the world prepared to greet the new century, Powell & Moya's Festival Theatre sat on its corner of Oaklands Park, a little battered perhaps, a little ragged round the edges, but with its doors open for any who might come. CFT had survived.

In the blue light of an afternoon in December, the foyer peaceful, quiet, it was a building given back to the silence before the Christmas show began. And at night, the floodlights continued to send the dancing shadow of Tom Merrifield's statue *Spartacus* up, up and over the brown and white and concrete façade of the building.

The 2000s

Artistic/Theatre Directors
ANDREW WELCH (1998 – 2002)
MARTIN DUNCAN, RUTH MACKENZIE and **STEVEN PIMLOTT** (2003 – 2005)
JONATHAN CHURCH (Artistic Director) and **ALAN FINCH** (Executive Director) (2006 – present)

*'For last year's words belong to last year's language
And next year's words await another voice.'*

'Little Gidding',
FOUR QUARTETS
T S Eliot

ndrew Welch launched the Millennium season at CFT with a community show, *The Barchester Chronicles*, in April: 'I was conscious that the Theatre had been through this difficult time. Clearly relationships with the community had been damaged, and I was well aware that even though there would be lots of people who might not normally go to the Theatre, there might be a way of engaging them and giving them more of a sense of ownership.'

Knowing it would involve a huge cast, music, musicians, adults and children, Welch invited Roger Redfarn – who had been responsible for some of CFT's most successful productions, not least of all *Underneath the Arches* and 1999's runaway hit, *Song of Singapore* – to direct: 'When I had been at Plymouth, we had done a large-scale community piece – *High Heels in the Rubble* – about Plymouth in the Blitz, by a local writer, Judith Cook, and directed by Roger Redfarn. It had been hugely successful. I asked Judith and Roger to be involved at Chichester and we chose the Trollope because we felt that this would have contemporary resonance – indeed I am a great Trollope fan... It was a nightmare of organisation, but Roger is enormously resilient, which is why he was just the person to do it. It proved to be a wonderful success.'

Sophie Ward and Janie Dee in *Three Sisters*, 2001
Photo: Clive Barda/ArenaPAL

The Community Cast of *The Barchester Chronicles*, 2000.

Photo: Clive Barda/ ArenaPAL

Welch's hope that it would engage many of the people who had drifted away from the Theatre was realised. With memories of *Cavalcade* and *Victory!* in people's minds, and supported strongly by the *Chichester Observer*, hundreds offered their services in all areas – singing, building, painting, leafleting, sewing, performing. The choir included several members of the new Trustee body, local teachers, doctors, lawyers, judges, as well as children (my nine year old daughter Martha among them). All the lead roles were taken by amateur actors too.

Christopher Doman, then Company Secretary, played Dr Septimus Harding. His wife Madeleine was one of the two Assistant Directors.

Doman remembers learning to play the cello – or, rather, pretending: 'They took the resin off the bow, so it didn't make any noise. Under my music stool, they placed a loudspeaker, so when I began to play, and the music started, it looked as though it was coming from the cello. Benedict Rogerson[1] came in for a few hours

and taught me enough to appear half-way convincing. It was a wonderful experience and I was in a state of blue funk before going on stage for every performance.'

Andy Brereton, then CFT Education Director, considers *Barchester* hugely important in rebuilding the relationship between the Theatre and Chichester: 'I remember standing on stage during the technical rehearsal, trying to keep over a hundred people dressed for the opening funeral scene happy while we sorted out yet another problem with the revolve. And one elderly woman said: "Do you know, Andy, I've never been on a stage before and look at me now!" That was a humbling moment – and a reminder that we have to share this amazing resource, this amazing theatre, with everyone, whoever they are and whatever their expertise.'

The 2000 Festival Season proper opened on Tuesday 16 May in the Main House with James Kerr's production of *The Recruiting Officer*, George Farquhar's popular Restoration comedy.

---

[1] Benedict Rogerson is the son of former General Manager Paul Rogerson, and a professional concert cellist. A member of the Irish Chamber Orchestra, Rogerson was one of the founder members of the Szabó Piano Trio in 2002.

It did not find much favour with the critics. For example, Lyn Gardner in *The Guardian*: 'The 2000 Chichester season begins with the beating of a military drum, but the overall effect is more of a whimper than a bang.'

The second play was George Bernard Shaw's apocalyptic *Heartbreak House*, commemorating the fiftieth anniversary of Shaw's death. It opened on Tuesday 30 May with an exceptional cast that included Joss Ackland, Clare Higgins, Anna Carteret, Christopher Benjamin and Susannah Wise. Directed by Christopher Morahan and with a wonderful set by John Gunter, the main room resembled a ship's quarters with decking and gangplank and a blindfolded figurehead. Despite praise for individual performances, overall again the production failed to please the critics and it played to little more than 40 per cent.

However, in the Minerva things were going very well. The opening production, another first for CFT, was Edward Bond's *The Sea*, directed by Sean Holmes, which brought in a new, younger audience. It was followed by CFT Associate Director Loveday Ingram's production of David Hare's *The Blue Room*.

A daisy chain of ten sexual trysts – played by two actors – Hare's updating of Arthur Schnitzler's

Susannah Fellows and Martin Crewes in *Pal Joey*, 2000.

Photo: Tristram Kenton/ Lebrecht Music & Arts

La Ronde had caused a storm when it was premiered at the Donmar Warehouse in 1998. Sam Mendes directed a (briefly) naked Nicole Kidman and Iain Glen as the lovers – cab driver, student, au pair, aristocrat, actress – and the production transferred to Broadway. Charles Spencer, writing in the *Daily Telegraph*, had reviewed it as 'pure theatrical Viagra'.

It was therefore something of a risk to programme the play a mere two years later – in Chichester and without star casting. In the event, Camilla Power and Michael Higgs both received excellent reviews. Ingram's production – each scene was punctuated by a gossipy projection that told the audience how long the sexual encounter actually took (zero seconds to 2 hours and 20 minutes!) – sold out and transferred to the Haymarket Theatre in London.

Ingram's next production was a Rodgers &

Hart musical, *Pal Joey*, which saw the beginning of the career of choreographer Craig Revel Horwood. The bitter-sweet tale of the rise and fall of Joey Evans – charismatic, womanising hoofer and hustler – was set in the dog-eat-dog night-club world of the late 1930s. *Pal Joey* opened in August and was an immediate hit with its toe-tapping numbers including 'Bewitched, Bothered and Bewildered' and 'I Could Write a Book'.

Ten years later, in an interview with Phil Hewitt for the *Chichester Observer* in December 2010, Revel Horwood said: 'Chichester can completely claim its part in everything that has happened to me. Without the support Andrew Welch gave me in *Pal Joey*, none of this would have been possible.'

Welch, too, remembers that early partnership: 'Craig was delightful to work with, great fun, full of jokes and a terrific choreographer. The

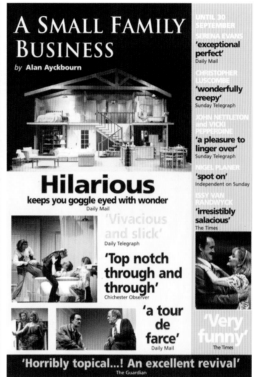

choreography had great energy, invention and excitement – lots of bums in the air and looking through the dancers' legs. The audiences adored it – risqué and rather sexy. He was clearly going to succeed as a choreographer, and as a person, so it was no great surprise when he turned up as a judge on *Strictly Come Dancing*.' *Pal Joey* was nominated for a Barclays' Theatre Award for Best Musical of the Year.

The fourth show in the Minerva was Brian Friel's *Aristocrats*, directed by Sean Holmes. The fifth was Terry Jones' *Hysteria*, again directed by Loveday Ingram, who was now billed as Associate Director for the Minerva.

Andrew Welch: 'By the end of that season, we were doing ninety per cent in the Minerva, which I felt was a real achievement. We had a loyal audience that was interested in the plays and you didn't have to star cast.'

Across the road in the Main House, things were progressing well, but without the sort of every-seat-sold hit that would transform the figures. The third production was Alan Ayckbourn's *A Small Family Business* with Nigel Planer in the lead. It was Planer's first time on stage at CFT, though he had a clear memory of coming to see *The Royal Hunt of the Sun* in 1964 when he was a child. Commissioned by Peter Hall, during Ayckbourn's two-year sabbatical away from Scarborough,[1] the play had premiered at the National Theatre in 1987.

The box office was steady rather than sensational and, once again, some critics were more

[1] Now called the Stephen Joseph Theatre since its reopening in new premises in 1996, Ayckbourn ran the company from 1972 to his retirement in 2009. All of his 61 plays – bar this – were premiered there during his period as Artistic Director.

Claire Cathcart and Billy Carter in *Aristocrats*, 2000.
Photo: Tristram Kenton/ Lebrecht Music & Arts

***A Small Family Business*, 2000.**
CFT Poster

Clive Swift, Guy Henry, Ian Bartholomew and Alison McKenna in *Hysteria*, **2000.**

Photo: Tristram Kenton/
Lebrecht Music & Arts

interested in reviewing the audience than the actors. The production was directed by Rachel Kavanaugh[1].

The final show in the Main House was Tom Stoppard's *Arcadia*. Premiered by Trevor Nunn at the National in 1993, it had been hailed by many as one of the most significant plays of the 20th century. The CFT production was the first major revival and was directed by veteran interpreter of Stoppard, Peter Wood. Set in an English country house, it is part-detective story,

part-meditation on science, part-romance, and juxtaposes the lives of two modern scholars and the house's contemporary occupants with the lives of those who had lived there 180 years before. Critically, it was well received.

When the season closed on Saturday 7 October, relations between City and Theatre were considerably better than they had been at the start of the year. The list of sponsors thanked in the programmes was growing and coverage in the local newspapers and radio stations was more about what was on the stage than what was happening behind the scenes.

However, although the Minerva had gained its

[1] Kavanaugh would go onto be Artistic Director of Birmingham Repertory company from 2006 – 2011. She returns to CFT in 2012 directing *The Way of the World*.

own momentum – radio plays, rehearsed readings, popular one-off performances and late-night sketches by young playwrights and directors – and there was a critical head of steam, it was clear that the Main House was struggling to rebuild a substantial enough audience to make the figures work. The finances were still fragile.

Over the course of the late summer and autumn, a series of meetings, meetings and more meetings – funding applications and assessment forms and feasibility studies, paper, paper, and more paper – had resulted in some support being allocated to CFT via the Arts Council Stabilisation Fund and a pledge to

pay off the large deficit. The City, District and County Councils were all still at the funding table, but there was still a sense that it might be too little, too late. The lack of regular Arts Council subsidy and the issues of the cost of both running two theatres and keeping them fit for purpose – as well as the fact that audiences, although growing, were not yet back to their mid-1990s levels – meant that the situation was still critical.

Lord Young, Chairman of the Productions Board: 'Although things were better, the year made a bigger loss than in 1999. Then, we started to run into serious trouble in the 2001 season.'

Jay Villiers, Pascal Langdale and Eleanor David in *Arcadia*, 2000.

Photo: Clive Barda/ ArenaPAL

2001

Janie Dee and Hilton McRea in *My One and Only,* **2001**

Photo: Clive Barda/ ArenaPAL

A range of building works and modifications were carried out over the autumn and winter, some required by new regulations that had been introduced, others down to simple wear and tear of a building starting to show its age.

But everything was ready for the Festival Season to open on Tuesday 31 May. It started where the 2000 season had left off, namely with Tom Stoppard in the Main House. *On the Razzle*, adapted from Johann Nestroy's 19th century comedy, had premiered at the National Theatre in 1981 with Peter Wood directing. Wood took charge of this CFT revival and with a strong cast that included Desmond Barritt and Daisy Donovan.

Charles Spencer took the occasion of his review of *On the Razzle* to preview the 2001 season as a whole: 'Chichester is routinely reviled by my more radical colleagues, but it is a theatre I always arrive at with a keen sense of anticipation. It is unashamedly middle class, the production standards are always high, and under its quietly determined director, Andrew Welch, it has become increasingly ambitious in its choice of repertoire.'

In addition to the Stoppard, the programme in the Main House was Rattigan's *The Winslow Boy*, the George Gershwin musical *My One and Only* and Brian Friel's adaptation of Chekhov's *Three Sisters*. As Spencer concluded in his *Daily Telegraph* piece: 'It is a programme of which any theatre could feel proud.'

Loveday Ingram directed the 'lost' Gershwin musical, *My One and Only*, with Tim Flavin and Janie Dee. Choreography was by Craig Revel Horwood and a fabulous design (not to mention a great deal of water!) by Lez Brotherston. Audiences loved it. The critics were won over too.

Dominic Cavendish in the *Daily Telegraph*: 'This tap-dancing extravaganza is hot... Loveday Ingram has already marked herself out as a young director with a bright future... Throughout, she displays a confident visual sense. Obviously a good deal of credit must go to the choreographer Craig Revel Horwood. He knows how to build from the simplest, slinkiest details – finger-clicks, hands-in-pockets insouciance – to full-blown, high-kicking riots.'

The final production in the Main House was *Three Sisters*. One hundred years after the first production of Chekhov's masterpiece, this new adaptation by Brian Friel was also directed by Loveday Ingram and starred Michael Siberry as Vershinin and Janie Dee, Sophie Ward and Susannah Wise as the Prozorov sisters.

The Minerva programme was ambitious and exciting. As well as a reprise of *Song of Singapore*, Welch programmed Catherine Johnson's outrageous comedy, *Shang-a-Lang*; David Storey's *In Celebration*; David Hare's *The Secret Rapture*; and a Sondheim revue, *Putting it Together*.

Education Director Andy Brereton directed Catherine Johnson's *Shang-a-Lang*. It caused, he remembers, a number of raised eyebrows: 'It was one of the rudest and funniest plays I've ever

Sean Gleeson and Susan Jameson, Adrian Bower in *In Celebration*, 2001.
Photo: Tristram Kenton/ Lebrecht Music & Arts

Niamh Linehan and Suzan Sylvester in *The Secret Rapture*, 2001.

Photo: Tristram Kenton/ Lebrecht Music & Arts

done, including directing several scenes with the actors in states of undress. One day during rehearsals in the draughty hall at Chichester Boy's Club [Little London, Chichester], we were working out how the two men could creep out of bed with the girls and get dressed on stage. Suddenly, the postman entered, looking for a signature for a parcel... To this day, I'm not sure what he thought we were doing – two men standing naked in the middle of the room, two partially clad women in bed, and two people sitting behind a desk obviously taking notes!'

But despite the successes on stage – and the growing audiences for the programme of talks and radio plays, one-offs and masterclasses – the bottom line looked as bad as ever. Lord Young remembers how frustrating it was that, despite everybody's hard work, CFT found itself back in crisis: 'In the first week of July, we got the auditors in... At the time, we had applied to the Arts Council for money, because I realised that we could not stay in the private sector any more. The auditors told us we could carry on trading until we got the result of our application to the Arts Council and, if it was negative, we would have to go in to receivership that day.'

Lord Young called an emergency meeting of the directors at his offices in Cavendish Square. The mood was pretty sombre. The meeting was interrupted by Lord Young's secretary explaining that a call had just come through from Harry Axton [still acting as an unofficial advisor to CFT] saying that a cheque had arrived for a £325,000 repayment of VAT. Having taken several deep breaths, Lord Young went back into the boardroom to deliver the news: 'The disbelief and the relief in that room! If that payment had come a day later, it would have been too late.'

The final show in the Minerva was Sondheim's *Putting it Together*. Directed by Edward Hall, the show is set in Manhattan, an undercurrent of the ennui of middle age behind the glamour and the glitz. The backdrop, poster and programme had the strong, instantly recognisable image of the twin towers of the World Trade Centre in New York. The production previewed from 6 September. And it was scheduled to open five days later.

Tuesday 11 September – now known as '9/11' – was destined to become a date engraved in everyone's memory. That morning, nearly 3000 people died in the worst terrorist attacks ever experienced on American soil. Four American passenger planes were hijacked and deliberately crashed, two into the Twin Towers of the

MINERVA
THEATRE

Chichester Festival Theatre presents

Putting it Together

A Musical Review
Music & Lyrics by STEPHEN SONDHEIM
Presented by arrangement with Cameron Mackintosh

World Trade Center. Both of the towers collapsed within two hours.

The world watched the horror of it all, and the devastation as it unfolded. The afternoon in Chichester was spent in discussions. Finally, after a great deal of debate, the decision was made that the show should still go ahead.

Just before 7:45pm, two members of the company came on to the Minerva Stage. They paid tribute to the suffering of New York, the courage of New York, then the house lights dimmed and the show began.

Michael Billington writing in *The Guardian* a few days later: 'Is it insensitive in present circumstances to enjoy the show? I don't think so, because it celebrates the imperishable values of wit, melody and an unsentimental realism about human relationships.'

Two-and-a-half weeks later, on Saturday 29 September, the 39th festival season came to a close. The reputation of the Theatre was improving and there was a sense of achievement in the work, but it was also clear that without a regular, secure funding package, it would be nigh on impossible to make the figures work. As for me, my three-year contract with CFT was over. The novel I had promised to my publisher some years before – *Labyrinth* – was waiting to be finished (in truth, waiting to be started!). But although it had been a tough three years, it was with a sense of great regret that I said goodbye and prepared to become just another member of the audience once again.

CLOCKWISE
Putting it Together,
2001.
CFT programme cover

Judy Flynn and Justine Glenton in *Shang-a-Lang*, 2001.
Photo: Tristram Kenton/ Lebrecht Music & Arts

CFYT's *Alice's Adventures*, 2001. Ella Bouquet, daughter of Tim Bouquet and RENEW Campaign Director, Sarah Mansell, is second from left.
Photo: Peter Langdown

2002

2002 was, of course, the fortieth anniversary year of CFT. Welch programmed a range of shows both to celebrate the achievements of the past and to look to the future. In the Minerva, Christopher Fry's *The Lady's Not for Burning* – last produced in the Main House with an all-star cast in 1972 – followed by *Up On the Roof* by Simon Moore and Jane Prowse. Then, two world premieres – Corin Redgrave performing in his own play, *Blunt Speaking*, and Christopher William Hill's *Song of the Western Men*, with Terry Johnson's *Dead Funny* to close the Minerva season in October. The list of directors included not only Loveday Ingram, but also up-and-coming directors, Sam West and Angus Jackson.[1]

As always, in terms of the box office, it was the figures for the Main House that mattered. The Festival season was to open with *The Front Page*, followed by Anouilh's *Wild Orchids*, in a new translation by Timberlake Wertenbaker. The fourth play was *Romeo and Juliet*, directed by Indhu Rubasingham, with London Newcomer of the Year, Emily Blunt, as Juliet and Lex Shrapnel as her Romeo.

But after the successes of *Song of Singapore*, *Pal Joey* and *My One and Only*, all eyes were on the third production, *Cabaret*. Scheduled to run from Wednesday 31 July to Saturday 5 October, everyone hoped it might be the kind of sell-out summer musical CFT needed. Lucy

---

[1]Angus Jackson, now CFT Associate Director, was Assistant Director at the Bush. After directing for Michael Grandage at Sheffield, he took on the musical *Desperately Seeking Susan* in the West End and Kwame Kwei-Armah's *Elmina's Kitchen* at the National in 2003.

Bailey – whose previous credits included *Baby Doll* for the Birmingham Rep, as well as work at the National and in the West End – was to direct. Alexandra Jay was to play Sally Bowles and Sarah Badel, Fraulein Schneider. But very quickly, disaster struck.

Sarah Badel explains: 'Lucy was remarkable and I really enjoyed the early rehearsals, because they were workshops, actors doing all sorts of incredible things. But we did not have very long to get a musical on and this is not an easy stage for all that is required for *Cabaret*. There was a danger that we would present a workshop rather than a finished play on stage. Apart from dinosaurs like me, the cast was very young. The atmosphere was getting increasingly fraught and alarm bells began ringing; then Lucy went.'

CFT was forced to issue a press release in early July citing 'artistic differences'.

Welch explains: 'We had to go our separate ways. As far as I was concerned [Bailey] was not taking into account what Chichester is. She was going to do a very risqué version where she had the principals without any clothes on. We reached an impasse... I brought in Roger Redfarn to rescue it.'

Sarah Badel again: 'Roger came in, redid the set on the back of an envelope, using the upper areas, whereas before it had been on the flat, and you need more perspective in that theatre, and we went on with rehearsals. We had got through

TOP LEFT
Adrian Lucas in
***Dead Funny*, 2002.**
Photo: Tristram Kenton/
Lebrecht Music & Arts

ABOVE
Lex Shrapnel and
Emily Blunt in
***Romeo and Juliet*,**
2002.
Photo: Clive Barda

Corin Redgrave in
***Blunt Speaking*,**
2002.
Photo: Tristram Kenton/
Lebrecht Music & Arts

one half of it and just about blocked the other. It was really very stressful. Rumours were going around about the state of the Theatre, it was incredibly serious.'

As if things were not difficult enough, there was worse to come for Badel herself: 'Then I got the news that I had breast cancer. They said we have to operate immediately – I heard just before we opened. I thought I can't come out of it until we have a replacement ready to go on. So I went on and it helped me enormously. I forgot everything else and just went on and did it. They did find somebody to take my place and I was operated on in London. When I came round, I heard the anaesthetist saying: "she was English when she came in here and now she's come round singing in German". Then the specialist came in and saw me raising my arm and he said: "What are you doing, you must be careful." I said: "I'm practising a Nazi salute, I must get back to the stage". I must have still been half-crazed with the anaesthetic.'

In the true 'show must go on' spirit, Badel did come back and the production was a great success: 'It was a wonderful part and I felt it was one of the best things I had ever done. It kept me going and I am forever grateful to it.'

Andrew Welch had already told the Board that this season – his fifth – would be his last and the newspapers were speculating as to who his successor might be.

Charles Spencer, writing in the *Daily Telegraph* in May 2002: 'Interviews will be held at the end of this month, with an appointment expected in June. Whoever inherits the theatre he [Welch] so stylishly brought back from the brink will have an exceptionally tough act to follow.'

Several months earlier, as part of being accepted by Arts Council England into the Stabilisation programme in 2001, ACE had asked for certain changes to structure and governance. The separate Trust and the Productions Company was to be replaced instead by a single Board. This was a decision Lord Young supports: 'It was ridiculous having this dual structure where only undertakers seemed to remove Board members and where you had so many Trustees that nobody took any responsibility. We had lots of meetings and there was a continuing rear-guard action – that is the only way to put it – from the old CFT who were very critical. We were sniped at morning, noon and night.'

Another condition of Arts Council funding was that the Theatre should be run jointly by an Artistic Director and an Executive Director. In May 2002, the Arts Council and CFT therefore jointly advertised for a new senior management team.

Ruth Mackenzie[1], now Director of the Cultural Olympiad, remembers the earliest conversations about Chichester: 'We [Martin Duncan[2] and Ruth

OPPOSITE

Julian Bleach in
***Cabaret**, 2002.*

Photo: Clive Barda/
ArenaPAL

***Cabaret**, 2002.*

Photo: Clive Barda/
ArenaPAL

[1]Mackenzie was the Co-Founder of Moving Parts, a socialist feminist company. She had been Chief Executive of Nottingham Playhouse, then General Director of Scottish Opera. After leaving CFT in 2005, she ran the Manchester International Festival and was an Expert Adviser to the Secretary of State for Culture, Media and Sport.

[2]Martin Duncan started his career at Lincoln Theatre Royal in 1968 as an Assistant Stage Manager. For the next 20 years, Duncan divided his time between acting and composing, then was appointed Artistic Director of the Nottingham Playhouse in 1994.

Mackenzie] were head-hunted by Caro Newling, who was on the Board just at the point we had persuaded Steven[1] [Pimlott] to join us and create a company, an ensemble of actors. Stephen was not at all keen to go to Chichester; he had just finished a stint at Stratford and he wanted to be freelance – and his family was sick of him being away. So we said to Caro, we would not apply or do an interview but we would come down and talk.'

Martin Duncan continues: 'We pre-met at Starbucks and said to one another, what if they ask us what we would do for a season? Literally half an hour before we went in. I said; "Let's flood the theatre and do a season all about Venice, or water or both. Then Steven said, "you could do *The Gondoliers,* I could do *The Merchant of Venice,* and we'll have a group of actors, an ensemble in rep". And that was it. In we walked."

Mackenzie continues: 'Water was our punchline. We said we were going to do lots of new plays and the ensemble in rep was going back to the founding principles of Olivier, and that's what made this place exciting. Education and community involvement was also something we wanted to concentrate on.'

As the 2002 Festival Season continued, the series of meetings and discussions intensified. Mackenzie again: 'We then moved to an interview with Lord Young, by which time Steven was wildly enthusiastic about coming to Chichester. The stabilisation team was all over the place and I remember Lord Young saying to us: "the Theatre is in the last-chance saloon and they have called last orders." So we said: 'hire us for four, five or six months and we will write you a plan.'

Mackenzie explains: 'We did an open meeting at the Theatre, to which hundreds of people came. I went round and talked to all the other arts organisations and to the local authorities and I did stuff in the *Chichester Observer*. We did a massive programme of engagement, talked to the Friends, talked to everybody. Having listened to everybody we wrote our plan – "Back to The Future" – which said, go back to the days of Laurence Olivier, look at the seasons he did... As we were writing it, in the summer of 2002, they were doing *Cabaret* and "Tomorrow Belongs to Me" came floating across the park. Lord Young and the Board bought the plan and off we went.'

Phil Hewitt of the *Chichester Observer*: 'When Ruth came in, it was a very difficult time for the Theatre. She was very cute in calling a number of public meetings. It was a very good PR move. It showed just how well considered the Theatre was that people came.'

When the cast of *Cabaret* took its final call on Saturday 5 October, it brought to an end Welch's five seasons in charge – a record only exceeded at that stage by John Clements and Patrick Garland.

Andrew Welch: 'My memory of Chichester is that there were some great moments and it was great fun, but it was also very difficult. David Young was a real rock. When we went to the Arts Council, he was incredibly supportive but the money we got was always too little, too late. My ambition was to try and rebuild the play audience in the Main House, and we had mixed success with that because it was clear that the appetite for big meaty plays wasn't there. Christopher Morahan did a fine *Heartbreak House*, but we sadly couldn't do the business with it; it played to around 40 per cent. Not good enough. Things like *My One and Only* were hugely popular and transferred to London – we transferred something every year,

[1] Steven Pimlott was a director of opera, musicals and theatre. Having begun his career at the English National Opera in 1976, he worked with Opera North and Scottish Opera, as well being responsible for many West End revivals of classic musicals included *Joseph and the Amazing Technicolor Dreamcoat*. He was Company Director of the Royal Shakespeare Company from 1996 – 2002 and Director of the Savoy Theatre Opera project in 2004.

barring my last year. Star casting was always difficult and it took a long time to get them to come. Theatre generally was going through a difficult stage. Actors were not so keen to come out of London, when there was a lot of telly being made and it was much more convenient than coming down to West Sussex – and better paid.'

The pros and cons of star casting – and how crucial it was to the CFT box office or not – was an issue that was to become even more acute in the next few years ahead.

Critic Michael Billington: 'I have to say that thanks to Andrew Welch I witnessed something I thought I would never live to see. An actor – Corin Redgrave – inviting the Chichester audience to stand up and sing the Internationale and join in the chorus in *Blunt Speaking* in the Minerva. And, somewhat sheepishly they did. This was something of a breakthrough, even though the whole play was an apologia for Blunt and his Marxist views.'

Lord Young concludes: 'In Andrew's fifth year we lost £1 million. But the subsidy was only few hundred thousand. If you take away our subsidy today we are losing £1 million, £1.5 million every year. Andrew did forty-three plays and two community plays[2] in his five seasons here.'

---

[2] The second community play was *The Devil's Dancing Hour*. Written by Nick Whitby, it was set during the siege of Chichester and involved many of the community performers who had taken part in *Barchester*.

The Community Cast in *The Devil's Dancing Hour – A City Under Siege*, 2002.

Photo: Unknown

2003

Ruth Mackenzie
Photo: Mike Eddowes

Stephen Pimlott
Photo: Clare Park

Martin Duncan
Photo: Clare Park

Having accepted the job, the artistic triumvirate – as Ruth Mackenzie, Stephen Pimlott and Martin Duncan were referred to in the press – got to work straight away. They were under no illusions about the challenge they were taking on.

Ruth Mackenzie: 'When we arrived finances were so bad we had to make a third of the people redundant and that was all of the technical team, because we moved back to a part-time model and closed the Theatre for five months. When we opened for our first Festival, new people came in who were up for adventure. It was the third time I had started with a major redundancy programme, which was miserable, but you have to do that when you start, so it is clear that it is finance that is motivating you, not spite. It is the only fair time to do it. We had inherited very desperate times. We had to get the costs down.'

Michael Billington remembers talking to the triumvirate prior to the 2003 season: 'I remember going to interview Ruth, Steven and Martin for *The Guardian* before they took over and thought they were very exciting in the way they talked about Chichester. I remember them all saying they had gone back to first principles, they had gone back to find out what drew people to Olivier's Chichester, and concluded it was the company, the ensemble, the regularity of actors. At the core of their philosophy was reaching out to the community... Not everything they did was artistically brilliant by any means, but I thought they had a purpose and a vision of what the Theatre could be again, an idea, even though the box office did not live up to their expectations.'

They hired a company of actors to do all the plays in the season and a team of Assistant Directors to work with Duncan and Pimlott – including Martin Constantine, Lucy Jameson, Joe McGann. They opened their first water-themed season in the Main House with *The Gondoliers* (directed by Duncan) followed by *The Merchant of Venice* (directed by Pimlott), then *The Water Babies* and *The Seagull* (Pimlott) while Edward Kemp's new version of Gotthold Lessing's *Nathan the Wise* (also directed by Pimlott) and *I Caught My Death in Venice* by Martin and John Marquez were in in the Minerva.

***The Gondoliers,
2003.***

Photo: Ivan Kync/ArenaPAL

The Gondoliers,
2003.

Photo: Ivan Kyncl/ArenaPAL

**CFYT director,
Dale Rooks.**

Photo: Mike Eddowes

It was a very different approach from the way CFT Festival Seasons had hitherto been programmed and it was a gamble. It was a way of working that required a huge commitment from the backstage teams too, as Martin Duncan points out: 'We rebuilt the stage every year, because we didn't quite get on with the shape of it. We wanted the audience to see something different every year so they would walk in and be endlessly surprised. Each show had to be struck or set up in half an hour. So we told designers that they could add bits and pieces to it but they could not be over-elaborate in what they did because there's no flying, there's no wing, no backstage, no pit, no sightlines and the acoustics are not brilliant. Also sets had to be simple because we did Festival weekends where all four plays would be performed Friday night, Saturday matinee, Saturday evening and Sunday matinee – four different shows in both theatres.'

Building on the success of the open public meetings, Mackenzie spent a deal of time thinking about how to engage with different sectors of the local community, not just the city of Chichester itself: 'We set out to share our education work with projects with refugees, people in Havant, Portsmouth, deprived rural communities. We tried to extend the Festival feeling and make it clear CFT was for everyone.'

Duncan takes up this theme: 'We had a huge tie-in with the Youth Theatre and the first thing

The Merchant of Venice, 2003.

Photo: Ivan Kyncl/ArenaPAL

was to give them a Festival show.'

In 2012, Dale Rooks, Director of the Youth Theatre, will celebrate ten years in the post. Rooks had been involved with CFT since 1993. Then Head of Performing Arts at St Cuthman's School, she came to Chichester to direct an opera called *Nowhere to Go* as part of the Drama Schools Festival, which featured 25 young people with learning disabilities.

After five years of doing the Drama Schools Festival, Rooks asked if some of her students might be involved with the Youth Theatre. The answer was 'yes', provided Rooks herself came to lead some of the sessions. So Rooks' association with CFT began.

In 1999, Rooks directed her first large-scale promenade show – *The Land of Oz* – with the Youth Theatre at St Cuthman's (both Tim Bouquet's daughter, Ella, and my daughter, Martha, were in it). In 2000, Rooks was appointed Assistant Director of CFYT and in 2002, offered the Youth Director's job full time.

Rooks takes up the story: 'When I arrived at CFT I remember being in a very cold office at the end of Gunter's, with the wind rattling the windows and no life and soul in the department. There was an Education Director [Andy Brereton], me and a part-time Youth Theatre leader who ran some of the sessions in the evening. I felt there were a lot more people in the community who could benefit, but it was difficult because we didn't have the space. We had

The Water Babies, 2003.

Photo: Ivan Kyncl/ArenaPAL

to hire school halls. My main ambition was to see many more young people engaging with the arts at CFT. And I was very keen to set up a technical side. The Youth Theatre had always done good work in the Theatre but there was no great engagement with the community outside.'

There is no audition process, but simply a random ballot of names, as Rooks explains: 'We do not cherry pick; people come to CFYT from all walks of life, all abilities. That is what I am proudest of. We have a diverse mix. That's what gives it its character. People come for all sorts of reasons. Some of them want to follow a career in theatre and get to drama school, others to enhance their drama work at school, some want to make friendships, and they all want to have fun.'

While Rooks was developing her ideas for the Youth Theatre, in the Main House and Minerva the 2003 Season was well under way. True to their policy as laid out in 'Back to the Future', the team was determined not to fall into the trap of casting names at the expense of the programme.

Highlights of the season were Edward Kemp's version of *Nathan the Wise* – with a towering performance from Michael Feast – and the UK premiere of Jeremy Sams' version of Fassbinder's *The Coffee House*. In the Main House, Pimlott's production of *The Water Babies*, with music and lyrics by Jason Carr, was based on an adaptation by Gary Yershon of Charles Kingsley's classic novel, a project Pimlott had commissioned from Carr during his time at the RSC. The world premiere, instead, took place at Chichester. The late night

TOP
I Caught My Death in Venice, 2003.
Photo: Clare Park

The Seagull, 2003.
Photo: Ivan Kyncl/ArenaPAL

Kay Curram,
Michael Feast and
Darlene Johnson in
Nathan the Wise,
2003.

Photo: Clare Park

LEFT

Michael Feast in
***Nathan the Wise*,**
2003.

Photo: Clare Park

RIGHT

Jonathan Cullen in
***Nathan the Wise*,**
2003.

Photo: Clare Park

and one-off programming was proving very successful – *Chic Cabaret*, with world class performers such as Maria Friedman, the commissioning circle and rehearsed readings – all of this was bringing new people to CFT. But, for all the razzamatazz, the issue was – as ever – the three Fs: figures, finance, funding... Most of all funding.

Lord Young, Chairman of the Board: 'Ruth is tremendous, she is sparky. She was very well connected in DCMS and also in the Labour Government. Although I was very friendly with Tony [Blair] and Gordon [Brown], because they were both against me when I was at the DTI,

I didn't carry much weight with the Labour Government. Ruth did. She got us the money.'

After months of meetings and proposals and discussions, Mackenzie's persistence paid off, as she explains: 'We had a triumph with the Arts Council and we doubled the funding from the local authorities. Andrew Welch did the brilliant thing of getting the Arts Council to commit to the Theatre in the first place, but they did that annoying thing of not giving him enough money. We managed to get it [CFT] to be the fifth-best funded theatre in the country, which was a real achievement.'

**Nicholas Colicos
and cast rehearse
Out of This World,
2004.**

Photo: Clare Park

2004

The 2004 Summer Festival was announced in January. Themed 'Out of this World', the season was scheduled to run from Thursday 29 April to Saturday 25 September. There were to be eight new productions (including two world premieres and two UK premieres), performed once again by a resident ensemble of more than 60 actors, directors, designers, choreographers, musicians.

In the Minerva, the Season was launched by a world premiere of Helen Cooper's *Three Women and a Piano Tuner*, followed by Jeremy Sams' new translation of Botho Strauss' *Seven Doors*. In May, Martin Crimp's scabrous *Cruel and Tender* (after Sophocles' *Women of Trachis*) was a co-production with the Wiener Festwochen and the Young Vic, the Théâtre des Bouffes du Nord and Ruhrfestspiele Recklinghausen. Directed by Luc Bondy and with Kerry Fox as Amelia, *The Stage* reviewed the production as: 'a must-see of European theatre.'

So far, so ambitious. The final show, mounted in association with Chichester Cathedral, was to be Christopher Marlowe's *Doctor Faustus*, which had elements of promenade as well as using the Minerva stage.

Youth Theatre Director, Dale Rooks: 'I was so proud of that. For me it brought together all the ingredients that make theatre. It was community based, it had professionals and it had the Youth Theatre with professional directors, stage managers. It is something I will never forget. For me personally, working on that with Steven Pimlott and Martin Duncan, was a great collaboration.

Simon Greiff and Fiona Dunn in *Out of this World*, 2004.

Photo: Clare Park

RIGHT

2004 Community Day, CFYT Soldiers.

Photo: Mike Eddowes

Ruth, Steven and Martin were huge supporters of the Youth Theatre and of us working with and in the community. That is one of their greatest and lasting contributions to CFT.'

The 2004 Main House season opened with the UK premiere of Cole Porter's *Out of This World*. The second show was *A Midsummer Night's Dream* and the third an exuberant, joyous version of Kipling's *Just So Stories,* with music by George Stiles and book and lyrics by Anthony Drew. Then, to close the Festival, the British premiere of Edward Kemp's brilliant adaptation of Bulgakov's brilliant, tricksy, satirical, mercurial novel, *The Master and Margarita.* With Michael

**Noma Dumezweni
in *A Midsummer
Night's Dream*,
2004.**

Photo: Clare Park

Feast, Samuel West, Steve Elias, Clare Holman[1] and Martin Duncan – together with a 20-strong cast of players – and directed by Steven Pimlott, Michael Billington reviewing in *The Guardian* gave the production five stars: 'With this kaleidoscopically inventive production Chichester, once the home of safe theatre, becomes a leader of the avant-garde.'

So far, so very ambitious. But if the critics were seduced, excited, engaged by what was hap-

pening on stage, audiences were not. Attendance was not growing in the way Mackenzie, Duncan, Pimlott and the Board had hoped.

Charles Spencer believes there was a mismatch between the productions on offer and the potential audience: 'Some of the work was good, but not the kind of thing Chichester wanted. Not rare plays by Lessing and ego trips for directors. You could see the audience draining away.'

Phil Hewitt at the *Chichester Observer* goes further: 'I think they had an unhealthy preoccupation with obscure directors and European co-productions and, frankly, I don't think anybody cared if something was co-produced in Vienna

---

[1] Clare Holman is the daughter of the former Chairman of the Theatre Society, Roy Holman, who played a key role in the recalibration of the Society and the Theatre in Andrew Welch's time.

TOP
Andrew Spillett in
Just So, **2004.**
Photo: Clare Park

Alexis Owen-Hobbs
and Simon Greiff in
Just So, **2004.**
Photo: Clare Park

CENTRE
Alexis Owen-Hobbs
and choreographer
Stephen Mears
rehearsing ***Just***
So, **2004.**
Photo: Clare Park

with some director nobody has ever heard of. This Theatre works best on big-name playwrights, not necessarily the big-name pieces. You can have an obscure Rattigan, Coward, or Shaw. But also you need big stars. Ruth got it wrong there – maybe she was making the best of a bad job – going on and on about this ensemble, this bunch of equals all working together, which is nuts really because CFT has never been about that. Olivier's ensemble was packed with megastars and those on their way to becoming stars later.'

Looking back, Michael Billington takes a different view: 'They brought a kind of European dimension because of all them, Steven Pimlott especially, were very European minded. They liked the great European classics, European directors, they brought a Polish director – Silviu Purcarete – to do *Scapino* [2005], which was a bold, expressionist production of the kind you had not seen at Chichester before. Maybe the audience didn't take to it, but I still think it was a very good thing to do.'

Mackenzie thinks comments about the perceived lack of big names are misleading: 'I can never understand this debate about stars or the suggestion that we didn't have any. When you look back at the Laurence Olivier seasons, yes the ensemble was full of stars, but they were not all stars at the time – Olivier and Plowright were stars, movie stars, and so was John Neville – but

others were yet to become the stars we regard them as now... We had perfectly good commercial names but we did not push them as 'Sam West is *Doctor Faustus*' or 'Alistair McGowan is *The Government Inspector*', because we wanted to build the kind of trust of the early days. Where you would not know what Keith Michell was going to put on stage for you, but you would go and see it all the same. We constructed that narrative. Above all our Festival was the star.'

At Christmas, the Youth Theatre produced another sell-out Christmas show in the Main House in the shape of *Oliver!* Once again, the costumes were designed by former CFYT member, Amy Jackson.

Clare Holman and Sam West in *The Master and Margarita*, 2004.
Photo: Clare Park

Director Silviu Purcarete (centre) rehearsing *Scapino*, 2005.
Photo: Clare Park

Poster image of Toby Sedgwick for *Scapino*, 2005.
Photo: Clare Park

2005

A blustery and stormy January, the coast of Scotland and of Northern Ireland were battered by winds. Closer to home, the finishing touches were being put to the 2005 season. As in 2003 and 2004, an ensemble of actors – including David Warner, James Bolam and Alistair McGowan. With a programme of new writing and European classics, the designers included Alison Chitty and Helmutt Sturmer, John Leonard. Directors included Pimlott, Duncan and Phyllis Nagy with her own adaptation of *The Scarlet Letter*.

The programming was again ambitious, but everyone knew that – subsidy or no subsidy – a significant increase in audience numbers was required to give CFT any chance of getting back on an even keel.

The Minerva season opened in May with a chamber production of *King Lear*, with David Warner making a long overdue return to the Shakespearean stage. Directed by Steven Pimlott and with an exquisite minimalist set design by Alison Chitty, the lighting was designed by Paul Pyant. The reviews were outstanding. Another world premiere followed, Edward Kemp's *Six Pictures of Lee Miller*, with music and lyrics by Jason Carr, then Nagy's *The Scarlet Letter*.

In the Main House, *How to Succeed in Business Without Really Trying*, Molière's *Scapino* – in a new version by Jeremy Sams – Nikolai Gogol's *The Government Inspector*, translated and adapted by Alistair Beaton, and the world premiere of Edward Kemp's *5/11*.

One of the highlights of the 2005 season was CFYT's promenade production of *Arabian Nights*, performed at Goodwood Estate. Dale Rooks considers it one of the best YT shows ever: 'It was really moving and each of the stories was told in such a perfect location. I remember Steven Pimlott crying at the end of the show. At first I thought I had done something wrong!'

But individual triumphs aside, by mid-sea-

son it was clear the finances were in trouble. Although Lord Young stresses the excellence of the work, he accepts that it did not deliver at the box office: 'Ruth had this commitment to European productions. Some of them were extremely good and I think the quality of the theatre really went up. We went from well prepared, popular but not outstanding productions, to rather obscure pieces really well done. I enjoyed them, but I was getting continuing complaints from all over, from people saying: "What's gone wrong at the Theatre? There is nothing there that I want to see." Ticket sales went down and down. Each year we got more subsidy, but it was

quite obvious that we were back in this position of not being able to continue any longer. I had intended to go at the end of Ruth's third year [2005], but I could see that we were heading for bankruptcy again. So I said to the Board there is no way I am going if the Theatre is going down, I want to see this through.'

Ruth Mackenzie looks backs at the achievements of their time at CFT: 'We built up the sponsorship, we started the capital scheme and we got the Theatre to a new mountain peak of funding. We got a new computerised box office, we started stabilising the audience, which had sunk gently downwards from the mid-1990s onwards.

LEFT
Elizabeth McGovern and Alan Williams rehearse *The Scarlet Letter*, **2005.**

Photo: Clare Park

RIGHT
Adrian Quinton, Lucy Betts, Emily Moseley and Ellie Price in CFYT's *Arabian Nights*, **2005.**

Photo: Mike Eddowes

**Alistair McGowan
in *5/11*, 2005.**

Photo: Clare Park

We stopped the decline, but what we didn't do was finally stabilise the place, because our plans were so ambitious.'

It was announced in August that Mackenzie, Pimlott and Duncan would move on at the end of the 2005 season when their contract came to an end, which meant that the Board found itself – for the third time in eight years – again needing to find a new artistic team to turn things around and take the Theatre forward. Enter stage left and stage right, Messrs Church and Finch.

For Alan Finch, this was actually his third attempt to work at CFT. Having worked as Production Manager at the Nottingham Playhouse, in 1994 he went to Plymouth as Technical Manager and became General Manager in 1999. Andrew Welch tried to entice him to

come to West Sussex, but Finch was on six months' notice so that hadn't been possible. In 2003, Ruth Mackenzie also tried to tempt him to Chichester.

Finch takes up the tale: 'I didn't end up coming to work for Ruth, at the beginning of their three-year tenure, which was the first conversation, because of a project I was doing down in Plymouth. But then I did come eventually, in their third year, albeit on a 35-week Festival contract. Then after six weeks, it all changed very quickly!'

Deputy Chairman of the Board, Clifford Hodgetts: 'Alan [Finch] is a first class Administrator and has got a very firm grasp of finance. He understands that if you raise money, you have to meet the obligations that you have set up. I think he's very good with staff too.'

5/11, 2005.

Photo: Clare Park

Jonathan Church also began his career back stage – as an electrician and stage manager – at the Dukes Playhouse, Lancaster, then at the Crucible Theatre, Sheffield, before being appointed Assistant Director at the Nottingham Playhouse in 1991. A four year spell as Artistic Director of the Triptych Theatre Company, was followed as Associate Director of the Derby Playhouse in 1994, then Artistic Director at the Salisbury Playhouse the following year. From 2001 – 2005, Church had been Artistic Director of the Birmingham Repertory Theatre and credited there with increasing audiences by some 92 per cent.

Lord Young says Church's reputation for saving theatres in trouble made him the ideal choice to take over at CFT: 'This was my business instinct kicking in, but I was very keen indeed on Jonathan because he had saved Salisbury and then saved Birmingham. Somebody who comes to a theatre with a big deficit, and leaves it with a surplus – and does it twice running – I thought could do it a third time!'

Charles Spencer agrees: 'I interviewed Jonathan Church when he was at Salisbury. He was incredibly candid about the mess the theatre was in and the fact that there was no money. You could see this guy was really bright… He only had enough money to do small cast plays and had the bright idea of doing *Educating Rita* and *Oleanna* by Mamet, which are both plays about a teacher and a girl, so you have a cast of two. Exactly the same set up, but completely different in tone and style. And suddenly those two incredibly cheap plays became an event and the two really played off each other.

Nobody had ever thought of that. He had the critics going down to Salisbury for the first time in years. Both plays transferred to the Minerva in 1996[1] and that's how he [Church] got his foot into CFT.'

Michael Billington also remembers Church transforming the audience figures at Salisbury, then at Birmingham: 'I remember going up to Birmingham Rep, a theatre that was actually on its last legs with derisory audiences and within the space of a season, he seemed to rediscover and bring back, not by being timorous, but by being bold… So I think he is the ideal figurehead for Chichester at this moment in time, because he is an artist with an artist's vision, but also a realist, a pragmatist with a sense of how much

the audience will take and at the same time be able to expand their horizons.'

But what were the attractions of taking over a theatre that had, over the previous ten years, produced a great deal of good work, but yet had failed to find audiences in sufficient quantities to sustain that work?

Jonathan Church explains: 'What persuaded me to come was the connection with Ruth. I had been down to see a couple of the shows, while she, Martin and Steven, were running it. Alan and I had worked for Ruth in Nottingham – she classes us as her graduates in many ways. Alan was doing a real job, I was training, so we had history… My connection with Martin and Steven went back even further actually, to Sheffield, so there was a great reason to come down here, partly to see what was going on, partly out of

---

[1] Duncan Weldon was responsible for the tour and the transfer.

loyalty to them, and actually to see the artistically challenging work they were doing. To see an ensemble doing something like *5/11* on the main stage was very interesting. I sort of got a glimpse, without knowing I was going to apply for it, how the mechanism could be made to work. I felt it was very clear if you combined some of the best of the artistic excellence, for want of a better phrase, provided by Ruth, Martin and Steven – but remembered that this was a 1200-seat theatre that needed a commercial driver to sustain the audience – then there was a solution.'

Finch agrees: 'Like Jonathan says, it seemed there was an opportunity to build on the foundation that Ruth, Martin and Steven had left... There had been a smattering of subsidy from the Arts Council during Andrew Welch's time, but the Arts Council wanted something really big, bold and brash to back. And I think, for right or wrong, what the triumvirate delivered was that, with all the redundancies and all the pain that went with it.'

It was also important to both Church and Finch that they would be joint Chief Executives. Church again: 'I have always worked in a joint structure, because I think it allows the financial and the artistic to work in perfect harmony.'

In the Main House, the Christmas Show was a Youth Theatre production of Adrian Mitchell's popular stage version of *The Lion, the Witch and the Wardrobe*. Directed by Dale Rooks, it involved nearly 100 young people from 11 up to 19 (my son Felix among them) – working backstage or performing on the stage. Rooks used every inch of the auditorium, every pocket-sized handkerchief corner of the thrust stage, the voms and upstage exits and entrances, to full and glorious effect.

For the long-serving (and long-suffering) staff, they were to be working under their fifth new management team in ten years. They had seen it all before. But at the same time, there was a sense that, finally, perhaps there might be a return to the glory days.

The Pevensey children and company in CFYT's *The Lion, The Witch and The Wardrobe*, 2011 – (centre) Jake Fieldhouse, Grant Harris, Poppy Crawford and Romina Hytten.
Photo: Mike Eddowes

2006

Church and Finch announced their first season in February. They were aware that Arts Council funding was only guaranteed for two years and that it was therefore essential that, from the get-go, audience figures grew and grew fast. By how much, and by how quickly, was a moot point. But the only way was up. Had to be up.

Jonathan Church describes how that first season began to take shape: 'The benefit of coming from running another theatre is that I was already in conversations with artists. I had been talking to David Edgar, who was a colleague at Birmingham, about doing *Nicholas Nickleby*[1].

---

[1] *The Life and Adventures of Nicholas Nickleby* is an eight-hour stage play, presented over two performances, adapted from the Dickens novel of the same name. Directed by John Caird and Trevor Nunn, it opened in June 1980 at the Aldwych Theatre in London, then was revived for the Royal Shakespeare Theatre, Stratford-upon-Avon, in January 1986.

Birmingham was inappropriate because (a) for the financial muscle it needed and (b) because of its proximity to Stratford. But I thought we might try it at CFT.'

Church had also been in conversation with David Hare, so he was able to quickly put *Pravda* in the schedule. But it was a conversation with one of CFT's most popular actresses, Penelope Keith – about the world premiere of a play by Richard Everett called *Entertaining Angels* – that Church credits with making the difference to that first season: 'It was one of those acts of goodwill. Penny's decision, at the last moment, to do the play – I believed she had turned it down before – signalled a turnaround. It was the sense of doing it here, as part of helping the Theatre she so loves. That single conversation and that single act of commitment from her meant that we had the right play to open the season.'

Entertaining Angels is a gentle, though sharp-edged, comedy about a recently-widowed vicar's wife, Grace, set in a vicarage garden complete with stream and wild flowers. The question asked by the play is what happens to a wife

Benjamin Whitrow and Penelope Keith in *Entertaining Angels*, 2006.

Photo: Robert Day

when her husband dies, and it struck a chord with audiences.

Penelope Keith elaborates: 'People said to me: "You don't want to go back there. There are no audiences, the audiences have gone." I've never been frightened of a challenge and I thought: "sod it, it's a good part". I'd worked with the director Alan Strachan before and it seemed a terribly good play for Chichester. Afterwards, I had a lot of letters from clergy widows who felt deep resentment. There are very few jobs where you lose everything – home, house, neighbours – when your husband dies.'

Charles Spencer agrees it was a wonderful piece of programming: 'Having Penelope Keith in *Entertaining Angels* was absolutely the right thing to do. It sent out a message that the place was safe to come back to, that it was under new management. And it sold out[1] ... I get tired of this attitude that theatre must be tough and challenging all the time. It doesn't have to be like that all the time, basically it is about entertainment.'

Acknowledging how Welch and the triumvirate had proved there was an audience for well-staged, large-scale musicals, Church programmed *Carousel* to follow *Entertaining Angels* in the Main House:

Church again: 'It wasn't my expertise producing musicals, although I had worked on them, but it was that – as part of the mix – that was very important. We didn't have long to ponder, but I suppose we wanted to do one of the

---

[1] *Entertaining Angels* sold out in 2006, ran for two sell-out UK tours – including a return to CFT in 2009 – playing to more than 100,000 people and grossing over £2million.

Carousel, 2006.

Photo: Catherine Ashmore

ten great musicals in Chichester and see what happened.'

The Life and Adventures of Nicholas Nickleby was the third production in the Main House. Slimmed down from its original eight hours to six-and-a-half and with a cast of a mere 23 (as against the RSC's forty-five), it was directed by CFT Associate Director Philip Franks.[1] The wonderful two-tiered set was designed by Simon Higlett, which made the audience feel they were, with the aid of props, in London or Yorkshire or Portsmouth.

However, the signs were not initially encouraging. Alan Finch recalls how the advance bookings for 'Nick Nick' – as it was affectionately known by – were dreadful: 'I remember sitting through previews with no more than 200 people in the auditorium – actually, we took too long to open it, but we so wanted to get it right; we previewed Part I, went back into the rehearsal room, then we previewed Part II. It was almost a month

before the press came in. Then it opened and it all ignited and we ran out of seats... It was thrilling, exciting and terrifying in equal measure.'

The critics loved it. Ian Shuttleworth in the *Financial Times*: 'One of the highest practical accolades I can offer is that I realised during Part Two I had stopped taking notes; I was simply caught up in the terrific storytelling, for which Dickens, Edgar and the directors must all take credit.'

Michael Billington in *The Guardian*: 'This revival of David Edgar's two-part version... is something of a triumph, which had the Chichester audience leaping to its feet... Church and Franks turn the long day into a celebration not just of Dickens but of performance itself.' It had been a gamble, but it had paid off. It also sold out.

The critics also admired, praised, celebrated *Pravda*, the revival of Hare and Brenton's 1980s satirical (and prescient) play about the corruptions and vagaries of the press.

In the Minerva, a mixture of artists that Church or Finch had a prior relationship with, as well as playwrights or performers who were familiar to the audience – Rattigan, Coward, Strindberg and a Youth Theatre production of Carol Ann Duffy's *Grimm Tales*. The directors

---

[1] In 2011, Franks directed my first-ever piece for theatre, *Endpapers*, commissioned by the Bush Theatre as part of a sequence of monologues reinterpreting all sixty-six books of the Bible. The actress was Zoe Waites, who played Nicholas' love interests in this production at CFT, from Fanny Squeers to put-upon Madeleine Bray.

included Lucy Bailey, Angus Jackson, Dale Rooks and Philip Wilson. Strindberg's *The Father* was the final production in the Minerva, closing a week after the Main House season finished on Saturday 30 September.

And when, on Sunday 1 October, the Youth Theatre took to the Main House stage to celebrate their 21st birthday, it was with the hope, expectation, a bubbling of anticipation that CFT might be around to celebrate other anniversaries yet to come.

Lord Young: 'To everybody's amazement, every production sold like mad. As a team, Alan and Jonathan are outstanding. Instead of ending the season with a deficit, we ended the year with a profit... Andrew [Welch] had done some very popular plays, but not always got the critical acclaim he should have done. Ruth [Mackenzie] got critical acclaim, but thumbs down from audiences. Jonathan seemed to get both.'

Jonathan Church reflects on that first season: 'The irony of the season that, arguably,

turned Chichester around is it contained Howard Brenton, David Hare and David Edgar, three of the foremost left-wing playwrights. We did try to engineer it to try and give two messages, and I think we were successful. What we could never have predicted was how quickly audiences would build up. We underestimated how much this city wanted the Theatre to work.'

Phil Hewitt adds: 'CFT is absolutely crucial to the wider community of Chichester. When the Theatre is going well there is a real feeling that Chichester is going well. When the Theatre is not going well it's all a bit grim. The saddest days were a couple of winters when the Theatre was closed and it just looked so awful to see that grey empty building, which even in the winter should be full to bursting. There is a genuine affection for the Theatre in Chichester, evidenced when it has almost gone to the wall. There has been a lot of soul searching, a lot of worry that we could have lost it, because CFT is essential to making Chichester "somewhere".'

Roger Allam, Bruce Alexander (seated), Nigel Hastings and Michael Begley in *Pravda*, 2006.

Photo: John Haynes/ Lebrecht Music & Arts

2007

After three years of stabilisation funding from the Arts Council, then a commitment to two years' funding to allow Finch and Church time to turn CFT's fortunes around, the issue was one of sustainability. To have more than just one good season and find a new way of working that secured the Theatre's long term future.

Church and Finch programmed the shape of the 2007 Main House season as they had done for 2006. Namely, that the first and the fifth productions were short, straight runs and the heart of the Festival Season – essentially the middle three months – with productions playing in rep. This enabled them to give a separate life to certain shows, should opportunities for transferring or touring arise, but also satisfy summer audiences who came wanting to take in three, even four shows, over the course of a long weekend.

So, with a second outing for *The Life and Adventures of Nicholas Nickleby* scheduled for the end of the Main House Season, the 2007 Season opened with *The Last Confession*, a world premiere of Roger Crane's play about behind-the-scenes shenanigans in the Vatican in the days leading up to the death of Pope John Paul I. Designed by William Dudley and directed by David Jones, David Suchet played Cardinal Bennelli. It opened in May, then transferred to the Haymarket in London in July.

The second Main House production was *Babes in Arms* by Rodgers and Hart. Directed by Martin Connor, it was a rare outing – despite the MGM movie starring Judy Garland and Mickey Rooney – for the musical about vaudeville performers. The audience was delighted and was swept away

by familiar songs such as 'The Lady is a Tramp' and 'My Funny Valentine'.[1]

Hobson's Choice, Harold Brighouse's 20th-century classic, was directed by Jonathan Church, with John Savident, a member of Olivier's second company at CFT, as Henry Horatio Hobson.

But it was *Twelfth Night* – directed by Philip Franks with Patrick Stewart as Malvolio and Kate Fleetwood as Olivia – that was destined to be one of the most talked about productions of the Main House season, thanks in part to its cross casting with *Macbeth* in the Minerva.

Franks situated Illyria in a pre-1914 Edwardian England. Laura Rees played Viola – the role taken by Michele Dotrice in 1975 – and Martin Turner was Orsino. Michael Feast played Feste, the part played by Tony Robinson thirty-two years before. The critics admired it, particularly Stewart's performance as the dour, sour steward.

The same company were working with Rupert Goold, Artistic Director of Headlong[2], in *Macbeth*

in the Minerva. Malvolio in the Main House, in the small theatre Patrick Stewart played Macbeth to Kate Fleetwood's Lady Macbeth.

It was, simply, a triumph. Word went round. The reviews were outstanding and it sold out. It was one of those occasions when a play is utterly transformed by the interpretation, by the performances. And the intimacy of the small space

---

[1] In the CFT production, Garland's daughter, Lorna Luft, played the pushy, showbiz Mother, who thinks her child should be a star.

[2] Originally called Anvil Productions, then the Oxford Stage Company, the company moved from Oxford to London in 2002. When Rupert Goold took over as Artistic Director in 2006, it changed its name to Headlong. A national and international touring theatre company, it is known both for reworking classic plays and for commissioning new work, also for blending elements of dance, circus and physical theatre skills, with more traditional aspects of theatre.

brought the horror of the piece home. When it transferred to London in October, there were the sorts of scenes for tickets and returns rarely seen with a 'straight' play.

Daily Telegraph critic Charles Spencer: 'It blew everyone away, the best *Macbeth* since Dench and McKellen.'

And Michael Billington agrees: 'Jonathan offered a roof to Headlong and to Rupert Goold, who is the most exciting director in Britain today, I think. Everything he does has a kind of visionary excitement and he uses stage spaces brilliantly... *Macbeth* was extraordinary because it took a play which critics and audience are familiar with and gave it a new dynamic by treating it as a Gothic horror piece.'

Church himself is characteristically modest: 'Anyone can get lucky. It was the combination of *Macbeth* and *Twelfth Night*. While *Nicholas Nickleby* had been well reviewed, that *Macbeth*

year to leave. We had hit the point we'd hoped to get to after five years by the end of only our second year, so we didn't know if the only way then was down!'

Lord Young, Chairman of the Board: 'I used to joke that I'd know when things were going well because people would ring me up because they couldn't get tickets. Well, that started to happen. And, what's more, I couldn't get them tickets either – even the house seats had gone!'

Other productions in the Minerva also performed excellently, both in critical and in box-office terms. The season opened with Alan Bennett's *Office Suite*, with the ever-popular Patricia Routledge. Jean Anouilh's *The Waltz of the Toreadors*, in a new translation by Ranjit Bolt, starring Peter Bowles and directed by Angus Jackson, opened in June. The final show was a piece conceived and written by Mark Rylance[1] and devised by the company, *I Am Shakespeare*.

Jonathan Church considers they learnt something about the CFT audience with this: 'It opened our eyes. On one level, it was a completely bonkers project. Mark Rylance had a conversation with us and said: "Is Chichester and your audience the place to do this, it's an internet-based show with live phone-ins, talking about who wrote Shakespeare's plays? Surely this needs to go to university towns, Liverpool, Oxford, Cambridge?" And we said: "No, let's try it here." And actually, it sold out. The audience wanted to engage with that debate. In no other city I've worked in, other than London, is there such a large part of the traditional audience that is not afraid of new work and I'm sure that's a legacy of Olivier somewhere in the DNA.'

was clearly – at that point – probably the best piece of work Rupert [Goold] had produced to date and its transfer to the West End, combined with what happened to *Nickleby* that previous year, gave the sense we had delivered both the commercial and that elusive thing, artistic quality as well. That was the year we said, actually it'll probably never get better than this.'

Finch agrees: 'We had a jokey conversation that, after the 2007 season, it was probably the

---

[1] Mark Rylance was the first Artistic Director of Shakespeare's Globe Theatre in London from 1995 – 2005. An award-winning actor on both screen and stage, in the UK and on Broadway, most recently in Jez Butterworth's *Jerusalem*.

2008

Six Characters in Search of An Author, 2008.

Photo: Manuel Harlan

TOP RIGHT

CFYT's *Toad of Toad Hall*, 2008 at Rolls-Royce, Goodwood.

Photo: Allan Hutching

Success brings its own burdens and, as Church and Finch said, the pressure to continue to deliver was always there. Fortunately, the season got off to a grand start in the Minerva. Charles Spencer: 'The opening of the Chichester season always signals summer, and what looks a tremendously promising Festival on paper gets off to a fizzily enjoyable start with *Funny Girl*... a high-octane revival directed by Angus Jackson.'

Samantha Spiro played the role made famous by Barbra Streisand in the 1960s. Equally highly acclaimed was Pirandello's *Six Characters in Search of an Author* in a new version by Rupert Goold and Ben Power. This was followed by the world premiere of Ronald Harwood's *Collaboration*, playing alongside *Taking Sides*[1].

In September, another world premiere, Martin Sherman's *Aristo* – based on Peter Evans biography of Artistotle Onassis – with Robert Lindsay, Diana Quick and Elizabeth McGovern. Although the production transferred to London, it was one of the rare productions of the 2008 season not to find favour with the critics.

[1] In the original production of *Taking Sides* in the Minerva in 1995, Daniel Massey and Michael Pennington took the roles of Interrogator and Furtwängler. This time round Pennington took the role of Furtwängler.

The Youth Theatre promenade production was *Toad of Toad Hall*. More than 60 CFYT performers and technicians took up residence at the Rolls-Royce head office and manufacturing site set in a 42-acre plot at Goodwood, Sussex. Running for two weeks at the beginning of August, the show was sold out before it had even opened.

CFYT director Dale Rooks: 'Initially they reacted cautiously to us coming on site for two weeks, while they were trying to make cars, but once they realised it would be totally outdoors and not in the factory, they were amazing. They gave us their managers' offices and suites as our dressing rooms, and even bravely allowed us to drive a Rolls at the concluding feast scene!'

In the Main House, the tried and tested formula of contemporary interpretations of classics, a new version of *The Cherry Orchard* and Somerset Maugham's *The Circle* – a large scale, all-singing, all-dancing musical. The popular television comedian and entertainer, Brian Conley (not to mention 76 trombones) brought the house down in *The Music Man*.

Last, but by no means least, was the premiere of Tim Firth's own stage adaptation of his film script *Calendar Girls*. Based on the real-life story of members of the Women's Institute in Yorkshire, who stripped off to raise money for leukaemia research, the production boasted an extraordinary cast of leading ladies including Patricia Hodge, Lynda Bellingham, Sian Phillips,

Brian Conley in
The Music Man,
2008.

Photo: Catherine Ashmore

LEFT MIDDLE
Natalie Cassidy
and Frank Finlay
rehearsing ***The***
Cherry Orchard,
2008.

Photo: Manuel Harlan

Gaynor Faye and Brigit Forsyth. Transferring into the West End in September, the production then toured to over 100 theatres in the UK and returned to CFT in the spring of 2012.

One of the most important creations in 2008 was the new Education and Rehearsal Centre, on the old Gunter's site at the southernmost tip of Oaklands Park. Intended to be both a home for the Youth Theatre and to provide professional rehearsal rooms and community spaces, during the late summer and autumn, the elegant building of glass and wood started to take on its finished shape.

The Duke of Richmond, a former CFT Trustee and long-term supporter of the Theatre, had agreed to be the President of the Appeal to help raise the £1.65million needed to realise architect Andrzej Blonski's design.

The Duke of Richmond: 'I was first deeply involved with the Theatre when I was asked to head up the appeal to raise the money to build the Pimlott Building.[1] It is very important for the Theatre to reach out to the community. It needs to make money by selling seats, but it is very important too that local people should appreciate it and see it as 'their' Theatre. Under Jonathan Church and Alan Finch it has extended much more into the community... The Pimlott Building is in use nearly all the time now and people in the park can see through those huge windows at the Theatre at work.'

---

[1] Shortly after leaving CFT, former Artistic Director, Steven Pimlott, had been diagnosed with lung cancer. He died in February 2007 and it was decided to name the building in his honour. Within it, there are two spaces. The larger room was named in recognition of the generous and passionate support of Dame Anita Roddick, who had died in September 2007. The second space, the Rehearsal Room, was to provide rehearsal space for the professional Festival companies.

The original WI Calendar Girls and CFT cast, 2008.
Photo: Allan Hutchings

Julia Hills, Gaynor Faye, Carl Prekopp and Patricia Hodge in rehearsals, *Calendar Girls*, 2008.
Photo: Catherine Ashmore

Gaynor Faye, Patricia Hodge, Sian Phillips, Lynda Bellingham, Elaine C Smith and Julia Hills in *Calendar Girls*, 2008.
Photo: John Swannell

The company warm-up for *The Music Man*, 2008.
Photo: Manuel Harlan

2009

Cyrano de Bergerac,
2009.

Photo: Catherine Ashmore

**Joseph Fiennes in
rehearsal for *Cyrano
de Bergerac,* 2009.**

Photo: Catherine Ashmore

**Trevor Nunn in
rehearsal for *Cyrano
de Bergerac,* 2009.**

Photo: Catherine Ashmore

So it was that on Friday 9 January 2009, some 150 guests gathered in the Steven Pimlott Building for the official opening. A bright winter day, the sun low in the sky and a brisk north-east wind whistling down Oaklands Park, there was a sense of achievement and community. Both Ruth Mackenzie and Martin Duncan were there, as was Gordon Roddick, together with many of the previous Artistic and Theatre Directors of CFT and the countless others who had, in cash or kind, supported CFT over many, many years.

Older members of the Youth Theatre – Alan Finch's daughter, Katie, among them – performed the 'laying out' scene from the CFYT Christmas production of *A Christmas Carol*. For those of us there, there could be no clearer representation of the past, the present and the future of CFT than this coming together in the new shared space.

Behind the scenes, of course, the same hugger-mugger finalising the season, printing the brochure, getting it out in time for advance booking. The usual last-moment panics when things fell to pieces or actors' availabilities turned out not to work with a director, a designer, a com-

poser, a choreographer. For Church, the same delicate act of balancing classic work with new commissions, famous names and those whose faces were yet to become familiar. For Finch, the same balancing of the books, the eternal battle between keeping the costs down and the quality of work up.

Jonathan Church: 'I think, for me, each year kept being special. The Theatre now had subsidy and had gained artistic credibility, so there was an absolute sense that, in terms of the industry, people now were interested in working here.'

The 2009 season was put on sale. Once more, five productions in the Main House – Joseph Fiennes in *Cyrano de Bergerac*, then *Oklahoma!* and Gelati's adaptation of Steinbeck's *The Grapes of Wrath* playing in rep during the summer, book-ended by Coward's *Hay Fever* in May and Rattigan's *Separate Tables* in September. The company of actors and directors included Trevor Nunn, Philip Franks, Stephanie Cole, Sorcha Cusack, Iain Glen, Gina McKee, Diana Rigg, Christopher Timothy, Simon Williams and Jonathan Church.

In the Minerva, the players included Isla Blair, Clare Holman, Felicity Kendal, Tim Piggott-Smith, Nicholas Le Prevost and Sam West. The line up of directors was extraordinary too – Howard Davies,

Oklahoma! **2009.**

Photo: Manuel Harlan

The Grapes of Wrath, 2009.

Photo: Manuel Harlan

Richard Eyre, Rupert Goold and Angus Jackson – and designers Simon Higlett and William Dudley, composer Matthew Scott and sound designer, John Leonard.

In the small theatre, a short run of Harwood's *Collaboration* and *Taking Sides* before they went in to the Duchess Theatre in London. There were also four world premieres, including a play that was to go on to take London by storm, Lucy Prebble's *ENRON*. This was only the second play by a young playwright, still in her twenties, about the collapse of the Enron Corporation and the accountancy firm Arthur Andersen. I saw it at a preview performance. Some of the older Youth Theatre members were there to boost the numbers – audiences hadn't been convinced about the idea of a play about the financial crash – and the Minerva was half empty. My husband was dreaming about a chocolate ice cream tub

in the interval, I was thinking of a glass of cold white wine and whether I could face cycling up the hill home after the show came down.

Then, the house lights dimmed and the most extraordinary piece of theatre began. Music, lights of the trading floor, raptors and light sabers, the most exhilarating piece of physical theatre I had ever seen. At the end, the Youth Theatre lads and lasses on their feet, cheering, shouting, knowing that they would be able to say that they had been there, right at the beginning, when something started. The reviews came out, pretty much a clean sweep. *ENRON* sold out – in the Minerva, at the Royal Court and in the West End – and became one of those shows people talked about even when they hadn't seen it. Became part of folk memory.

For Jonathan Church, it illustrates both the sophistication of the audience and the way

that CFT was now able to invest in a company, develop ideas, make extraordinary things possible: 'There are not that many theatres – outside of the National and the RSC – where Headlong could come and say: "We want to do a new play, with nobody cast in it, in the studio with seventeen people, marauding dinosaurs and video." We want to fund that artistic inspiration.'

The old links with the National were very much to the fore in the summer of 2009 through the Youth Theatre. For some years, under Andy Brereton and then Dale Rooks, CFYT had entered the National Connections competition. In 2009, the play chosen was Lisa McGee's *The Heights*. Holly Mirams was one of the members of the first ever Technical Youth Theatre group, which concentrates on providing training in all aspects of production, lighting, sound, costumes and stage management.[1] She was Stage Manager for the show, which was chosen to be performed at the National Theatre in London.

Holly looks back on the production: 'It was

[1] Holly's parents are Amanda and Patrick Mirams, who had met when working in stage management at CFT – in The Tent – in the 1980s.

the best experience of my entire life. We started in January, doing it first at Havant Arts Centre, then the Minerva. Then in July we got to go to the National for a week and work with the professionals. In rehearsals, I made notes of all the blocking, where everyone moved, and all the cues, kept lists of props. Then you get into technical rehearsals. You have to tell people where to go, from cue to cue, making sure things run as smoothly as possible. Then in the actual show

Sam West and Tom Goodman-Hill in rehearsal for *ENRON*, 2009.
Photo: Manuel Harlan

Tim Pigott-Smith in *ENRON*, 2009.
Photo: Manuel Harlan

ENRON, 2009.

Photo: Manuel Harlan

you are controlling what happens, telling lighting when to go, telling sound when to go, cueing the actors. Pretty scary!'

CFYT was one of the rare youth companies to have young people fulfilling all the roles backstage as well as on the stage. When it was over, the technical crew at the National commented on how well trained CFYT were, how professionally they behaved. One of the reasons for this, many CFYT members past and present were keen to point out, was the steadfast support and enthusiasm of CFT stage manager, Sally Garner-Gibbons. Another long-term member of YT, Jonny Boutwood – who appeared in many CFYT productions, including *The Heights* – has in 2012 started his professional career in producing/casting. He is one of many young people to begin their training at CFT.

Holly concludes: 'I don't think I would have got this experience anywhere else. All my closest friends are through Youth Theatre. And there are not many theatres that have such an outreach in to the community; the Street Art[1] and the different satellite groups.'

Back at CFT, the summer season was the most successful to date. The final shows in both the Minerva [*ENRON*] and the Main House [*Separate Tables*] garnering the sorts of reviews that look as if they must have been written by a relative of the director or leading lady.

When CFT shut its doors on Saturday 3 October, Jonathan Church and Alan Finch could comfortably feel that they had put CFT

[1] The Street Art Company, for older YT members, is formed every year. Pieces are created for performances at different festivals and open-air events.

back on the map. The finances looked healthy, the Theatre's artistic reputation was as high as it had been for some years, the very best actors and directors, designers and choreographers, musicians and artists, all now wanted to come to Chichester.

Michael Billington: 'There used to be a time when as a critic going to Chichester there was an element of "Oh, Chichester …", an element of the routine about it, quite truthfully. Now one goes down with an air of expectation, with a spring in our step rather than getting ready to dust off the old clichés about the Bentleys, stockbrokers, the dressy ladies, the hats – all that, that's all pretty much in the past, and I think this is the real breakthrough.

'We have stopped reviewing the audience and we are now reviewing the plays and the productions. That didn't happen twenty, thirty years ago. That's progress.'

The decade was done, but the story was far from over. In two years time, CFT would celebrate its fiftieth birthday. And in theatre, as in life, two years can be a long time.

'Old Year! upon the Stage of Time
You stand to bow your last adieu;
A moment, and the prompter's chime
Will ring the curtain down on you.
Your mien is sad, your step is slow;
You falter as a Sage in pain;
Yet turn, Old Year, before you go,
And face your audience again.'

The Passing of the Year
ROBERT W SERVICE, 1912

**Edward Eustace,
Nell Underwood,
Florence Christie
and Felix Mosse in**
The Heights, **2009.**
Photo: Mike Eddowes

**Holly Mirams,
stage managing**
The Heights, **2009.**
Photo: Dale Rooks

The Story Continues

Artistic Directors & Executive Directors
JONATHAN CHURCH and **ALAN FINCH** (2006 – present)

'As happens sometimes, a moment settled and hovered and remained for much more than a moment. And sound stopped and movement stopped for much, much more than a moment.'

OF MICE AND MEN
John Steinbeck

Since we are now so very nearly up to date, I'll spend less time remembering, reminiscing about the individual productions, performances, of the past two years. Each of us has our own memories, our own favourite scenes, moments – whether it is Adam Cooper swinging from the lamppost in the rain or Michael Ball dispatching another hapless victim into the bloody furnace.

Suffice to say that, of course, the 2010 and 2011 seasons, because they are so recent, fresh, of course seem the strongest, better, the best. It is also true that one of the joys of theatre is that, when it is going well, success does of course breed success. Since their arrival in 2006, Church and Finch – backed by the Board, by the critics, by the hard-working, committed CFT staff, by actors and designers and creative teams of such quality – have made the Theatre a place where audience and critics alike feel that outstanding work is being done.

The trick is, of course, to keep moving forward, to keep finding the perfect balance of new and old, breaking new ground and revisiting familiar spaces. If you like, to provide a narrative of what theatre is – and what it can be – for the audiences.

Michael Billington: 'What Chichester needs is that constant injection of a big new play if they can find one, and smaller scale new plays in the Minerva. Keeping the momentum going and keeping the air of excite-

Adam Cooper in *Singin' in the Rain*, 2011.

Photo: Manuel Harlan

Patrick Stewart in
Bingo, **2010.**

Photo: Catherine Ashmore

**Michael Xavier and
Emma Williams in**
Love Story, **2010.**

Photo: Manuel Harlan

**Jonathan Church in
rehearsal for** ***The
Critic,*** **2010.**

Photo: Manuel Harlan

ment means that all theatre these days has to be an event, there is no room for anything that is routine or run of the mill, everything has to be an special in some way, and in Chichester that can be lots of different ways, either the star, the director, the choreographer, you have got to have something to make it look good for an audience.'

The 2010 season, when announced in February, had that and in spades. Top-level casting, top-level writers, world premieres and reinterpretations. So, in the Main House, a world premiere of *Yes, Prime Minister* – with David Haig and Henry Goodman – followed by one of the biggest tap shows of them all, *42nd Street*. *Pygmalion* next, with all-star casting in the shape of Rupert Everett and Honeysuckle Weeks, herself a former member of CFYT, then a short run of *ENRON* before it transferred to the Royal Court in London. Finally, Brian Friel's adaptation of *A Month in the Country* with Janie Dee and Michael Feast, popular CFT actors from the Welch and the Mackenzie/Pimlott/Duncan eras.

In the Minerva, Patrick Stewart in Edward Bond's *Bingo*, followed by the world premiere of a musical version of *Love Story*; a double bill of Tom Stoppard's *The Real Inspector Hound* and Richard Brinsley Sheridan's *The Critic* (which was, for my money, quite the funniest thing I'd watched in the Minerva for some time), then Howard Brenton's adaptation of Tressell's *The Ragged Trousered Philanthropist* and David Edgar's new version of Ibsen's seminal *The Master Builder*, with Michael Pennington, to close the 2010 season. So, Brenton, Stoppard, Bond, Prebble and Edgar. Stop for a moment, to take a breath. Also Turgenev, Shaw, Ibsen and Sheridan.

Advance booking was brisk (though 2011 and 2012 were to be even livelier), the figures were promising and, of course, on paper, it looked perfect. A season just right. Of course the reality, as every Artistic Director knows, is that one never can be sure about what will catch, what will be the surprise hit or what might disappoint. Which productions the critics will admire or love or hate, which the audiences will take to their hearts.

CFYT's *The Firework-Maker's Daughter*, 2010.

Photo: Mike Eddowes

Jonathan Church: 'Things like *Yes, Prime Minister* or more particularly *Calendar Girls* actually aren't necessarily obvious, but they were two of our biggest successes. Again, it's about the diversifying of the audience. I am not convinced that Rupert Everett falls slap-bang into the middle of what we would call an obvious Chichester Festival Theatre star. But what I thought was exciting was the combination of the actors we had in that, the combination of Shaw with Rupert who, I suspect, appeals to a slightly younger audience because of the diversity of the work he does. I think the magic moments are when we hit all those audiences rather than when you just hit one. But you can't always plan those things.'

A few miles north of Oaklands Park, the Youth Theatre summer promenade performance was to take place in the historic 50 acres of the Weald and Downland Open Air Museum nestling in the Sussex Downs. One of only a few such living museums in the world – some 45 houses and agricultural buildings, a working farm, dating from the 13th century to Victorian Times – CFYT filled it with colour and light and puppetry, magical animals to bring to life Philip Pullman's *The Firework-Maker's Daughter*. Jonathan Church's daughters, Beth and Olivia, were in the company.

Dale Rooks: 'It was so memorable, because it introduced puppetry and a different style of music, and different professionals coming in to work with the young people.'

Holly Mirams was, on this occasion, a performer: 'I was one of the puppeteers of the Big White Elephant. That was really interesting,

because we got to work with one of the lead puppeteers on *War Horse*, Toby Olié. It was amazing to work with someone so expert in their field.'

Behind the scenes, discussions were beginning to take place about the fiftieth anniversary, fast approaching. More important, though, than merely thinking about what form that might take and what might be celebrated – or not – was the issue about the physical state of the building. The Main House had been built on a shoestring. For nearly fifty years, there had been running repairs. Each decade had seen additions, modifications, changes to purpose and to design in line with the changing needs of a growing theatre staff and population. Duncan Weldon had been forced into the position of having to spend a great deal of money repairing the roof of the Main House in 1993 and in 1999. Andrew Welch had put in train re-seating the auditorium (in a frantic ten days between the closing of the 1999 summer season closing and the autumn touring programme opening). But although these works were not cosmetic, at the same time they didn't address the fundamental issue, which was that the Powell & Moya building, beautiful as it was, had been built on a wing and a prayer and a great deal of goodwill.

A new major Capital Appeal to restore, refurbish and renovate CFT to make it ready for the next fifty years was about to be launched. Part of the honouring of the past was to provide a theatre fit for the future. So while plans were in action for the 2011 season, as well as the anniversary year, Jonathan Church, Alan Finch and the Board were beginning conversations about how much money might be needed and what the priorities should be. How to involve the local community and business beyond asking them to dig deep, once more, into their pockets? What about the design, the desires, the dreams? What did Chichester want to see on the green patch of land to the north of the city centre?

42nd Street, 2010.

Photo: Johan Persson

There was a strong sense that CFT had a huge chance to get it right, but that the devil would be in the detail.

As Tom Stoppard says in *Rosencrantz and Guildenstern are Dead* – the play scheduled to open the 2011 season in the Main House: 'We cross our bridges when we come to them and burn them behind us, with nothing to show for our progress except a memory of the smell of smoke, and a presumption that once our eyes watered.'

Nobody wanted the opportunity to be missed. So, ready to announce with the 2011 season, was a declaration of the fiftieth anniversary Capital Project. Haworth Tompkins Architects were commissioned to identify what needed to be done to make the buildings fit for purpose, appropriate. An explanation of why this was the time to launch such a major fundraising appeal was laid out in the brochure: 'Our national artistic profile, together with the re-emergence of an Arts Council capital programme, provide the foundations for a successful campaign to raise the necessary funds and our public appeal will be driven by the impetus and focus of our fiftieth anniversary celebrations in 2012. Ten years ago it wouldn't have been possible; in ten years' time the opportunity will almost certainly have passed.'

Michael Billington, considering the 2011 season, agreed that the time was right: 'I think Jonathan Church got the balance almost perfectly right in that in 2011 he would give us three musicals that would do very nicely at the box office, but also give us lots of other things which are slightly more unpredictable and at the same time have the backing of good actors. If you can get McKellen and Pennington to do an Eduardo De Filippo play [*The Syndicate*] you will get a sell-out in advance – and I think Jonathan Church has been a quite admirable figure at Chichester.'

2011

While Finch and Church and the Board considered what could be achieved in Chichester itself, in the wider world – London, New York, on tour – CFT productions were everywhere, or so it seemed: *Yes, Prime Minister*, *ENRON*, *Macbeth*, *Calendar Girls*. The idea of 'taking CFT to the world' that had been so important in the past – from Michell to Garland, Weldon and Welch – was writ large in neon lights and banners on the side of red London buses and on flyers crammed in to racks at the airports.

The 2011 season – which was to run from Monday 9 May to Saturday 5 November – was announced in February 2011. In the Main House, Trevor Nunn directing *Rosencrantz and Guildenstern Are Dead*, followed by Jonathan Church directing Adam Cooper in *Singin' in the Rain*. Philip Franks, one of theatre's foremost interpreters of Terence Rattigan, was to direct *The Deep Blue Sea* and a world premiere of Nicholas Wright's *Rattigan's Nijinksy* as a dou-

ble bill. The final production in the Main House, running worryingly late into November, was Sondheim's fiendish, challenging *Sweeney Todd*, starring Michael Ball and Imelda Staunton.

In the Minerva, the tried and tested formula of new writing, top names and revivals: Masteroff's *She Loves Me*, followed by Max Stafford-Clark directing the first major revival of Caryl Churchill's *Top Girls* since he had first staged the play at the Royal Court twenty years before. The third play was Eduardo de Filippo's *The Syndicate*. Directed by Sean Mathias, it starred Ian McKellen and Michael Pennington. Finally, in the hands of Angus Jackson, Rattigan's *The Browning Version* playing in a double bill with a world premiere of David Hare's *South Downs*, directed by Jeremy Herrin.

Jonathan Church explains how, although it's always complicated putting a season together, often it is a matter of the luck of timing – people's diaries, commitments, availabilities, all the pieces of a jigsaw falling into place at just the right time: 'It's never simple. It's easier now to have the conversations, because people realise they can create great work here. We can transfer and create international opportunities. Sometimes, though, the higher up the tree you get to talk the less chance there is of it delivering. Mike Poulton had sent the script of the *The Syndicate* to us a couple of years ago. I was talking to Sean Mathias and there had been a reading with Ian [McKellen], but Ian was going into filming and that looked like something we wouldn't be able to consider. Then suddenly Ian had a gap in filming and we had to move the whole season around to accommodate it.'

Alan Finch agrees and makes the point that the fact CFT now has significant public funding helps makes the possibilities so much the greater: 'If you look at the Minerva with sixteen or seventeen actors in *She Loves Me* or in *The Syndicate*, it is a delicate balance. Actually the core funding that comes to us from the Arts Council – from the tripartite funding arrangement – is what allows us to, if you like, pay for the complexity of work. When the box office is good, it's quite a complicated message about the importance of that foundation of public subsidy, because that's where the possibility of taking risks comes from.'

And, of course, just as Weldon and Welch said before them, it is essential to have this sort of cushion to guard against a situation where things might go wrong – illness, acts of God in the wider world, life.

By these lights, the 2011 season got off to a bad start in the Main House, with one of the leads of *Rosencrantz and Guildenstern Are Dead* – Tim Curry – becoming ill and being unable to go on. On the day I saw it, a chilly Saturday matinee in May, the actor playing Rosencrantz (or was it gentle Guildenstern) was with his wife in hospital, where she was giving birth to their second child, so there were two understudies out of the three leads. The audience figures, perhaps, reflect the fact that the production never quite found its feet.

Joseph Drake in *Rattigan's Nijinsky*, 2011.

Photo: Manuel Harlan

Malcolm Sinclair and director Philip Franks in rehearsals for *Rattigan's Nijinsky*, 2011.

Photo: Manuel Harlan

It was the centenary of Rattigan's birth and CFT intended to celebrate it properly. Developing further the concept of an ensemble company set in place by Mackenzie, Pimlott and Duncan – and done successfully with the two Shakespeares in 2007 – the actors in Franks' Rattigan double bill played younger and older roles, played dancers and lovers, and brought a new audiences to the work of a playwright who had, in recent years, fallen so far out of favour. Amanda Root in *The Deep Blue Sea* was exquisite, perfectly composed, clipped and despairing, the period detail perfect. The second play, by Nicholas Wright, was based on a 'discovered' screenplay by Rattigan himself.

Across the road, in the Minerva, Angus Jackson directed *The Browning Version* in a double bill with a brand new one-act play from David Hare, *South Downs*. Commissioned by the Rattigan Trust as a response to *The Browning Version*, it is set in 1962 in a public school in Sussex – perhaps based on Hare's own school, Lancing College – and was directed by Jeremy Herrin.

But the triumphs of the 2011 season were to be – as so often at CFT – the musicals. *She Loves Me* in the Minerva, then astonishing productions of *Singin' in the Rain* and *Sweeney Todd* in the Main House. Directed by Church himself, *Singin' in the Rain* was, in some respects, a gamble. One of those musicals that everybody knows from the film – Gene Kelly, that 104°F temperature, that sequence and the lamp post – the challenge is how to make so magical a screen memory work on stage. The Palladium version with Tommy Steele in the 1980s had played to good houses, but to so-so reviews.

In the event, the genius of casting star of the Royal Ballet, Adam Cooper, was a piece of inspiration that paid dividends. A world class ballet dancer, on the stage of CFT, the critics adored it. Charles Spencer reviewing for the *Daily Telegraph*:

'It was chucking it down on my way to Chichester, the traffic crawled, and I was too late for a much-needed pre-show supper. I can tell you one thing, I wasn't singin'. But as soon as this stage version of perhaps the greatest of all Hollywood musicals gets under way, the anxieties of the outside world are forgotten in an evening of pure joy.'

The audience loved the playful, gleeful performances – even if those in Row A and B had to be given plastic macs to keep the hoofers from kicking rain in their faces. Katherine Kingsley, Scarlett Strallen and Daniel Crossley, almost every member of the company was picked out for praise in one review or another. And with Higlett's joyous set and the on-stage band, despite the grim July and August weather, it was the perfect CFT summer show.

As Quentin Letts in the *Daily Mail* put it: 'Five stars all round.'

And as I was finishing this book in January 2012, I happened to be walking past the Palace Theatre at Cambridge Circus. There, in the bitter

TOP
Scarlett Strallen and company in rehearsal for *Singin' in the Rain*, 2011.
Photo: Manuel Harlan

Scarlett Strallen, Daniel Crossley and Adam Cooper in *Singin' in the Rain*, 2011.
Photo: Manuel Harlan

Bradley Hall and Alex Lawther in *South Downs*, 2011.
Photo: Johan Persson

north-east wind, was being constructed a riot-ous display of yellow and red and blue and white umbrellas, ready for the London opening on Wednesday 15 February 2012. As Holly Mirams says: 'As somebody who loves Chichester, both working at CFT and being part of the Youth Theatre it makes me proud when I go to London and see shows that started here that have trans-ferred to the West End and to know that that quality of work began here.' I feel the same. I think, perhaps, we all feel the same.

The atmosphere created on site by both the runaway success of *Singin' in the Rain* and the company itself looked hard to beat. So, the *Sweeney Todd* company, which had been rehearsing in London rather than Sussex, had quite something to look up to and when they arrived, at the beginning of October, there was a distinct snap of autumn in the air.

Sweeney Todd had, in some ways, the same issue to overcome as had Cooper, Strallen and Crossley. Namely, that many members of the audience would have a classic film version fixed in their minds. In 2007, Tim Burton had pro-duced a dark, surreal vision of *Sweeney Todd: The Demon Barber of Fleet Street*, starring Johnny Depp and Helena Bonham-Carter.

At CFT, blue-eyed, golden boy of the stage, Michael Ball, with lank hair and dirty finger-nails, was a bitter, deranged, menacing Sweeney, returning from deportation half-crazed and seeking revenge. On the night I saw it, two ladies behind me simply would not believe it was Michael Ball at all. In his hands, the cut-throat razor looked vicious, lethal, not a stage prop. Imelda Staunton as Mrs Lovett was simply magnificent. Manipulative and bustling, mis-tress of a thousand tiny moments of comic tim-ing. With an extraordinarily complicated set by Anthony Ward – a semi-derelict 19th-century Fleet Street, all belching chimneys and broken shutters and wire mesh – Jonathan Kent intro-duced elements of the early 20th century into the mid-Victorian mix.

Audiences adored it, the bleakness, the black-ness, the surreal horror of the piece somehow striking a mood. And Stephen Sondheim him-self, in Chichester for a few days in October 2011 to see the show, is said to have commented it was the finest production of *Sweeney* he had ever seen.

The critics, almost without exception agreed: 'A magnificent production, easily the finest I've seen, of Stephen Sondheim's master-

piece' (*Evening Standard*). Or the *Daily Mail*: 'A world-class production featuring two world-class performances.' And the *Sunday Express*: 'A comic triumph.'

Sweeney Todd opened at the Adelphi Theatre, London, in March 2012 for a limited run until September. Again, a string of four- and five-star reviews followed. *Bingo* – the 2010 production with Patrick Stewart – opened a few weeks earlier, in February 2012, at the Young Vic. Max Stafford-Clark's revival of *Top Girls* played at the Trafalgar Studios in the Autumn of 2011 and *Yes, Prime Minister* and *Calendar Girls* were both back on the CFT stage as part of their UK touring schedule. As I was finishing this book *The Browning Version* and Hare's *South Downs* opened at the Harold Pinter Theatre in April 2012 to five star reviews too.

As Michael Billington says: 'In his years at Chichester, Church has put the Theatre back on an even financial keel. He has made it credible with the Arts Council and he hasn't done it by compromising. He has done everything from *Calendar Girls* to big productions like *Nicholas Nickleby*, wonderful musicals and that dotty Mark Rylance play *I Am Shakespeare*. I think he is astonishing as a producer.'

TOP
Imelda Staunton and James McConville in *Sweeney Todd*, **2011.**
Photo: Catherine Ashmore

Imelda Staunton and Michael Ball in *Sweeney Todd*, **2011.**
Photo: Catherine Ashmore

Michael Ball in rehearsal for *Sweeney Todd*, **2011.**
Photo: Catherine Ashmore

2012

The *Uncle Vanya* Company in rehearsal, March 2012.

Photo: Johan Persson

So what does the fiftieth anniversary year hold for CFT? The programme was announced in February 2012. Paying tribute to the past, as well as looking to the future, there are actors and directors and designers from all decades of CFT's long and distinguished, sometimes difficult, history – Derek Jacobi, Patricia Routledge, Penelope Keith, Henry Goodman, Toby Stephens making his CFT debut on stage (rather than backstage), Roger Allam, Michael Pennington. Directors Trevor Nunn, Angus Jackson, Rachel Kavanaugh, Jonathan Kent and Alan Ayckbourn. Designers Simon Higlett and Gareth Valentine, Matthew Scott.

In the Main House, modern interpretations of works that been played on the wonderful thrust stage before – *Heartbreak House*, *The Way of the World*, *Antony and Cleopatra*. Echoes in the air, ghosts and a shimmering of the light. Three new plays – Hugh Whitemore's *A Marvellous Year for Plums* and, in the Minerva, Alan Ayckbourn's *Surprises* and Michael Wynne's *Canvas*. In the Minerva, too, a new version of the play that secured CFT's future back in 1962, *Uncle Vanya*.

The story is yet to be written. The particular character of the 2012 season is yet to be felt, tasted, smelt, imagined.

At the end of October 2012, the wonderful Powell & Moya building might close its doors. Perhaps for a year, perhaps for 18 months, perhaps not yet a while. The Capital Appeal, launched at the beginning of the fiftieth anniversary year, is already full steam ahead. And, as Finch and Church wrote in the *RENEW* brochure, when better to launch an appeal than when the city and the park are working so well together, when Chichester is proud of its Theatre, when audiences and critics, the local authorities and the national funding bodies, are all – extraordinarily – in agreement as to the value, the pur-

50 | CHICHESTER FESTIVAL THEATRE

FESTIVAL 2012

30 MARCH - 27 OCTOBER

01243 781312 CFT.ORG.UK

Supported by ARTS COUNCIL ENGLAND · Chichester District Council · West Sussex County Council

FESTIVAL THEATRE

13 APRIL - 5 MAY
PENELOPE KEITH
THE WAY OF THE WORLD
By **WILLIAM CONGREVE**
Director **RACHEL KAVANAUGH**
Sponsored by Bramshott Place, Durrants Village and Vintage TV
Supported by The Way of the World Commissioning Circle

11 MAY - 2 JUNE · WORLD PREMIERE
A MARVELLOUS YEAR FOR PLUMS
By **HUGH WHITEMORE**
Director **PHILIP FRANKS**
Sponsored by Reynolds Fine Furniture
Supported by the A Marvellous Year for Plums Commissioning Circle

18 JUNE - 1 SEPTEMBER
KISS ME, KATE
Music and lyrics **COLE PORTER**
Book by **SAM** and **BELLA SPEWACK**
Director **TREVOR NUNN**
Sponsored by Henry Adams, Oval Insurance Broking, Seaward Properties and John Wiley & Sons
Supported by the Kiss Me, Kate Commissioning Circle

6 JULY - 25 AUGUST
DEREK JACOBI
HEARTBREAK HOUSE
By **BERNARD SHAW**
Director **RICHARD CLIFFORD**
Sponsored by Thomas Eggar
Supported by the Heartbreak House Commissioning Circle

7 - 29 SEPTEMBER
KIM CATTRALL & **MICHAEL PENNINGTON**
ANTONY AND CLEOPATRA
By **WILLIAM SHAKESPEARE**
Director **JANET SUZMAN**
Co-produced with **LIVERPOOL EVERYMAN**
and **PLAYHOUSE THEATRE**
Sponsored by Jackson-Stops & Staff and Lockheed Martin

MINERVA THEATRE

30 MARCH - 28 APRIL
ROGER ALLAM, DERVLA KIRWAN & **TIMOTHY WEST**
UNCLE VANYA
By **ANTON CHEKHOV**
Translated by **MICHAEL FRAYN**
Director **JEREMY HERRIN**
Sponsored by Kenwood

18 MAY - 16 JUNE · WORLD PREMIERE
CANVAS
By **MICHAEL WYNNE**
Director **ANGUS JACKSON**
Sponsored by Pridewatch Events and Graylingwell Park
Supported by the Canvas Commissioning Circle

29 JUNE - 28 JULY
HENRY GOODMAN
THE RESISTIBLE RISE OF ARTURO UI
By **BERTOLT BRECHT**
In a translation by **GEORGE TABORI**
Director **JONATHAN CHURCH**
Sponsored by Hentys Corporate
Supported by the Arturo Ui Commissioning Circle

8 AUGUST - 8 SEPTEMBER · WORLD PREMIERE
SURPRISES
By **ALAN AYCKBOURN**
Director **ALAN AYCKBOURN**
Co-produced with **STEPHEN JOSEPH THEATRE SCARBOROUGH**
Sponsored by Baker Tilly and Oldham Seals Group

10 AUGUST - 8 SEPTEMBER
ABSURD PERSON SINGULAR
By **ALAN AYCKBOURN**
Director **ALAN AYCKBOURN**
Co-produced with **STEPHEN JOSEPH THEATRE SCARBOROUGH**
Sponsored by Baker Tilly and Oldham Seals Group

21 SEPTEMBER - 27 OCTOBER
ANNA CHANCELLOR & **TOBY STEPHENS**
NOËL COWARD'S
PRIVATE LIVES
Director **JONATHAN KENT**
Sponsored by Harwoods
Supported by the Private Lives Commissioning Circle

OAKLANDS PARK / THEATRE ON THE FLY

27 JULY - 11 AUGUST
CHICHESTER FESTIVAL YOUTH THEATRE presents
NOAH
A new adaptation by **RACHEL BARNETT**
Director **DALE ROOKS**
Sponsored by Criterion Ices, Mercer and Pall Corporation
Supported by the Noah Commissioning Circle

Dervla Kirwan in rehearsal for *Uncle Vanya*, 2012.

Photo: Johan Persson

pose, the joy of the fact that world-class theatre is being produced in the heart of this modest market town in West Sussex.

What has come through to me most strongly, while writing this book, is how every Director of CFT, however long or short their tenure, has felt the responsibility of being a custodian. Has felt responsible for the past, as well as the future – from Olivier and Clements in the 1960s, Michell and Dews in the 1970s, Garland and Gale in the 1980s, Rudman, Weldon, Jacobi and Welch in the

1990s, Mackenzie, Duncan, Pimlott in the early years of this century and, since 2006, Finch and Church. That sense of feeling part of a tradition, part of the story of the building.

As Church puts it: 'One of the first bits of advice given to us by Patrick Garland when we started was that "artistic directors come and go but Duncan Weldon is, and has always been, there for Chichester". It was hard to imagine how true this observation was to become. Through all of our seasons many of the key introductions to actors and many of the highest profile commercial transfers of our work have been led – or partnered – by Duncan.'

Executive Director, Alan Finch, says this: 'There's a sense of pride, yes. I think it's an honour to run an organisation like this, given its reputation and the wealth of its history.'

And Church adds how this sense of history, of legacy, did play a part when they were deciding how best to rebuild and refurbish the buildings: 'There's always that sense of Olivier. We talked a lot with the architects whether the point on the stage is very illogical. Most thrusts don't have points, most theatre consultants that looked at it said, if you build a theatre in a hexagon, you should put the stage on a flat bit, not on a point, which is what creates the corner. We debated long and hard whether the points should go, whether that slightly strange pointy relationship at the front should give way to a more conventional one. And, jokingly – without knowing what we would end up deciding – we kept coming back to: "but Olivier stood on that point". Then, sitting down with Derek Jacobi, he said: "I remember watching *Uncle Vanya*. The lights went down, for what seemed like fifteen seconds, then they came up and there he was on that point." There are spaces you go into where the hair goes up on the back of your neck before the show has even started. We have two such spaces here.'

Seamed into the DNA of the building is that

legacy of Olivier's first companies, the drama of creating something new, building something from scratch, generations of fathers and daughters, mothers and sons, actors and writers, technicians and production staff, directors and designers, administrators and musicians. CFT is more than the building, more than the sum of its parts. Memory and moment, concrete and glass, the black-and-white photographs that grin, glower, grimace, smile down on audiences in the foyer, all of it both a living history and a blank canvas on which the stories of the next fifty years might be written.

From the first instant when Olivier stepped out onto the spotlit stage, through fifty years to the arrival of the company of 2012 taking up residence in the labyrinth of dressing rooms backstage, everywhere are the ghosts of the past and the shimmering possibilities of the future.

It is this, then – this shared experience – that makes CFT, the 'impossible theatre', what it is. And it is this determination and affection for what CFT might be in the future, that makes this fiftieth anniversary year and the thought of the years ahead, so very wonderful to imagine.

Not so impossible after all...

After the performance...

Photo: Manuel Harlan

Main House Productions 1962 – 2012

As First Dayman Andy Neal says (page 105) 'theatre is a team game', so we very much regret that lack of space means we cannot manage to list everybody who has worked at CFT over the past fifty years – actors, actresses, singers, dancers, choreographers, designers (of costume, set, lighting, sound, fights), stage management, production, front of house, maintenance, administration, catering. Over the decades, CFT has put on more and more work and the seasons have grown longer. The sheer numbers of people employed has grown so the full list would run to thousands of names and many pages. We have been forced, therefore, to restrict ourselves to listing artistic directors, directors and plays in the Festival Season (though we have put full creative teams on the CFT website – www.cft.org.uk – as well as the very many outstanding concerts, recitals and Sunday/Gala revue shows). We apologise to anyone disappointed not to find their name here.

The 1960s

1962

The Chances –
John Fletcher
The Broken Heart –
John Ford
Uncle Vanya –
Anton Chekhov
(translated by
Constance Garnett)

1963

Saint Joan –
George Bernard Shaw
Uncle Vanya –
Anton Chekhov
(translated by
Constance Garnett)
The Workhouse Donkey –
John Arden

1964

*The Royal Hunt of
the Sun* –
Peter Shaffer
The Dutch Courtesan –
John Marston
Othello –
William Shakespeare

1965

*Armstrong's Last
Goodnight*
John Arden
Trelawny of the 'Wells' –
Arthur Wing Pinero
Miss Julie –
August Strindberg
(translated by
Michael Meyer)
Black Comedy –
Peter Shaffer

1966

The Clandestine Marriage
George Colman &
David Garrick
The Fighting Cock –
Jean Anouilh
(translated by Lucienne Hill)
The Cherry Orchard –
Anton Chekhov
(translated by Elisaveta Fen)
Macbeth –
William Shakespeare

1967

The Farmer's Wife –
Eden Phillpotts
The Beaux' Stratagem –
George Farquhar
Heartbreak House –
George Bernard Shaw
An Italian Straw Hat –
Eugène Labiche &
Marc-Michel
(translated by
Theodore Hoffman/
music by André Cadou)

1968

*The Unknown Soldier
and his Wife* –
Peter Ustinov
The Cocktail Party –
T S Eliot
The Tempest –
William Shakespeare
The Skin of Our Teeth –
Thornton Wilder

1969

The Caucasian Chalk Circle
Bertolt Brecht
(translated by James &
Tania Stern with W H Auden)

The Magistrate –
Arthur Wing Pinero
The Country Wife –
William Wycherley
Antony and Cleopatra –
William Shakespeare

The 1970s

1970

Peer Gynt –
Henrik Ibsen
(English version by
Christopher Fry based
on a first translation
by Johann Fillinger)
Vivat! Vivat Regina! –
Robert Bolt
The Proposal –
Anton Chekhov
(translated by
Constance Garnett)
Arms and the Man –
George Bernard Shaw
The Alchemist –
Ben Jonson

1971

The Rivals –
Richard Brinsley Sheridan
Dear Antoine –
Jean Anouilh
(translated by Lucienne Hill)
Caesar and Cleopatra –
George Bernard Shaw
Reunion in Vienna –
Robert E Sherwood

1972

The Beggar's Opera –
John Gay
The Doctor's Dilemma –
George Bernard Shaw

The Taming of the Shrew –
William Shakespeare
The Lady's Not for Burning –
Christopher Fry

1973

The Director of the Opera –
Jean Anouilh
(translated by Lucienne Hill)
The Seagull –
Anton Chekhov
(translated by Elisaveta Fen)
R loves J –
Peter Ustinov
(music by Alexander Faris,
lyrics by Julian More)
Dandy Dick –
Arthur Wing Pinero

1974

Tonight We Improvise –
Luigi Pirandello
(translated by
Samuel Putnam)
The Confederacy –
John Vanbrugh
Oedipus Tyrannus –
Sophocles
(adapted by
Gail Rademacher)
A Month in the Country –
Ivan Turgenev
(translated by
Ariadne Nicolaeff)

1975

Cyrano de Bergerac –
Edmond Rostand
(translated by
Christopher Fry)
An Enemy of the People –
Henrik Ibsen
(English version by

John Patrick Vincent)
Made in Heaven –
Andrew Sachs
Othello –
William Shakespeare

1976
Noah –
André Obey
(English text
by Arthur Wilmurt)
Twelfth Night –
William Shakespeare
The Circle –
W Somerset Maugham
Monsieur Perrichon's Travels
Eugène Labiche &
Edouard Martin
(English version by
R H Ward)

1977
Waters of the Moon –
N C Hunter
In Order of Appearance –
Wally K Daly & Keith Michell
(music by Jim Parker)
Julius Caesar –
William Shakespeare
The Apple Cart –
George Bernard Shaw

1978
A Woman of No Importance –
Oscar Wilde
The Inconstant Couple –
from *L'Heureux Strategème*
by Pierre Carlet Marivaux
(translated & adapted
by John Bowen)
The Aspern Papers –
Henry James
(adapted for the theatre by

Michael Redgrave)
Look After Lulu –
Noël Coward
(based on *Occupe-toi
d'Amélie* by
Georges Feydeau)

1979
The Devil's Disciple –
George Bernard Shaw
The Eagle Has Two Heads –
Jean Cocteau
(adapted by Ronald Duncan)
*The Importance of
Being Earnest* –
Oscar Wilde
*The Man Who Came
to Dinner* –
Moss Hart & George
S Kaufmann

The 1980s

1980
The Last of Mrs Cheyney –
Frederick Lonsdale
Terra Nova –
Ted Tally
Much Ado About Nothing –
William Shakespeare
Old Heads and Young Hearts
Dion Boucicault
(freely adapted by
Peter Sallis)

1981
The Cherry Orchard –
Anton Chekhov
(translated by David
Magarshack, revised by
Philip Roth)
Feasting with Panthers –
Peter Coe

The Mitford Girls –
Caryl Brahms &
Ned Sherrin
(music by Peter Greenwell)
Underneath the Arches –
Patrick Garland, Brian
Glanville & Roy Hudd

1982
On the Rocks –
George Bernard Shaw
Valmouth –
Sandy Wilson
(from the novel by
Ronald Firbank)
Cavell –
Keith Baxter
Goodbye, Mr Chips –
based on the novel
by James Hilton
(book by Roland Starke,
music & lyrics by
Leslie Bricusse)

1983
A Patriot for Me –
John Osborne
Time and the Conways –
J B Priestley
As You Like It –
William Shakespeare
The Sleeping Prince –
Terence Rattigan

1984
Forty Years On –
Alan Bennett
Oh, Kay! –
music by George Gershwin,
lyrics by Ira Gershwin,
book by Tony Geiss &
Ned Sherrin (based on the
original by Guy Bolton &

P G Wodehouse)
The Merchant of Venice –
William Shakespeare
The Way of the World –
William Congreve

1985
Cavalcade –
Noël Coward
Antony and Cleopatra –
William Shakespeare
The Philanthropist –
Christopher Hampton
The Scarlet Pimpernel –
book by Baroness Orczy
(revised by Beverley Cross)

1986
Annie Get Your Gun –
music & lyrics by
Irving Berlin
(book by Herbert
& Dorothy Fields)
The Chalk Garden –
Enid Bagnold
The Relapse –
Sir John Vanbrugh
Jane Eyre –
Charlotte Bronte
(adapted for the stage
by Peter Coe)
*A Funny Thing Happened on
the Way to the Forum* –
book by Burt Shevelove
& Larry Gelbart
(music & lyrics by
Stephen Sondheim)

1987
Robert and Elizabeth –
book & lyrics by Ronald Millar
(music by Ron Grainer)
An Ideal Husband –

Oscar Wilde
A Man for All Seasons –
Robert Bolt
Miranda –
Beverley Cross after
Carlo Goldoni

1988

Hay Fever –
Noël Coward
Major Barbara –
George Bernard Shaw
The Royal Baccarat Scandal –
Royce Ryton
(based on the book by
Michael Havers &
Edward Grayson)
Ring Round the Moon –
Jean Anouilh
(translated by
Christopher Fry)

1989

Victory! –
Patrick Garland
(adapted from *The Dynasts*
by Thomas Hardy)
The Heiress –
Ruth & Augustus Goetz
London Assurance –
Dion Boucicault
A Little Night Music –
music & lyrics
Stephen Sondheim
(book by
Hugh Wheeler)

The 1990s

1990

The Merry Wives of Windsor
William Shakespeare
The Power and the Glory –

from the novel by
Graham Greene, adapted
by Denis Cannan
The Silver King –
Henry Arthur Jones &
Henry Herman
Rumours –
Neil Simon
Born Again –
music by Jason Carr,
libretto by Julian Barry
& Peter Hall
(based on the play
Rhinoceros by
Eugene Ionesco)

1991

Arsenic and Old Lace –
Joseph Kesselring
Henry VIII or *All is True* –
William Shakespeare
& John Fletcher
Tovarich –
Jacques Deval
(English version by
Anthony Wood)
Preserving Mr Panmure –
Arthur Wing Pinero

1992

Coriolanus –
William Shakespeare
Venus Observed –
Christopher Fry
King Lear in New York –
Melvyn Bragg
She Stoops to Conquer –
Oliver Goldsmith

1993

Getting Married –
George Bernard Shaw
Relative Values –

Noël Coward
Pickwick –
based on Charles *Dicken's
Posthumous Papers
of the Pickwick Club*
(book by Wolf Mankowitz,
lyrics by Leslie Bricusse,
music by Cyril Ornadel)
The Matchmaker –
Thornton Wilder

1994

The Rivals –
Richard Brinsley Sheridan
Pygmalion –
George Bernard Shaw
The Schoolmistress –
Arthur Wing Pinero
Noël/Cole: Let's Do It! -
a Celebration of the
Works of Noël Coward
& Cole Porter compiled
by David Kernan, written
by Robin Ray &
Dick Vosburgh

1995

Hadrian VII –
Peter Luke
(based on *Hadrian the
Seventh* & other works by
Frederick Rolfe)
Hobson's Choice –
Harold Brighouse
The School for Scandal –
Richard Brinsley Sheridan
The Miser –
Molière
(new version by Ranjit Bolt)
The Visit –
Friedrich Dürrenmatt
(adapted by
Maurice Valency)

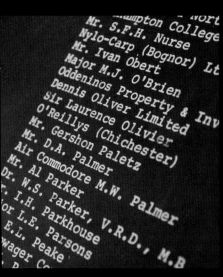

1996

Love for Love –
William Congreve
Mansfield Park –
Jane Austen
(adapted by Willis Hall)
Beethoven's Tenth –
Peter Ustinov
When We Are Married –
J B Priestley
Fortune's Fool –
Ivan Turgenev (adapted
by Mike Poulton)
Lock Up Your Daughters –
adapted by Bernard Miles
from Henry Fielding's
comedy (music by
Laurie Johnson, lyrics
by Lionel Hart)

1997

The Admirable Crichton –
J M Barrie
Lady Windermere's Fan –
Oscar Wilde
Blithe Spirit –
Noël Coward
Divorce Me, Darling! –
Sandy Wilson
Our Betters –
W Somerset Maugham
The Magistrate –
Arthur Wing Pinero

1998

*Saturday, Sunday …
and Monday* –
Eduardo de Filippo (new
version by Jeremy Sams)
Racing Demon –
David Hare
Chimes at Midnight –
written & adapted by Orson

Welles from Shakespeare
Katherine Howard –
William Nicholson

1999

*The Importance
of Being Earnest* –
Oscar Wilde
Semi-Detached –
David Turner
Easy Virtue –
Noël Coward
*The Man Who Came
to Dinner* –
Moss Hart &
George S Kaufman

The 2000s

2000

The Recruiting Officer –
George Farquhar
Heartbreak House –
George Bernard Shaw
A Small Family Business –
Alan Ayckbourn
Arcadia –
Tom Stoppard

2001

On the Razzle –
Tom Stoppard (adapted
from *Einen Jux Will Er Sich
Machen* Johann Nestroy)
The Winslow Boy –
Terence Rattigan
My One & Only –
music & lyrics by George
& Ira Gershwin (book Peter
Stone & Timothy S Mayer)
Three Sisters –
a version of Anton Chekhov's
play by Brian Friel

2002

The Front Page –
Ben Hecht & Charles
MacArthur
Wild Orchids –
Jean Anouilh (in a
new translation by
Timberlake Wertenbaker)
Cabaret –
book by Joe Masteroff, music
by John Kander, lyrics by
Fred Ebb, based on the play
by John van Druten & stories
by Christopher Isherwood
Romeo and Juliet –
William Shakespeare

2003

The Gondoliers –
book & lyrics by W S Gilbert,
music by Arthur Sullivan
The Merchant of Venice –
William Shakespeare
The Water Babies –
book by Gary Yershon,
lyrics & music by Jason Carr
(based on *The Water Babies*
by Charles Kingsley)
The Seagull –
Anton Chekhov (a new
version by Phyllis Nagy,
based on a literal translation
by Helen Molchanoff)

2004

Out of this World –
music & lyrics Cole Porter,
book by Dwight Taylor
& Reginald Lawrence,
revised by Greg MacKellan
incorporating material by
Howard Ashman and Jeremy
Sams, based on Plautus'

Amphitryon
A Midsummer Night's Dream –
William Shakespeare
Just So –
music by George Stiles, book
& lyrics by Anthony Drewe,
inspired by the stories of
Rudyard Kipling
The Master and Margarita –
Mikhail Bulgakov
(a new adaptation by
Edward Kemp)

2005

*How to Succeed in Business
Without Really Trying* –
music & lyrics Frank Loesser,
book by Abe Burrows,
Jack Weinstock
& Willie Gilbert
Scapino or *The Trickster* –
Les Fourberies de Scapin by
Molière in a new
English translation by
Jeremy Sams
The Government Inspector –
Nikolai Gogol
(a new English version by
Alistair Beaton)
5/11 –
Edward Kemp

2006

Entertaining Angels –
Richard Everett
Carousel –
music Richard Rodgers
& lyrics Oscar Hammerstein,
based on the play *Liliom*
by Ferenc Molnar,
adapted by Benjamin
F Glaser
The Life and Adventures of

Nicholas Nickleby –
Charles Dickens
(adapted for the stage in
two parts by David Edgar,
music & lyrics by
Stephen Oliver)
Pravda –
Howard Brenton
& David Hare

2007

The Last Confession –
Roger Crane
Babes in Arms –
music by Richard Rodgers,
lyrics by Lorenz Hart,
book by George
Oppenheimer based
on the original by
Rodgers & Hart, adapted
by Martin Connor
Twelfth Night –
William Shakespeare
Hobson's Choice –
Harold Brighouse
*The Life and Adventures of
Nicholas Nickleby* –
Charles Dickens
(adapted for the stage in
two parts by David Edgar,
music & lyrics by
Stephen Oliver)

2008

The Cherry Orchard –
Anton Chekhov
(version by
Mike Poulton)
The Music Man –
books, music & lyrics
by Meredith Willson,
story by Meredith Willson
& Franklin Lacey

The Circle –
W Somerset Maugham
Calendar Girls –
Tim Firth

2009

Hay Fever –
Noël Coward
Cyrano de Bergerac –
Edmond de Rostand
(translated & adapted by
Anthony Burgess)
Oklahoma! –
music by Richard Rodgers,
book & lyrics by Oscar
Hammerstein II, based
on Lynn Rigg's *Green Grow
the Lilacs*, original dances
by Agnes de Mille)
The Grapes of Wrath –
adapted by Frank Gelati,
based on the novel by
John Steinbeck
Separate Tables –
Terence Rattigan

2010

Yes, Prime Minister –
Antony Jay &
Jonathan Lynn
42nd Street –
music by Harry Warren,
yrics by Hal Dubin,
book by Michael Stewart &
Mark Bramble, based on the
novel by Bradford Ropes
Pygmalion –
George Bernard Shaw
ENRON –
Lucy Prebble
A Month in the Country –
Ivan Turgenev
(adapted by Brian Friel)

2011

*Rosencrantz and
Guildenstern Are Dead* –
Tom Stoppard
Singin' in the Rain –
based on the MGM
film screenplay, adaptation
by Betty Comden &
Aldoph Green, songs
by Nacio Herb Brown
& Arthur Freed
The Deep Blue Sea –
Terence Rattigan
Rattigan's Nijinsky –
Nicholas Wright, based
on a screenplay by
Terence Rattigan
*Sweeney Todd: The Demon
Barber of Fleet Street:* –
music & lyrics Stephen
Sondheim, book by
Hugh Wheeler, from
an adaptation by
Harold Prince, original
orchestrations by
Jonathan Tunick

2012

The Way of the World –
William Congreve
*A Marvellous Year
for Plums*
Hugh Whitemore
Kiss Me Kate –
music & lyrics Cole
Porter, book by Sam &
Bella Spewack, based on
Shakespeare's
The Taming of the Shrew
Heartbreak House –
George Bernard Shaw
Antony and Cleopatra –
William Shakespeare

Minerva Festival Productions 1989 - 2012

Although the Minerva has only been open for twenty-two years – as against the Festival Theatre's fifty – the volume of work, one-off performances, charity galas, late-night revue shows, Sunday concerts, platform events, 'solo' events means we don't have the pages available to list everything. We have therefore only been able to list plays presented in the summer festival seasons, though again a comprehensive list appears on the CFT website, as well as community plays and youth theatre productions. On two occasions, the Minerva has had its own Artistic Director – Sam Mendes in 1989 and Caroline Sharman in 1991 – otherwise the Minerva has come under the auspices of the Artistic/Theatre Director of CFT. We have put full creative and backstage teams on the CFT website.

1989

Summerfolk –
Maxim Gorky
(in a version by Botho
Strauss & Peter Stein,
translated by
Michael Robinson)
Culture Vultures –
Robin Glendinning
Warrior –
Shirley Gee
The Triumph of Love –
Marivaux (translated
by Guy Callan)
Cloud Nine –
Caryl Churchill
Love's Labour's Lost –
William Shakespeare
The Purity Game –
Gillian Plowman
(music by Corin Buckeridge,
lyrics by Will Cohu)
War and Peaces –
a revue devised by Will
Cohu & Stefan Bednarczyk

1990

Thérèse Raquin –
Emile Zola
(translated by
Nicholas Wright)
Eurydice –
Jean Anouilh
(translated by Peter Meyer)
70, Girls, 70 –
book by David Thompson
& Norman L Martin,
music by John Kander,
lyrics by Fred Ebb,
based on *Breath of Spring*
by Peter Cole, adapted by
Joe Masteroff
My Mother Said I –

Never Should –
Charlotte Keatley
Scenes from a Marriage –
Ingmar Bergman
(translated by Alan Blair)

1991

Pont Valaine –
Noel Coward
The Sisterhood –
Molière
(translated & adapted
by Ranjit Bolt)
Valentine's Day –
book adapted by
Benny Green &
David William, lyrics by
Benny Green, music
by Denis King
Adam Was a Gardener –
Louise Page
Talking Heads –
Alan Bennett

1992

Me and My Friend –
Gilliam Plowman
Double Take –
Deborah Moggach
Vita and Virginia –
Eileen Atkins
(adapted from the
correspondence between
Virginia Woolf
& Vita Sackville-West)

1993

Carrington –
Jane Beeson
Rope –
Patrick Hamilton
Elvira '40 –
Brigitte Jacques

(English version by
David Edney)

1994

A Doll's House –
Henrik Ibsen
(new version
by Christopher Hampton)
Dangerous Corner –
J B Priestley
Three Sisters –
Anton Chekhov
(translated by
Michael Henry Heim)

1995

Taking Sides –
Ronald Harwood
A Word from Our Sponsor –
Alan Ayckbourn
(music by John Pattison)
Playing the Wife –
Ronald Hayman
The Hothouse –
Harold Pinter
Monsieur Amilcar –
Yves Jamiaque
(adapted by George Gonneau
& Norman Rose)

1996

Simply Disonnected –
Simon Gray
Talking Heads –
Alan Bennett
Uncle Vanya –
Anton Chekhov
(English version by
Mike Poulton)
Hedda Gabler –
Henrik Ibsen
(adapted by Helen Cooper)
Beatrix –

adapted from the writings
of Beatrix Potter by
Patrick Garland &
Judy Taylor
The Handyman –
Ronald Harwood
It Could Be Any One of Us –
Alan Ayckbourn
Educating Rita –
Willy Russell
Oleanna –
David Mamet
*Whom Do I Have the
Honour of Addressing?* –
Peter Shaffer

1997

After October –
Rodney Ackland
Nocturne for Lovers –
Bruno Villien
(English version by
Gavin Lambert)
Tallulah! –
Sandra Ryan Heyward
Suzanna Adler –
Marguerite Duras
(translated by Barbara Bray)
Misalliance –
George Bernard Shaw
Electra –
Sophocles
(in a new version by
Frank McGuinness)

1998

Loot –
Joe Orton
Song of Singapore –
book by Alan Katz,
Erik Frandsen, Robert
Hipkens, Michael Garin
& Paula Lockheart,

music & lyrics by Erik
Frandsen, Robert Hipkens,
Michael Garin &
Paula Lockheart
The Glass Menagerie –
Tennesse Williams

1999
The King of Prussia –
Nick Darke
Insignificance –
Terry Johnson
Nymph Errant –
music & lyrics Cole Porter,
book by Steve Mackes
& Michael Whaley,
based on the novel by
James Laver
The School of Night –
Peter Whelan
The Retreat from Moscow –
William Nicholson

2000
The Sea –
Edward Bond
The Blue Room –
freely adapted from Arthur
Schnitzler's *La Ronde* by
David Hare
Pal Joey –
music by Richard Rodgers,
lyrics by Lorenz Hart,
book by John O'Hara,
based on his series of short
stories in the *New Yorker*
Aristocrats –
Brian Friel
Hysteria –
Terry Johnson

2001
Song of Singapore –

book by Alan Katz,
Erik Frandsen, Robert
Hipkens, Michael Garin
& Paula Lockheart,
music & lyrics by Erik
Frandsen, Robert Hipkens,
Michael Garin & Paula
Lockheart
Shang-a-Lang –
Catherine Johnson
In Celebration –
David Storey
The Secret Rapture –
David Hare
Putting it Together –
a musical revue by
Stephen Sondheim

2002
*The Lady's Not
for Burning* –
Christopher Fry
Up On the Roof –
Simon Moore & Jane Prowse
Blunt Speaking –
Corin Redgrave
Song of the Western Men –
Christopher William Hill
Dead Funny –
Terry Johnson

2003
Nathan the Wise –
Gotthold Lessing
(in a new version by
Edward Kemp)
Holes in the Skin –
Robert Holman
The Coffee House –
Rainer Werner Fassbinder
(after *La Bottega del
Caffé* by Goldoni, translated
by Jeremy Sams)

*I Caught My Death
in Venice*
Martin Marquez &
John Marquez

2004
*Three Women and
a Piano Tuner* –
Helen Cooper
Seven Doors –
Botho Straus
(translated by
Jeremy Sams)
Cruel and Tender –
Martin Crimp
(after Sophocles' *Women
of Trachis*)
Doctor Faustus –
Christopher Marlowe

2005
King Lear –
William Shakespeare
Six Pictures of Lee Miller –
music & lyrics by
Jason Carr, book by
Edward Kemp, inspired
by *The Lives of Lee Miller*
by Antony Penrose
The Scarlet Letter –
Phyllis Nagy
(adapted from the
novel by Nathaniel
Hawthorne)

2006
In Praise of Love –
Terence Rattigan
Tonight at 8.30 –
Noël Coward
The Father –
August Strindberg
(adapted by Mike Poulton)

2007
Office Suite –
Alan Bennett
Macbeth –
William Shakespeare
The Waltz of the Toreadors –
Jean Anouilh
(translated by Ranjit Bolt)
I Am Shakespeare –
conceived & written
by Mark Rylance

2008
Funny Girl –
music by Julie Styne,
lyrics by Bob Merrill,
book by Isobel Lennart
Collaboration –
Ronald Harwood
Taking Sides –
Ronald Harwood
*Six Characters in
Search of An Author* –
Luigi Pirandello
(in a new version by
Rupert Goold & Ben Power)
Aristo –
Martin Sherman

2009
The Last Cigarette –
adapted from Simon Gray's
The Smoking Room
by Simon Gray
& Hugh Whitemore
Taking Sides –
Ronald Harwood
Collaboration –
Ronald Harwood
Wallenstein –
Friedrich Schiller
(adapted by Mike Poulton)
The House of Special

Purpose –
Heidi Thomas
ENRON –
Lucy Prebble

2010
Bingo –
Edward Bond
Love Story –
Erich Segal, music composed
by Howard Goodall,
bookby Stephen Clark,
lyrics by Stephen Clark
& Howard Goodall
The Critic –
Richard Brinsley Sherridan
The Real Inspector Hound –
Tom Stoppard
*The Ragged Trousered
Philanthropists* –
Robert Tressell
(a new
adaptation by
Howard Brenton)
The Master Builder –
Henrik Ibsen
(a new adaptation by
David Edgar)

2011
She Loves Me –
book by Joe Masteroff,
music by Jerry Bock,
lyrics by Sheldon Harnick,
based on a play by
Miklos Laszlo
Top Girls –
Caryl Churchill
The Syndicate –
by Eduardo de Filippo
(new English version
by Mike Poulton)
South Downs –

David Hare
The Browning Version –
Terrence Rattigan

2012
Uncle Vanya –
Anton Chekhov
(new translation by
Michael Frayn)
Canvass –
Michael Wynne
*The Resistible Rise
of Arturo Ui* –
Bertolt Brecht
(in a translation by
George Tabori
Surprises –
Alan Ayckbourn
Absurd Person Singular –
Alan Ayckbourn
Private Lives –
Noël Coward

Community Productions
Cavalcade –
Chichester & Festival
Theatre (1985)
The Spershott Version –
Chichester (1986)
Victory! –
Chichester & Festival
Theatre (1989)
The Barchester Chronicles –
Festival Theatre (2000)
The Devil's Dancing Hour –
Festival Theatre (2002)
Doctor Faustus –
Chichester Cathedral (2004)

Youth Theatre Productions

CFYT is now one of the
most thriving, most
respected, youth
companies in the country,
with some 600 young
people and some 500 on
the waiting list. From the
earliest days performing
in The Tent to being
responsible for the Main
House Christmas Show
since 2003, CFYT has
appeared at the Minerva
Theatre, Havant Arts
Centre, the National
Theatre and the Festival
Theatre, taken part in
competitions such as
the National Theatre
Connections and the
Shakespeare Schools
Festival, at the Brighton
and Edinburgh Festivals,
as well as undertaking
promenade performances in
a range of venues including
Chichester Cathedral; the
Bishop's Palace Gardens;
St Cuthman's School,
Midhurst; Goodwood Estate;
Rolls-Royce Motor Cars at
Goodwood; and the Weald
& Downland Open Air
Museum, Singleton.
Sadly, once again because
of limited space, we cannot
list all the productions here.
A comprehensive list of
productions 1993 - 2012
appears on the CFT website,
www.cft.org.uk

Photograph credits

We are very grateful to all the photographers and picture libraries who have allowed us to reproduce their work in this book. These beautiful images play a vital part in retelling the Chichester Festival Theatre story and without their time and support the book would be much the poorer.

However, in spite of our best endeavours to trace copyright holders, the Chichester Festival Theatre archive does have a few gaps and there are some production photos without credits. Where these photographs have been used, we have marked them as Photo: Unknown. We would like to rectify this in any further printings, so Chichester Festival Theatre would be very grateful for any information helping us to identify photographs and credits. Please contact us via the website www.cft.org.uk or email photo@cft.org.uk.

Numbers refer to pages

Endpapers show a selection of programmes and telegrams. Evershed-Martin Family archive and other collections

Front Cover, back cover and all part title mages Lee Hind, 2012 ©Chichester Festival Theatre Archive.

Singin' in the Rain, 2011. Photo: Manuel Harlan Chichester Festival Theatre, 1962. Reproduced by permission of English Heritage.
Richard McCabe, Derek Griffiths and Nicholas Le Prevost in *The Critic*, 2010. Photo: Manuel Harlan

Interviews

Rex Harrison in *Monsieur Perrichon's Travels*, 1976. Photo: Zoë Dominic

Acknowledgements

P1 John Standing and Sarah Badel in *The Farmer's Wife*, 1967. Photo: John Timbers/ ArenaPAL
P2 *42nd Street*, 2010. Photo: Johan Persson Committee in session, Arundel Castle Ball programme, May 1961. West Sussex Record Office
P3 Penelope Keith in *Entertaining Angels*, 2006. Photo: Robert Day

Foreword

P4 Joan Plowright and Laurence Olivier at the Chichester Festival Theatre Thanksgiving Service, June 3 1962. Photo: Chichester Photographic Collection/West Sussex Record Office
P6 Arundel Castle Ball programme, May 1961. West Sussex Record Office
Joan Plowright in *Saint Joan*, 1963. Angus McBean Photograph (MS THR 581.) © Harvard Theatre Collection, Houghton Library, Harvard University
P7 Joan Plowright and Laurence Olivier in *Uncle Vanya*, 1962. Angus McBean Photograph (MS THR 581.) © Harvard Theatre Collection, Houghton Library, Harvard University
Joan Plowright and Anthony Hopkins in *The Taming of the Shrew*, 1972. Photo: John Timbers/ ArenaPAL

Introduction

P8 Chichester Festival Theatre Foyer, 1975. Photo: Sam Lambert. Architectural Press Archive / RIBA Library Photographs Collection
P10 Joss Ackland and Susannah Wise in *Heartbreak House*, 2000. Photo: Clive Barda/ ArenaPAL
Hannah Yelland and Daniel Weyman in *Nicholas Nickleby Part 2*, 2006. Photo: Robert Day
P11 Set design for 'Scott Writes' *Terra Nova*, 1980. © Designer: Pamela Howard
P12 Michele Dotrice and Jeanette Sterke in *Twelfth Night*, 1976. Photo: Anthony Crickmay/Victoria and Albert Museum, London. Courtesy of Keith and Jeanette Michell
P13 Issy van Randwyck in *Song of Singapore*, 1998. Photo: Nigel Norrington/ArenaPAL

The Story Begins

P14 Andre Morell and Joan Greenwood, Tatler, 4 July 1962. Tatler/ Mary Evans Picture Library
P16 The Theatre Shop by the Cross, Arundel Castle Ball programme, May 1961. West Sussex Record Office
David and Sophie Shalit, 1960. Courtesy of

Mr and Mrs Shalit
P17 The roof structure being built, winter 1961. West Sussex Record Office/Chichester Photographic Collection
P18 Princess Alexandra performs Stone Laying Ceremony, May 12 1961. Evening Argus, Brighton/ West Sussex Record Office
Vivien Leigh at Mason's, Pulborough fundraising event, 1961. Courtesy of Evershed-Martin Family archive
P19 Minerva, a symbol for the Theatre. Arundel Castle Ball programme, May 1961. West Sussex Record Office
P20 Laurence Olivier at the Topping Out Ceremony, November 1961. Chichester Photographic Collection/West Sussex Record Office
P23 Scenic Artist Vanessa Clarke flat out after hectic last minute preparations. Tatler, 4 July 1962. Courtesy of Tatler/ Mary Evans Picture Library
P24 Chichester Photographic Collection/West Sussex Record Office
P25 VIP guests leaving Gunter's for the First Night performance, 3 July 1962. Chichester Photographic Collection/West Sussex Record Office

The 1960s

P26 Laurence Olivier directing *The Chances*, 1962. Angus McBean Photograph (MS THR 581) © Harvard Theatre Collection, Houghton Library, Harvard University
P28 Keith Michell in *The Broken Heart*, 1962. Angus McBean Photograph (MS THR 581.) © Harvard Theatre Collection, Houghton Library, Harvard University. Duncan Weldon collection
P29 Courtesy of The News, Portsmouth, 4 July 1962/West Sussex Record Office
P30 *Uncle Vanya* company and theatre staff, July 1962. Angus McBean Photograph (MS THR 581.) © Harvard Theatre Collection, Houghton Library, Harvard University. Duncan Weldon collection
P31 *Uncle Vanya*, July 1962. Angus McBean Photograph (MS THR 581.) © Harvard Theatre Collection, Houghton Library, Harvard University
Alexander Hanson, Timothy West, Roger Allam, Dervla Kirwan, Maggie Steed, Lara Pulver and Anthony O'Donnell in Uncle Vanya, 2012. Photo: Johan Persson
P32 *Saint Joan* costume swatches 1963. Designer: Michael Annals/National Theatre Archive
Michael Billington. Photo courtesy of the Guardian
P33 Joan Plowright in *Saint Joan*, 1963. Angus McBean Photograph (MS THR 581.) © Harvard Theatre Collection, Houghton Library, Harvard University/National Theatre Archive
P34 Joan Plowright in *Saint Joan*, 1963. Angus McBean Photograph (MS THR 581.) © Harvard Theatre Collection, Houghton Library, Harvard University/National Theatre Archive
P35 *The Workhouse Donkey*, 1963. Angus McBean Photograph (MS THR 581.) © Harvard Theatre Collection, Houghton Library, Harvard University
P37 *The Royal Hunt of the Sun*, 1964. Angus McBean Photograph (MS THR 581.) © Harvard Theatre Collection, Houghton Library, Harvard University
P38 Robert Stephens in *The Royal Hunt of the Sun*, 1964. Photo: Chris Arthur/National Theatre Archive
P39 Laurence Olivier removing his makeup after a performance of *Othello*, 1964. Photo: Gareth McDowell/National Theatre Archive
P40 Laurence Olivier, *Othello*, 1964. Angus McBean Photograph (MS THR 581.) © Harvard Theatre Collection, Houghton Library, Harvard University/ National Theatre Archive
Frank Finlay and Laurence Olivier, *Othello*, 1964.

Angus McBean Photograph (MS THR 581.) © Harvard Theatre Collection, Houghton Library, Harvard University/ National Theatre Archive
P41 Courtesy of The News, Portsmouth, 28 July 1964/West Sussex Record Office
Maggie Smith in *Black Comedy*, 1965. Angus McBean Photograph (MS THR 581.) © Harvard Theatre Collection, Houghton Library, Harvard University
P42 Maggie Smith and Jeanne Watts in *Miss Julie*, 1965. Angus McBean Photograph (MS THR 581.) © Harvard Theatre Collection, Houghton Library, Harvard University/ National Theatre Archive
Albert Finney and Derek Jacobi in *Black Comedy*, 1965. Angus McBean Photograph (MS THR 581.) © Harvard Theatre Collection, Houghton Library, Harvard University
P43 Alastair Sim and Margaret Rutherford rehearsing a scene from *The Clandestine Marriage*, 1966. Photo: Zoë Dominic
P44 Celia Johnson (seated centre) in *The Cherry Orchard*, 1966. Photo: Zoë Dominic
P45 John Clements and Margaret Johnston in *Macbeth*, 1966. Photo: Zoë Dominic
Patrick Stewart and Kate Fleetwood in *Macbeth*, 2007. Photo: Manuel Harlan
P46 Courtesy of the The News, Portsmouth, 29 August 1966/Evershed-Martin Family archive
Ben Kingsley as 1st Murderer (left) *Macbeth*, 1966. Photo: Zoë Dominic
P47 Michael Aldridge, Irene Handl and Bill Fraser at the 1967 press launch of *The Farmer's Wife*. Photo: Zoë Dominic
P48 *An Italian Straw Hat*, 1967. Photo: Zoë Dominic
P49 Simon Ward and Prunella Scales in *The Unknown Soldier and His Wife*, 1968. Photo: John Timbers/ArenaPAL
Alec Guinness and Eileen Atkins in *The Cocktail Party*, 1968. Photo: John Timbers/ArenaPAL
P50 Topol in *The Caucasian Chalk Circle*, 1969. Photo: John Timbers/ArenaPAL
P51 Maggie Smith in *The Country Wife*, 1969. Photo by John Timbers/ArenaPAL
Alastair Sim and Patricia Routledge in T*he Magistrate*, 1969. Photo: John Timbers/ArenaPAL
John Clements and Margaret Leighton in *Antony and Cleopatra*, 1969. Photo: John Timbers/ ArenaPAL

The 1970s

P53 Sarah Miles and Eileen Atkins in *Vivat! Vivat Regina!* 1970. Photo: John Timbers/ArenaPAL
P54 John Clements. Courtesy of The News, Portsmouth, 13 May 1970/West Sussex Record Office
P55 Princess Margaret in bomb scare. The Argus, Brighton 13 May 1971/West Sussex Record Office
P56 John Gielgud in Caesar *and Cleopatra*, 1971. Photo: John Timbers/ArenaPAL
P57 Edith Evans in *Dear Antoine*, 1971. Photo: John Timbers/ArenaPAL
P58 Joan Plowright and Robin Phillips in *The Doctor's Dilemma*, 1972. Photo: John Timbers/ ArenaPAL
P59 Richard Chamberlain and Michael Aldridge in *The Lady's Not For Burning*, 1972. Photo: John Timbers/ArenaPAL
Millicent Martin, Maggie Fitzgibbon and Harold Innocent in *The Beggar's Opera*, 1972. Photo: John Timbers/ArenaPAL
P60 Topol (centre) in *R Loves J*, 1973. Photo: John Timbers/ArenaPAL
P61 John Clements in *The Director of the Opera*, 1973. Photo: John Timbers/ArenaPAL
P62 Patricia Routledge and Alastair Sim in *Dandy Dick*, 1973. Photo: John Timbers/ArenaPAL
P63 The News, Portsmouth, 20 November 1973/

West Sussex Record Office
Leslie and Carol Evershed-Martin. Courtesy of the Evershed-Martin Family Archive
Keith Michell and John Clements at Chichester Festival Theatre, 1973. Courtesy of Keith and Jeanette Michell
Keith and Jeanette Michell and their children Helena and Paul, Funtington, 1970s. Courtesy of Keith and Jeanette Michell
P64 Press launch of 1974 Festival Season. Photo: CFT
P65 *Tonight We Improvise*, 1974: Photo: John Timbers/ArenaPAL
In rehearsal for *Six Characters in Search of An Author*, 2008. Photo: Manuel Harlan
P66 *The Argus*, Brighton. 27 December 1974/ West Sussex Record Office
P67 *Oedipus Tyrannus*, 1974. Photo: Mark Gudgeon
P68 Keith Michell preparing for *Cyrano de Bergerac*, 1975. Photo courtesy of Keith Michell
P70 *Cyrano de Bergerac*, 1975. Photo: Zoë Dominic
P71 Donald Sinden and Barbara Jefford in *An Enemy of the People*, 1975. Photo: John Timbers/ArenaPAL
Joseph Fiennes (centre) in *Cyrano de Bergerac*, 2009. Photo: Catherine Ashmore
P72 Hannah Gordon and Topol in *Othello*, 1975. Photo: John Haynes/Lebrecht Music and Arts
P73 Hannah Gordon and Patricia Routledge in *Othello*, 1975. Photo: John Haynes/Lebrecht Music and Arts
P75 Rex Harrison and Tony Robinson in *Monsieur Perrichon's Travels*, 1976. Photo: Zoë Dominic
P76 Ingrid Bergman in *Waters of the Moon*, 1977. Photo: Zoë Dominic
P77 Keith Michell and Penelope Keith in *The Apple Cart*, 1977. Photo: John Timbers/ ArenaPAL
P78 Paul Rogerson welcomes Princess Alexandra to Chichester Festival Theatre, Sunday 12 June 1977. Photo: CFT
Penelope Keith in *The Apple Cart*, 1977. Photo: John Timbers/ArenaPAL
P79 *Murder in the Cathedral*, 1977. Photo: not known/West Sussex Record Office
P80 Clive Francis, Geraldine McEwan and Fenella Fielding in *Look After Lulu*, 1978. Photo: John Timbers/ArenaPAL
P82 John Clements, Christine McKenna, Ian Ogilvy and Brian Blessed in *The Devil's Disciple*, 1979. Photo: John Timbers/ArenaPAL

The 1980s

P84 Joan Collins in *The Last of Mrs Cheyney*, 1980. Photo: John Timbers/ArenaPAL
P85 Stage crew in the dock, *Terra Nova*, 1980. Photo: Andy Neal
P87 Peter Birch, Benjamin Whitrow, Hywel Bennett, Christopher Neame, David Wood and Martin Sadler in *Terra Nova*, 1980. Photo: Zoë Dominic
P88 Patricia Hodge and Christopher Timothy launching 1981 Festival Season at The Millstream Hotel, Bosham. Photo: Chichester Observer
Gemma Jones, Briony McRoberts, Jessica Turner and Alexa Provah in *Much Ado about Nothing*, 1980. Photo: Sophie Baker
P89 Charlotte Riley, Diana Rigg and Jemma Redgrave in *The Cherry Orchard*, 2008. Photo: Manuel Harlan
Claire Bloom in *The Cherry Orchard*. 1981. Photo: Zoë Dominic
P90 Jeremy Anthony, Stephen Bone, Jonathon Morris, Gary Fairhall and Tom Baker in *Feasting with Panthers*, 1981. Photo: Reg Wilson/ *The Mitford Girls*, 1981. Photo: Patrick Lichfield.

P91 Linda Williams, Rachel Izen, Annette Lyons and Amanda Holmes in *Underneath the Arches*, 1981. Photo: Reg Wilson/Rex Features
Stage Crew blowing up balloons for *Underneath the Arches*, 1981. Photo: Andy Neal
P92 Christopher Timothy and Roy Hudd in *Underneath the Arches*, 1981. Photo: Reg Wilson/Rex Features
The Crazy Gang. West Sussex Gazette, July 1981/ West Sussex Record Office
P93 Festival Season launch, 1982. All photos: CFT
P94 Joan Plowright and Dulcie Gray in *Cavell*, 1982. Photo: Reg Wilson/Rex Features
Bertice Reading in *Valmouth*, 1982. Photo: Zoë Dominic
P95 Colette Gleeson and John Mills in *Goodbye Mr Chips*, 1982. Photo: Reg Wilson/Rex Features
John Mills and Nigel Stock in *Goodbye Mr Chips*, 1982. Photo: Reg Wilson/Rex Features
P96 Michael G Jones, Jonathon Morris, Patricia Hodge and Lucy Fleming in *As You Like It*, 1983. Photo: Reg Wilson/Rex Features
P97 Omar Sharif and Debbie Arnold in *The Sleeping Prince*, 1983. Photo: Reg Wilson/ Rex Features
P98 David Yelland and Alan Bates in *A Patriot for Me*, 1983. Photo: Reg Wilson/Rex Features
The Drag Ball, *A Patriot for Me*, 1983. Photo: Reg Wilson/Rex Features
P99 Bognor Regis Post, 13 August 1983. West Sussex Record Office
Jonathon Morris directs *Final Furlong* in rehearsal in The Tent, 1983. Photo: Diane Goodman
P100 Paul Eddington in *Forty Years On*, 1984. Photo: Reg Wilson/Rex Features
Forty Years On, 1984. Photo: Reg Wilson/ Rex Features
Stephen Fry in *Forty Years On*, 1984. Photo: Reg Wilson/Rex Features
P102 Alec Guinness in *The Merchant of Venice*, 1984. Photo: Stephen MacMillan
P103 *The Scarlet Pimpernel*, 1985. Photo: Reg Wilson/Rex Features
P104 *Cavalcade*, 1985. Photo: John Haynes/ Lebrecht Music and Arts
Joanna McCallum and Simon Chandler with Alastair Brett in *Cavalcade*, 1985. Photo: John Haynes/ Lebrecht Music and Arts
P105 Donald Sinden and Joanna McCallum in *The Scarlet Pimpernel*, 1985. Photo: Reg Wilson/ Rex Features
P106 *Peter Pan*, 2006. Photo: Mike Eddowes
Chichester Festival Youth Theatre performing *Ragged Streets*, 1985. Photographer: Unknown
Celia Imrie and Edward Fox in *The Philanthropist*, 1985. Photo: Reg Wilson/Rex Features
P107 Frankie Howerd in *A Funny Thing Happened on the Way to the Forum*, 1986. Photo: Reg Wilson/Rex Features
Sophie Thompson and Dorothy Tutin in *The Chalk Garden*, 1986. Photo: Reg Wilson/Rex Features
P108 Richard Briers in *The Relapse*, 1986. Photo: Reg Wilson/Rex Features
Lucy Briers and Catherine McCormack in *Top Girls*, 2011. Photo: John Haynes/Lebrecht Music and Arts
Keith Michell and Jenny Seagrove in *Jane Eyre*, 1986. Photo: Reg Wilson/Rex Features
P109 Tony Britton and Gordon Chater in *A Man for All Seasons*, 1987. Photo: Reg Wilson/ Rex Features
Roy Kinnear in *A Man for All Seasons*, 1987. Photo: Reg Wilson/Rex Features
P110 Joanna Lumley and June Whitfield in *An Ideal Husband*, 1987. Photo: Reg Wilson/Rex Features
P113 CFT Cricket Team, 1985. Courtesy of Jeannie Brook Barnett
Sam Mendes, Bill Bray and Patrick Mirams at CFT cricket match, 1988. Photo: Amanda Mirams
P114 Keith Michell, Jeanette Sterke and Gerald

Harper in *The Royal Baccarat Scandal*, 1988. Photo: Reg Wilson/Rex Features
P115 Googie Withers and Ruth Hudson in *Hay Fever*, 1988. Photo: Reg Wilson/Rex Features
Minerva Theatre being built, 1988. Photo: Amanda Mirams
The Tent repositioned behind the administration block 1988. Photo: Amanda Mirams
P116 Tom Hollander in *Cloud Nine*, 1989. Photo: Paul Carter
P117 *Summerfolk* company , 1989. Photo: Amanda Mirams
Sam Graham in *Love's Labour's Lost*, 1989. Photo: Paul Carter P118 *A Little Night Music*, 1989. Photo: Michael Le Poer Trench
P119 James Bolam in *Victory!* 1989. Photo: Reg Wilson/Rex Features
James Bolam on horseback in *Victory!* during the promenade to CFT, 1989. Photo: Janet Capelin
Phyllis Calvert and Nichola McAuliffe in *The Heiress*, 1989. Photo: Reg Wilson/Rex Features
P120 The Founder and former and current Artistic Directors, 1989. Photo: CFT
P121 Paul Eddington in *London Assurance*, 1989. Photo: Reg Wilson/Rex Features

The 1990s

P122 *Born Again*, 1990: Poster, copyright and courtesy of Gerald Scarfe
P124 Simon Ward and Hilary Drake in *Rumours*, 1990. Photo: John Haynes/Lebrecht Music and Arts
P125 Phyllida Law, Bill Maynard and Penelope Keith in *The Merry Wives of Windsor*, 1990. Photo: John Haynes/Lebrecht Music and Arts
Alan Howard and Penny Downie in *Scenes from a Marriage*, 1990. Photo: Paul Carter
P126 Mandy Patinkin in *Born Again*, 1990. Photo: John Haynes/Lebrecht Music and Arts
P127 Peter Davison and Elizabeth Spriggs in *Arsenic and Old Lace*, 1991. Photo: Simon Annand
Sharon Maughan and Simon Dormandy in *Adam was a Gardener*, 1991. Photo: John Harding
P128 Keith Michell and Tony Britton in *Henry VIII*, 1991. Photo: Robert Workman
P129 Robert Hands, Gemma Lowy, Fiona Fullerton and Judy Parfitt in *Valentine's Day*, 1991. Photo: John Haynes/Lebrecht Music and Arts
Preserving Mr Panmure, 1991. Photo: John Haynes/Lebrecht Music and Arts
P130 Maggie Smith in *Bed Among the Lentils*: *Talking Heads*, 1991. Photo: John Timbers/ ArenaPAL
Alan Bennett, Maggie Smith and Margaret Tyzack, *Talking Heads*, 1991: Photo: John Timbers/ ArenaPAL
P131 Natalia Markova and Robert Powell in *Tovarich*, 1990. Photo: John Haynes/Lebrecht Music and Arts
Natalia Markova in *Tovarich*, 1990. Photo: John Haynes/Lebrecht Music and Arts
P132 Judi Dench and Richard Briers in *Coriolanus*, 1992. Photo: Richard H. Smith
P133 Kenneth Branagh in *Coriolanus*, 1992. Photo: Richard H. Smith
P134 Eileen Atkins and Penelope Wilton in *Vita and Virginia*, 1992. Photo: John Timbers/ArenaPAL
Jonathon Morris and Tom Hollander in *Me and My Friend*, 1992. Photo: Paul Carter
P135 *King Lear* in New York, 1992. Photo: John Timbers/ArenaPAL.
The cast of *She Stoops to Conquer* raise a toast to Her Majesty on Chichester Festival Theatre's thirtieth anniversary, 1992. Photo: Louise Adams/ Chichester Observer
P136 Tony Britton and Christopher Benjamin in *Getting Married*, 1993. Photo: John Timbers/ ArenaPAL

Prunella Scales in *The Matchmaker*, 1993. Photo: John Timbers/ArenaPAL
P137 Susan Hampshire in *Relative Values*, 1993. Photo: John Timbers/ArenaPAL
Toyah Wilcox in *Carrington*, 1993. Photo: Paul Carter
Anthony Head and John Barrowman in *Rope*, 1993. Photo: John Timbers/ArenaPAL
P139 The cast of *Pickwick*, 1993. Photo: John Timbers/ArenaPAL
P140 Peter McEnery and Sharon Maughan in *A Doll's House*, 1994. Photo: John Timbers/ ArenaPAL
P141 Peter Greenwell, Liz Robertson, David Kernan, Pat Kirkwood, Robin Ray and Louise Gold in *Noël: Cole Let's Do It*, 1994. Photo: John Timbers/ArenaPAL
Peter Bowles and Fiona Fullerton in *Pygmalion*, 1994. Photo: John Timbers/ArenaPAL
Rupert Everett and Honeysuckle Weeks in *Pygmalion*, 2010. Photo: Manuel Harlan
P142 Dulcie Gray and Michael Denison in *The School Mistress*, 1994. Photo: John Timbers/ArenaPAL
P143 Patricia Routledge in *The School Mistress*, 1994. Photo: John Timbers/ArenaPAL
Timothy West and Patricia Routledge in *The Rivals*, 1994. Photo: John Timbers/ArenaPAL
P144 Cartoon of the Board, 1974. Artist: P. Cole. Courtesy of Barbara Mosse
P145 Derek Jacobi in *Playing the Wife*, 1995. Photo: Alastair Muir
Lois Harvey, Penelope Keith and Keith Michell in *Monsieur Amilcar*, 1995. Photo: John Timbers/ArenaPAL
P146 Lauren Bacall and Joss Ackland in *The Visit*, 1995. Photo: Ivan Kyncl/ArenaPAL
Celia Imrie and Harold Pinter and in *The Hothouse*, 1995. Photo: Ivan Kyncl/ArenaPAL
P147 Michael Pennington and Daniel Massey in *Taking Sides*, 1995. Photo: Ivan Kyncl/ArenaPAL
Michael Pennington as Furtwängler in *Taking Sides*, 2008. Photo: Manuel Harlan
P148 Derek Jacobi in *Hadrian VII*, 1995. Photo: Ivan Kyncl/ArenaPAL
P149 Ian Richardson in *The Miser*, 1995. Photo: Ivan Kyncl/ArenaPAL
Leo McKern and Nichola McAuliffe in *Hobson's Choice*, 1995. Photo: John Timbers/ArenaPAL
P150 Dawn French in *When We are Married*, 1996. Photo: Robbie Jack/Corbis
P151 Dawn French, Alison Steadman, Annette Badland and Paul Copley, Gary Waldhorn, Roger Lloyd Pack in *When We Are Married*, 1996. Photo: Robbie Jack
Peter Ustinov and John Neville in *Beethoven's Tenth*, 1996. Photo: John Timbers/ArenaPAL
P152 Gawn Grainger and Alan Bates in *Simply Disconnected*, 1996. Photo: Ivan Kyncl/ArenaPAL
Derek Jacobi in *Uncle Vanya*, 1996. Photo: Nobby Clark /ArenaPAL
P153 Harriet Walter in *Hedda Gabler*, 1996. Photo: Ivan Kyncl/ArenaPAL
Frank Finlay in *The Handyman*, 1996. Photo: John Timbers/ArenaPAL
Edward Kemp, 2004. Photo: Clare Park
P154 Patricia Routledge in *Beatrix*, 1996. Photo: John Timbers/ArenaPAL
Tabitha Wady, Juliet Mills, Jon Strickland, Richard Derrington and Malcolm Rennie in *It Could Be Any One Of Us*, 1996. Photo: Adrian Gatie
P155 Alan Bates and Rachel Pickup in *Fortunes Fool*, 1996. Photo: Ivan Kyncl/ArenaPAL
P156 Kathleen Turner, Leslie Caron, Twiggy and Maureen Lipman at 1997 Festival Season launch. Photo: Ivan Kyncl/ArenaPAL/ Duncan Weldon collection
P157 Zoe Wanamaker in *Electra*, 1997. Photo: Ivan Kyncl/ArenaPAL/Duncan Weldon collection
Julie Christie in *Suzanna Adler*, 1997. Photo: Ivan

Kyncl/ArenaPAL
Stephanie Beecham at 1997 Festival Season launch. Photo: Ivan Kyncl/ArenaPAL/Duncan Weldon collection
P158 Ian McShane and Michael Denison in *The Admirable Crichton*, 1997. Photo: John Timbers/ArenaPAL
Dora Bryan and Twiggy in *Blithe Spirit*, 1997. Photo: John Timbers/ArenaPAL
P159 Rula Lenska and Stephen Billington in *Our Betters*, 1997. Photo: Ivan Kyncl/ArenaPAL
P160 Ruthie Henshall, Ann Sidney and Samantha George in *Divorce Me, Darling!* 1997. Photo: Ivan Kyncl/ArenaPAL
P161 Dorothy Tutin in *After October*, 1997. Photo John Timbers/ArenaPAL
P162 The cast of *Mother Goose*, Christmas 1997. Photo: Chichester Observer
P163 Andrew Welch. Photo: Chichester Observer
Issy van Randwyck in *Song of Singapore*, 1998. Photo: Nigel Norrington/ArenaPAL
P164 *Saturday, Sunday... and Monday*, 1998. Photo: Clive Barda/ArenaPAL
Simon Callow in *Chimes at Midnight*, 1998. Photo: Clive Barda/ArenaPAL
P165 Denis Quilley, Mark Kingston, Paul Venables and John Harding in *Racing Demon*, 1998. Photo: Clive Barda/ArenaPAL
P166 Denis Quilley and Richard Griffiths in rehearsals for *Katherine Howard*, 1998. Photo: The News, Portsmouth
Richard Griffiths in *Katherine Howard*, 1998. Photo: Clive Barda/ArenaPAL
P167 Emilia Fox and Julian Rhind-Tutt in rehearsals for *Katherine Howard*, 1998. Photo: The News, Portsmouth
Tracy-Ann Oberman in *Loot*, 1998. Photo: Tristram Kenton/Lebrecht Music and Arts
P168 Patricia Routledge in *The Importance of Being Earnest*, 1999. Photo: Clive Barda/ ArenaPAL
P169 James Bolam and Anna Carteret in *Semi-Detached*, 1999. Photo: Clive Barda/ArenaPAL
P170 *The King of Prussia*, 1999. Photo: Tristram Kenton/Lebrecht Music and Arts
The Man who came to Dinner, 1999. Programme cover image. Photo: Unknown
P171 Sharon Small and Martin Marquez in *Insignificance*, 1999. Photo: Tristram Kenton/ Lebrecht Music and Arts
P172 Janet Suzman and Edward Hardwicke in *Retreat from Moscow*, 1999. Photo: Tristram Kenton/Lebrecht Music and Arts
P173 Joss Ackland in *Heartbreak House*, 1999. Photo: Clive Barda/ArenaPAL

The 2000s

P174 Sophie Ward and Janie Dee in *Three Sisters*, 2001. Photo: Clive Barda/ArenaPAL
P176 The Community Choir in T*he Barchester Chronicles*, 2000. Photo: Clive Barda/ArenaPAL
The Community Cast of The Barchester Chronicles, 2000. Photo: Clive Barda/ArenaPAL
P177 Nicholas Tennant and Kevin Bishop in *The Recruiting Officer*, 2000. Photo: Clive Barda/ArenaPAL
Michael Gould, Peter Bourke, Elizabeth Edmonds and Kali Peacock in *The Sea*, 2000. Photo: Tristram Kenton/Lebrecht Music and Arts
Camilla Power and Michael Higgs in *The Blue Room*, 2000. Photo: Tristram Kenton/Lebrecht Music and Arts
P178 Susannah Fellows and Martin Crewes in *Pal Joey*, 2000. Photo: Tristram Kenton/Lebrecht Music and Arts
P179 Claire Cathcart and Billy Carter in *Aristocrats*, 2000. Photo: Tristram Kenton/Lebrecht Music and Arts

A Small Family Business, 2000. CFT Poster.
P180 Clive Swift, Guy Henry, Ian Bartholomew and Alison McKenna in *Hysteria*, 2000.
Photo: Tristram Kenton/Lebrecht Music and Arts
P181 Jay Villiers, Pascal Langdale and Eleanor David in *Arcadia*, 2000. Photo: Clive Barda/ArenaPAL
P182 Hilton Mcrea and Janie Dee in *My One and Only*, 2001. Photo: Clive Barda/ArenaPAL
P183 Susan Jameson, Sean Gleeson and Adrian Bower in *In Celebration*, 2001.
Photo: Tristram Kenton/Lebrecht Music and Arts
P184 Niamh Linehan and Suzan Sylvester in *The Secret Rapture*, 2001. Photo: Tristram Kenton/Lebrecht Music and Arts
P185 *Putting It Together*, 2001. CFT programme cover image
Judy Flynn and Justine Glenton in *Shang-a-Lang*, 2001. Photo: Tristram Kenton/Lebrecht Music and Arts
CFYT's *Alice's Adventures*, 2001.
Photo: Peter Langdown
P186 Jessica Oyelowo, Giles Terera, Gordon Cooper, Madeleine Worral and Mark Stobbart in *Up on the Roof*, 2002. Photo: Tristram Kenton/Lebrecht Music and Arts
P187 Adrian Lucas in *Dead Funny*, 2002.
Photo: Tristram Kenton/Lebrecht Music and Arts
Lex Shrapnel and Emily Blunt in *Romeo and Juliet*, 2002. Photo: Clive Barda/ArenaPAL
Corin Redgrave in *Blunt Speaking*, 2002.
Photo: Tristram Kenton/Lebrecht Music and Arts
P188 Julian Bleach in *Cabaret*, 2002. Photo: Clive Barda/ArenaPAL
P189 *Cabaret*, 2002. Photo: Clive Barda/ArenaPAL
P191 The Community Cast in *The Devil's Dancing Hour – A City Under Siege*, 2002, Photo: Unknown
P192 Ruth Mackenzie. Photo: Mike Eddowes
Martin Duncan. Photo: Clare Park
Stephen Pimlott. Photo: Clare Park
P193 *The Gondoliers*, 2003. Photo: Ivan Kyncl/ArenaPAL
P194 *The Gondoliers*, 2003. Photo: Ivan Kyncl/ArenaPAL
Dale Rooks. Photo: Martin Eddowes
P195 *The Merchant of Venice*, 2003.
Photo: Ivan Kyncl/ArenaPAL
P196 *The Waterbabies*, 2003. Photo: Ivan Kyncl/ArenaPAL
P197 *I Caught My Death in Venice*, 2003.
Photo: Clare Park
The Seagull, 2003. Photo: Ivan Kyncl/ArenaPAL
P198 Kay Curram, Michael Feast and Darlene Johnson in *Nathan the Wise*, 2003.
Photo: Clare Park
Michael Feast in *Nathan the Wise*, 2003.
Photo: Clare Park
Jonathan Cullen in *Nathan the Wise*, 2003.
Photo: Clare Park
P199 Nicholas Colicos and cast rehearse *Out of this World*, 2004. Photo: Clare Park
P200 Simon Grieff and Fiona Dunn in *Out of this World*, 2004. Photo: Clare Park
2004 Community Day, CFYT Soldiers. Photo: Mike Eddowes
P201 Noma Dumezweni in *A Midsummer Night's Dream*, 2004. Photo: Clare Park
P202 *Just So*, 2004. Photo: Clare Park
Alexis Owen and Simon Grieff in *Just So*, 2004.
Photo: Clare Park
Alexis Owen and choreographer Stephen Mears rehearsing *Just So*, 2004. Photo: Clare Park
P203 Clare Holman and Sam West in *The Master and Margarita*, 2004.
Photo: Clare Park
Director Silviu Purcarete (centre) rehearsing

Scapino, 2004. Photo: Clare Park
Poster image of Toby Sedgwick for *Scapino*, 2004. Photo: Clare Park
P204 John Ramm in *King Lear*, 2005. Photo: Clare Park
Jo Stone-Fewings and David Warner in rehearsal for *King Lear*, 2005. Photo: Clare Park
P205 *How To Succeed In Business Without Really Trying*, 2005. Photo: Clare Park
Elizabeth McGovern and Alan Williams rehearse *The Scarlet Letter*, 2005. Photo: Clare Park
Adrian Quinton, Lucy Betts, Emily Moseley and Ellie Price in CFYT's *Arabian Nights*, 2005.
Photo: Mike Eddowes
P206 Alistair McGowan in *5/11*, 2005. Photo: Clare Park
P207 *5/11*, 2005. Photo: Clare Park
P208 The Pevensey children in CFYT's *The Lion, the Witch and the Wardrobe*, 2005
Photo: Mike Eddowes
P209 The Pevensey children and company in CFYT's *The Lion, The Witch and The Wardrobe*, 2011. Photo: Mike Eddowes
P210 David Dawson in *Nicholas Nickleby, Part I*, 2006. Photo: Robert Day
P211 Penelope Keith and Benjamin Whitrow in *Entertaining Angels*, 2006. Photo: Robert Day
P212 *Carousel*, 2006. Photo: Catherine Ashmore
P213 Roger Allam, Bruce Alexander, Nigel Hastings and Michael Begley in *Pravda*, 2006.
Photo: John Haynes/Lebrecht Music and Arts
P214 *Babes in Arms*, 2007. Photo: Catherine Ashmore
P215 *Babes in Arms* in rehearsal, 2007.
Photo: Catherine Ashmore
Patrick Stewart in *Macbeth*, 2007. Photo: Manuel Harlan
P216 Alex Hassell, Roddy Maude-Roxby and Mark Rylance in *I Am Shakespeare*, 2007.
Photo: Alistair Muir
P218 *Six Characters in Search of An Author*, 2008. Photo: Manuel Harlan
CFYT's *Toad of Toad Hall*, 2008 at Rolls-Royce, Goodwood. Photo: Allan Hutching
Natalie Cassidy and Frank Finlay rehearsing *The Cherry Orchard*, 2008.
Photo: Manuel Harlan
P219 Brian Conley in *The Music Man*, 2008.
Photo: Catherine Ashmore
P220 *Calendar Girls*, 2008. The original WI Calendar Girls and CFT cast.
Photo: Allan Hutchings
Julia Hills, Gaynor Faye, Carl Prekopp and Patricia Hodge in rehearsals, *Calendar Girls*, 2008.
Photo: Catherine Ashmore
Gaynor Faye, Patricia Hodge, Sian Phillips, Lynda Bellingham, Elaine C Smith and Julia Hills in *Calendar Girls*, 2008. Photo: John Swannell
P221 The company warm-up for *The Music Man*, 2008. Photo: Manuel Harlan
P222 *Cyrano de Bergerac*, 2009. Photo: Catherine Ashmore
Joseph Fiennes in rehearsal for *Cyrano de Bergerac*, 2009. Photo: Catherine Ashmore
Trevor Nunn in rehearsal for *Cyrano de Bergerac*, 2009. Photo: Catherine Ashmore
P223 *Oklahoma!* 2009. Photo: Manuel Harlan
P224 *The Grapes of Wrath*, 2009. Photo: Manuel Harlan
P225 Sam West and Tom Goodman-Hill in rehearsal for *ENRON*, 2009. Photo: Manuel Harlan
Tim Pigott-Smith in *ENRON*, 2009 Photo: Manuel Harlan
P226 *ENRON*, 2009. Photo: Manuel Harlan
P227 Edward Eustace, Nell Underwood, Florence Christie and Felix Mosse in *The Heights*, 2009.
Photo: Mike Eddowes
Holly Mirams, stage managing *The Heights*, 2009.
Photo: Dale Rooks

The Story Continues

P228 Adam Cooper in *Singin' in the Rain*, 2011.
Photo: Manuel Harlan
P230 Patrick Stewart in *Bingo*, 2010.
Photo: Catherine Ashmore
Michael Xavier and Emma Williams in *Love Story*, 2010. Photo: Manuel Harlan
Jonathan Church in rehearsal for *The Critic*, 2010.
Photo: Manuel Harlan
P231 CFYT's *The Firework-Maker's Daughter*, 2010. Photo: Mike Eddowes
P232 Richard McCabe and Nicholas Le Prevost in *The Real Inspector Hound*, 2010. Photo: Manuel Harlan
David Haig and Henry Goodman in *Yes, Prime Minister*, 2010. Photo: Manuel Harlan
P233 *42nd Street*, 2010. Photo: Johan Persson
P234 Amanda Root in T*he Deep Blue Sea*, 2010.
Photo: Manuel Harlan
P235 *Rattigan's Nijinsky*, 2011.
Photo: Manuel Harlan
Director Philip Franks and Malcolm Sinclair in rehearsal for *Rattigan's Nijinsky*, 2011.
Photo: Manuel Harlan
P236 Michael Pennington and Ian McKellen in rehearsal for *The Syndicate*, 2011. Photo: Manuel Harlan
Michael Pennington and Ian McKellen in *The Syndicate*, 2011. Photo: Manuel Harlan
Cheri Lunghi in *The Syndicate*, 2011. Photo: Manuel Harlan
P237 Scarlett Strallen and Company in rehearsals for *Singin' in the Rain*, 2011. Photo: Manual Harlan Bradley Hall and Alex Lawther in *South Downs*, 2011. Photo: Johan Persson
Scarlett Strallen, Daniel Crossley and Adam Cooper in *Singin' in the Rain*, 2011.
Photo: Manuel Harlan
P238 Stella Gonet, Laura Elphinstone, Olivia Poulet, Lucy Briers, Suranne Jones, Catherine McCormack in *Top Girls*, 2010. Photo: John Haynes/Lebrecht Music and Art
Cast of *Sweeney Todd* in rehearsal, 2011.
Photo: Catherine Ashmore
P239 Imelda Staunton and James McConville in *Sweeney Todd*, 2011. Photo: Catherine Ashmore
Imelda Staunton and Michael Ball in *Sweeney Todd*, 2011. Photo: Catherine Ashmore
Michael Ball in rehearsal for *Sweeney Todd*, 2011. Photo: Catherine Ashmore
P240 The *Uncle Vanya* Company in rehearsal, 2012. Photo: Johan Persson
P241 2012 poster ©CFT
P242 Dervla Kirwan in rehearsal for *Uncle Vanya*, 2012. Photo: Johan Persson (B/C)
P243 After the performance, *Music Man*, 2008.
Photo: Manuel Harlan

With thanks to:

Phillimore and Co Ltd for permission to reproduce various quotes from Leslie Evershed-Martin's *The Impossible Theatre* (1986); to ACTAC (Theatrical and Cinematic) Ltd for permission to quote from Christopher Fry's 'Sonnet for the Oration' and 'Prologue for Chichester Festival Theatre' (1962); to ICM for permission to quote from Ted Tally's *Terra Nova* (1977); to Faber and Faber for permission to quote T.S. Eliot's 'Little Gidding' from Four Quartets (1942) and from Samuel Beckett's *Murphy* (1938); and to the estate of Robert W. Service for permission to quote from 'The Passing of the Year' (1912).

List of Supporters

CFT itself was built by crowd-funding – although the phrase was yet to be invented in 1962. Individuals pledging their support to see a magnificent, modern theatre, fit for the 20th century, built in the cathedral city of Chichester. Fifty years later, this book – through the crowd-funding publisher, Unbound – has been made possible on the same basis. I would like to thank all those who pledged their support including:

Margaret Abel

Mrs Margaret A'court

Cheryll Adams

Barbara Adams

Peter & Janet Adams

Mrs B Allen

Georgina Allman

Robert Allnutt

John Allum

Trish Allwood

Tim Andrews

Barbara & Ralph Ansley

Janet Anthony

Clare Apel

Matt Applewhite

Dora Archer

John C Armstone

Ms V M Arnold

Sally Atkins

Alison Atkinson

Steven Atkinson

Patricia Attree

Viv Aylward

Mrs J Azis

Mrs Helen Bailey

John A R Bailey

John Bailey

Michael Baker

Sue Baldwin

W E Ball

Anne Barry

Mrs Victoria Barton

Carole Beaves

Ian & Gill Beavis

Trevor Beckett

Kate Beeby

Emma Bendon

Tony Bennett

Charles Collingwood
& Judy Bennett

Valery Benson

Elaine Bentley

Charlie Bentley

Jean Berrisford

Nicholas Betteridge

Antony Bignell

Mrs Beckwith née Bird

Mr David Blake

William & Christine Bodey

Anne Bohbot

Betty Saunders & Val Bond

Mr D Bosdet

Tim Bovis

Mrs Margaret Bowden

Mr Pat Bowman

Ian Brachi

Francis Breame

Julian Breare

Andy Brereton

Therese Brook

James Brookes

Mr D A Brooks

Paul Brotherton

Ms Julia M Brough

Ken & Sylvia Brown

Richard & Sue Brownfield

Peter & Angela Bunker

Rebecca Bunting

Mr M B Bunting

Margaret Burbidge

Heather Burch

Dan Burch

Miss P Burdock

David MacDonald Burns

Alan Butland

Clive Butler

Mrs Audrey Butler

Peter & Melanie Byrom

Catriona Cahill

George & Madeleine Cameron

Jean Campbell

Mrs Wanda Canwell

Ralph Lucas & Stuart Carter

Mike Carvil

Mr David Casher-Soffe

Wilfred Cass

William Castell

Richard Chalk

Edward Chambers

Noelle Chase

Bill & Beryl Cheale

H P Chetwynd-Stapylton

Deborah Owen-Ellis Clark

Mr H G Clark

Peter Clayton

Patricia Clayton

Julian Clayton

Bruce Cleave

Christina Cobden

John Coldstream

Mrs G A Collins

Valerie Conduct

Mr B Cook

Mrs S J Cook

David & Joyce Cooling

Lorna & Roger Cooper

David & Valerie Cope

Derek Cornelius

Richard Cossens

Mr A Cowell

Josephine Cranston-Burgess

Carole Cregeen

Mrs Elizabeth Croughan

Dizzy & Jules Dalziel

Andrew Dascalopoulos

Michael Davall

Anthony Davies

Alison Dea

Stuart Dean

Christopher & Madeline Doman

Jackie Donnelly

Susan Douglas

Peter & Ruth Doust

Edward Dowling

Mrs J A Downes

Lawrence T Doyle

Miss S Durrant

Paul Easton

Mr D Eatock

Mrs G Eckenstein

Alan & Jennie Edwards

Mr Lance Edynbry

Mrs R Edynbry

Betty & Ian Elliott

Mike Elsley

Dr B S Ely

Susan Emery

David Epstein

Douglas & Jacqui Erskine Crum

Susan Espanola

Mr Michael Etheridge

Mrs G E Etherington

Therese Evans

Mrs Meg Everitt

Mr Barry Evershed-Martin

Mr Philip Evershed-Martin

Alfred Fairman

Christopher Farries

Ruth Faulkner

Brian Faulkner

Mrs M Featherstonhaugh

Stewart Ferris

Paul Fischer

Bernard Fleckley

Beryl Fleming

Barry Fletcher

Mrs G J Flude

Mr Michael & Mrs Alison Follis

Peter Foster

Victor Foulks

Paul & Odette Franks

Mr A J French

Jean Fricker

Miss M H Frost

Mrs Helen Frost

Anthony Fry

Mrs Vivienne Fulda

Alison Fulton

Stella & Stephen Funnell

Robert Furnell

Justin Gamblin

Mrs Susan Gambold

Pirjo Gardiner

Jackie Gauntlett

Ollie Geering

Ben Geering

Lilli Geissendorfer

Mr & Mrs Goodchild

Mr Garry Goodey

John Gordon

Emily Jennett Gower
Ian & Jean Graham-Jones
Nicholas Granatino
Ray & Barbara Greatorex
Alan Green
Yvonne Green
Angela Greenwood
Ian & Elizabeth Gregory
Jill Gregory
Mr & Mrs J Gregory
David Guest
Robert Gunnell
Liz Guy
Lawrence & Ruth Guyer
Simon Hadley
Mrs V Hadley
Lorraine Haines
Alan Hakim
Charles Halford
Ron Hall
Ros Hall & the late Mr Tom Hall
Miss R Hambrook
Sarah Hammett
Kathy Hammond
Ian Hammond
Douglas Hammond
Mr N J Harding
Mrs Jill Harding
Maureen Hare
Grant Harris
Elizabeth Harris
Tony Hart
Mr M Hart
Mrs A M Haskell
Paul Hathway
Mrs Valia Hedley
Richard & Moira Hemmett
Brian Henham
Jemima Henstridge-Blows
Mark Hepworth
Richard Heslop
Mrs Judith Hewins
Mrs H Hibbert
B R Higgins
Anthony & Jeanette Higham

Philip & Sue Hill
Richard Hoare
Anthea Hodgetts
Chris & Barbara Hodson
Matthew Hoggarth
Harold Penderel Holding
Vic & Jill Holloway
Mr Roy Holman, MBE, JP
John & Janet Holt
Reg Hook
Beatrice Hook
Dina Hoskins
Antony Howard
Ms P Howard
Mrs V E Howland
Matthew P Hoy
Peter Hubbard
Caroline Hughes
Ian Hunter
Michael & Janet Hutchinson
Saud iAspire
Raynor Isted
Majeed Jabbar
David Jack
Ronald Jacobs
Julia Janiec
Steven Jeram
Angela Jeremy
Barrie Jerram
Iain Jessup
Margaret Johnson
Roger Jones
Mr John Jones
Ms Jane Jones
Mr & Mrs C G Jones
Lynda & Joe Kearns
Ms Carol Kemm
Henry Kemme
Jeannie Kemnitzer
& Bryan Kemnitzer
Rodney Kempster
Gary Kench
Mr Roger Keyworth
Dan Kieran
Neville Lacey

Dr Patrick Lacey
Brian Lake
Alison & Michael Lane
Matthew Laza
Mr John Leeson
Roger Leggett
Kim Leslie
Frank & Freda Letch
Graham Lewis
Melissa Lewis
Paul Lewis
David & Shirley Linford
Mr Timothy Linnell
Eddie & Janet Lintott
Miranda Litchfield
Keith Lomas
Terry & Thora Loseby
Sue Love
Paul Lyness
Mrs J D Macbride
Amanda MacNally
Robert Macnaughtan
Nick & Carol Manley
John Manning
Charles March
Fiz Marcus
Janet Marsh
Mr Peter Marsh
Mr Stuart Martin
Mrs Sarah Martin
Dennis Martin
Brenda Mathers
Roger Matthews
Sidonie & Tabitha McBain
Ms Barbara McDonough
Mr J D McGurk
John McKerchar
Stephen Mear
Mr G E Merrick
Mrs A M Merriman
Ken & Joyce Miles
Dr & Mrs Mick Milligan
Vivien Mills
Roger & Linda Mills
Edward Milward-Oliver

Denise Milward-Oliver
Mrs S EN Mitchell
Mrs Sheila Mitchell
Miss Helen Moakes
Clare Moat
Colin & Chrissie Molyneux
Diane Moody
Angela Moore & Lindsay Vass
Katie Angela Morgan
James Morgan
Mr J Morgan
JP Morgan
Amanda Morgans
Mike Morten
Mrs Sarah Mulhall
Mrs J Munro
Miss Patricia Murphy
John Murphy & Tim Randall
Mrs Stella Murray
Mr P G Murrells
Mrs R Musker
Caro Newling
Stephen Nicholls
Angela Nye
Jacquie Ogilvie
Catherine O'Hanlon
Phil & Ghilaine Ower
Pat Packham
Graham & Sybil Papworth
Richard Parish
David Park
Mrs Sylvia Parnell
Arthur & Winifred Parr
Simon & Claire Parsonage
Janice Parsons
Clare Parsons
Christine Pashby-Taylor
Mr E Pattison
Graeme Payne
Mr Sam Peake
Mrs E Peart
Miss Sarah Pegram
Julie & Stuart Pembery
Arabella Peniston
Charlotte Peniston

Lyana Peniston
Guy Peters
Mrs Celia Peters
Ryan Petersen
Mrs Sheila Pettifer
Andrea Phillips
Anna Place
Mr H Plowden-Roberts
Mrs A Plyming
Kevin Pointer
Heidi Pointet
Justin Pollard
Maggie Pollock
Robert & Larraine Poole
Margret Preece
Edwin Prince
Pam & David Priscott
Mike & Eve Pritchard
Caroline Procter
Kim Protheroe
Becky Purcell
Megan Purdie
Michael Rangos
Michael D Read
Christopher Redknap
Anne Renshaw
Nigel Reynolds
Malcolm Reynolds
Adam Rice
Carole Richmond
Mrs Sally Rieder
Paul Rigg
John Rimmer
Miss Helen Robathan
Elizabeth & David Robinson
Dale Rooks
Elizabeth Rosoman
Betty & Tony Rowthorn
Peter Ruddick
W B Rymer
Cherry Sadler
Christoph Sander
Rhona Scott
David Seager
Joan Secombe

Mr C E Sedgwick
David & Sophie Shalit
Jonathan Shapiro
Amanda Sharp
Colin Shearing
Barry Sheppard
Tony & Pauline Short
Norman & Jean Siviter
Skaptason
Brian & Sarah Skilling
Mr Bernard Slatter
Greg & Katherine Slay
Lynne Smith
Mark Smith
Anne & David Smith
Christine & Dave Smithers
Peter Spence
Miriam Stephenson
Colin Stepney
Ms Jenny Stewart
Lorna Still
Jane Stoggles
Adam Stuart
David & Inge Sumner
Anthony Sumner & Victor Poole
Miss E M Sutter
Andre Tammes
Alan Tapp
Mrs Christine Taylor
Louise Thomas
Julia Thomson
Mr David Thornley
Lois Tibbetts
Mr James Tice
Monica Timms
Phil Tite
James, Jen & Harry Tod
Sam Tod
Christopher Tod
Mr John Toll
Annie Tomkins
Graham Tomlinson
Mr T F Tott
Ann & Bob Travis
Deborah Trollope

Geoffrey Tudor
Mr David Turner
Karen Tyler
Richard & Helen Tyrrell
Andrew Vance
Mr & Mrs A Walsh
Elizabeth Walter
Phill Ward
Ian & Alison Warren
Professor D W Warwick
Mr Mark Waters
Brian & Pat Waters
Tina & Martin Webb
Richard Webber
Susie Wells
Carla White
Mrs Stella Whitelock
Kerry Whiting
Brigid & Robert Whyte
Stephen Wickham
Mrs Josephine T Willday
Rob Williams
Carole Williams
Mrs Angela Williams
Robin & Gillian Wilson
Robin Wilson
Doris Wilson
Mrs Karin Mackenzie Wilson
Yvonne Wilkinson
Suzanne Wilson-Higgins
John & Claire Wilton
Stephanie Winter
Stephen Wise
John & June Witham
S Wood
Mr J Wood
Angela Wormald
Diana Wray
Alan Wright
Mr J Wright
Jonathan Mark Wright
Mrs Deborah Wyman
Ernest Yelf
Alan Yentob
Sheila Young